THE  TIMES

GOOD UNIVERSITIES GUIDE

About the authors

John O'Leary is Education Correspondent of *The Times*. He joined the paper in 1990 as Higher Education Correspondent and assumed responsibility for the whole range of education coverage in 1992. Previously the deputy editor of *The Times Higher Education Supplement*, he has been writing on the subject for more than a decade. He has a degree in politics from Sheffield University.

Tom Cannon is visiting professor of corporate responsibility at Manchester University and a former director of Manchester Business School. He was previously professor of business management at Stirling University. He maintains strong links with policy-makers in government and industry in many countries and was founding director of the Scottish Enterprise Foundation and the International Institute for Corporate Responsibility. As well as being the author of 10 books, he writes regularly on marketing, enterprise development and innovation in many newspapers and magazines.

The guide features additional contributions from Matthew D'Ancona and Daniel Rosenthal

THE  TIMES

GOOD UNIVERSITIES GUIDE

**The Definitive Guide to Britain's Universities
Edited by JOHN O'LEARY and TOM CANNON**

TIMES BOOKS
A Division of HarperCollinsPublishers

First published by Times Books
A Division of HarperCollins*Publishers*
77–85 Fulham Palace Road
London w6 8jb

© Times Newspapers 1993

British Library Cataloguing in Publication Data
O'Leary, John
'Times' Good Universities Guide
Definitive Guide to Britain's Universities
I. Title II. Cannon, Tom
378.41

ISBN 0 7230 0597 4

Typeset by Rowland Phototypesetting Limited
Bury St Edmunds, Suffolk

Printed in Finland

Cover photograph: Rex Features Limited

CONTENTS

PREFACE

Early in 1992, an apparently inconsequential change of government policy altered the map of British higher education for ever. The 34 English and Welsh polytechnics along with four Scottish institutions acquired the right to university status. One college of higher education followed later. The promotions were a reward for several years' unstinting service to the widening of educational opportunities. At last, the confusing distinction between the major providers of higher education was to be abolished, putting all the institutions on an equal footing.

In reality, however, the confusion deepened. By the end of the year, not only were applicants confronted with an array of new names for familiar institutions, it had become obvious that all universitites were by no means equal in the new higher education world. Some were destined to become the research powerhouses of the 21st century, while others among the traditional universities would become more like the old polytechnics, teaching many more students to compensate for a loss of research income.

A British university degree, with few exceptions, has always been of roughly equal standing. Oxford and Cambridge may have been in a class of their own, parts of London may have conferred significant advantages, but few employers could or would discriminate between Aberdeen and York for example. This is almost certain to change. Not because the new universities' standards are any lower, but because the existence of more than 90 diverse universities and an ever-growing pool of graduates will make a pecking order inevitable.

An elite group, with the lion's share of the research work to attract top academics, is already beginning to emerge. Some universities will concentrate on developing a reputation in particular subjects, while others continue to spread their resources more widely. At the same time, the government's temporary brake on university expansion will force up entry requirements, while high levels of graduate unemployment demand an informed choice of course. All of which makes a route map of higher education more necessary than ever.

The Times Good Universities Guide is intended as a starting point. The rankings will not identify the most suitable university for you, but they will provide an indication of each university's standing on a range of significant indicators. Many in higher education insist that such comparisons are meaningless – that all universities are unique. But choices have to be made, both by students and employers. Better that they should be on the basis of open information than on dated, often inaccurate impressions of distant institutions.

INTRODUCTION
The changing face of higher education

Any attempt to profile Britain's new unified system of higher education faces a number of problems, the result principally of the range and the scale of the changes prompted by the government's 1992 shake-up. All must be faced if a rounded portrait of Britain's universities at a critical point in their evolution is to be given. So what are these changes? They include:

- The expansion of student numbers
- The elimination of the division between universities and polytechnics
- The attempt to open up university education to groups previously excluded from it
- The reinforcement of links between universities and employers, especially in the private sector
- More local orientation in universities
- An increased emphasis on quality and performance

The student going to university in 1994 will be joining a higher education system in considerable flux. In part, today's changes reflect the increased demands being placed on higher education as Britain adjusts to a world in which knowledge and knowledge-based industries lie at the heart of industrial competitiveness. The decision to abolish the distinction between universities and polytechnics is part of a systematic attempt to increase student numbers while acknowledging the diversity of university education. The new universities – the former polytechnics – add an extra and distinct dimension to the country's university system.

These and other changes reflect deep technological, economic and social processes. As Sir Douglas Hague, one of the most radical thinkers on the issue, argued in 1991 in *Beyond Universities,*

> In the 1990s and 2000s, people outside the universities will increasingly be working in similar ways and with similar talents to those within; and they will often do so more innovatively and with greater vigour, because they will come to what they do untrammelled by academic traditions, preconceptions and institutions. The pioneers of the knowledge society will increasingly be able to compete with the universities and, increasingly, will do so . . . To avoid being driven out of activities which they have

imagined their own by right, the universities will have to make substantial changes in what they do and how they do it.

Thus universities themselves have found themselves obliged to work to a new agenda. Its salient points are:

- The increased importance of knowledge-based industries
- New technologies
- New methods of communication
- Increased expectations of rights and responsibilities
- Access to national and international universities
- Recognition of the value of life-long learning

Few aspects of student life are unaffected. The student population will be much larger – well over a million full-time students by the time you graduate. Even more students will be studying part-time or on non-traditional courses. More will be older – many with work experience – and from a far wider range of classes and ethnic and other groups than in the past. Many will live at home. Technology will play a much larger role in the arts as well as in the sciences. You will probably have a chance to study abroad for at least part of your course. Your graduation will no longer be the end of your studies but the start of a different pattern of life-long learning.

These transformations are far from a simple tinkering with Britain's higher education but a reflection of much wider changes in the country's economic and social life – and of a determination that universities must be part of this revolution. Economic recession and social change can best be tackled in an advanced industrial country if the university system plays its full part.

What is this part? Universities lie at the heart of any effort to transform our technological base. They are vital to attempts to appreciate the cultural, natural or built environment. The skills, knowledge and expertise of staff, students and graduates provide the primary means to understand and develop our communities. Their contribution is crucial if we are to move from recession and pessimism to prosperity and confidence. Research provides the key to unlocking potential; education, training and development, the means to mobilise potential.

The nature and impact of change

Looking more closely at the changes, five basic issues will affect the nature of the university experience for those entering in 1994. These are growth, change, diversity, resources and quality. All universities and their courses will be affected.

Growth creates opportunities and poses challenges. Vice-chancellors and principals are facing up to these in a number of ways. Professor John

Forty, principal and vice-chancellor of Stirling University, has commented that,

> The greater income associated with a bigger number of students reduces the relative burden of central overheads, and a greater overall intake of students allows the various academic departments to expand staff and their range of academic interests . . . Growth also provides the university with an opportunity to introduce new academic subjects thereby extending the breadth of subjects it can offer to students.

Professor Gordon Higginson, vice-chancellor of Southampton University, developed this theme in acknowledging that 'all higher education institutions will have more students', reinforcing the point with the observation that 'the status quo is not an option'.

Professor Neil Buxton, vice-chancellor of the University of Hertfordshire, highlighted the opportunities inherent in change when he identified 'significant new course developments and new opportunities'. Professor William Turmeau, principal of Napier University, sees change as the means by which institutions can push 'forward the frontiers of education and knowledge by introducing new courses and delivery methods, the key and cornerstone to all our work'.

Increased diversity is an integral part of this process of change. This will be seen in the nature of the student population as well as in the organisation and structure of the universities and the courses they provide. For example, the University of Central England in Birmingam saw the number of 'first-year women students increase from 44% in 1989–90 to 47% in 1990–91'. It also took 'pride in the numbers of students recruited from ethnic minorities'. Indeed universities in general are seeking to make higher education available to a much broader range of the population and to invite applications from all social classes and ethnic groups.

What is also beyond question, however, is that change can be expensive. Professor J. Quayle, vice-chancellor of the University of Bath, points out that the funding mechanism employed by the government 'is an ingenious ratchet . . . mainly directed towards the objective of driving down costs'. Many of these costs, however, are outside the direct control of university authorities: books, periodicals, residential facilities, health services and student facilities, for example. And as costs rise, so universities can find themselves obliged to pass them on to students. A cut in library expenditure on books means that students will probably need to spend more themselves – out of a shrinking grant. Professor Gareth Roberts, vice-chancellor of Sheffield University, draws these topics together when he points out that 'a central issue . . . during the next decade will be how to maintain quality while expanding rapidly and economically'.

This theme of quality was reinforced by Dr Anne Wright, vice-chancellor of the University of Sunderland, in her comment that 'we regard our students as valued customers deserving the highest quality of service who, in turn, will themselves become committed to quality as employees and employers. This, the ultimate 'quality circle', is essential for all our futures'. It seems inevitable that students will be expected to play a fuller role in shaping and evaluating the ability of universities to enhance the quality of the education they offer.

The effectiveness with which all British universities perform one of their prime tasks – helping students to finish their studies successfully – vividly illustrates the core strength throughout higher education in Britain. This emerges in all institutions throughout the *Times Guide*. If anything, the quality of universities is understated.

Their accomplishments raise wider questions. It is clear that additional finance is essential if these changes are to be implemented. This is a problem above all for the new universities, whose resource bases are much smaller than those of the traditional universities. As well as more money for staff, additional finance is needed for areas such as libraries, equipment and accommodation. A similar issue faces the civic, redbrick and metropolitan universities. These have been at the sharp end of many of the changes in resourcing of the last decade. They are, however, the guardians of the nation's science and technology base. Costs have increased faster than income. The imbalances this has created must be addressed if the country has any serious ambition to remain a prosperous, mature industrial economy.

Other sources of information

There are many sources of information on the issues and challenges facing universities and their students over the next few years. Most universities issue an annual report in which the vice-chancellor comments on the challenges faced. Many of the comments above were culled from these documents. The determined student might want to consult:

Higher Education: A New Framework, HMSO Cm 1541, 1991

Education and Training for the 21st Century, HMSO Cm1536, 1991 vols 1 & 2

Beyond Universities, Sir Douglas Hague, Institute for Economic Affairs, 1991

PART 1
THE BACKGROUND

1 ORGANISE YOURSELF

There is a Chinese proverb that the longest journey starts with the first step. The trick is to make sure that this step is in the right direction. Decisions about going to university, about when to go, which university to go to, what course to take, come thick and fast during the six or nine months before applications are sent off.

For the 1993–94 academic year, these questions will be harder to answer than ever. The greatly increased number of universities has made what was always an important decision much harder simply by virtue of the greater choice available. Furthermore, the mechanics of applying have changed. Whereas universities and polytechnics had their own systems of entry through their own clearing houses – the Universities Central Council on Admissions (UCCA) and the Polytechnics Central Admissions System (PCAS) – now there is just one body, the Universities and Colleges Admissions Service (UCAS).

The best approach to what, by any standard, is the hugely important decision facing you is to get organised yourself. Develop your own, well-thought-out systems. Plan ahead. Otherwise, you risk becoming increasingly confused – and making decisions you may regret.

There are three basic keys to success:

- Be clear about your objectives
- Establish a clear strategy
- Work systematically. Tackle each problem in turn and refuse to be overwhelmed

Objectives

It is important to be clear about what you want to achieve from the next stage in your education and your working life. Today's choices are not just going to shape the next two, three or four years. They are going to influence the rest of your life. Though it is possible to change direction, the costs can be high and the dislocation considerable. So list your objectives at an early stage. These should be split into the short, medium and long term and drawn up with a clear understanding of your personal circumstances and capabilities. There is little point in getting locked into a set of choices which your likely qualifications, talents and interests preclude. Objectives should be:

- Based on a clear understanding of your current situation
- Realistic
- Stimulating

These latter two may seem conflicting. Won't 'realistic' objectives be pretty boring? In practice, no. Most people want to achieve as much as they can – not as little as they need.

It is a good idea to get into the habit of keeping notes of the processes followed, the information gathered and the choices made. Your objectives can be listed as:

Long term These are sometimes called life goals. They might refer to the type of career you hope to follow, how mobile you want to be or issues about security or risk.

Medium term These are often closely linked to 'life goals' and might be staging posts on the way to their achievement. In its simplest form, if your long-term goal is to be a barrister, a good law degree is an important first step.

Short term These are generally about how you want to spend the next few months or years. But don't underestimate them. Because these are the goals that will be encountered first, they are the least likely to change or be overtaken by events.

Make a point of spelling out these goals. Discuss them with others. Not only will you be able to eliminate inconsistencies, thinking about them seriously and systematically is crucial in helping you decide if you are going in the right direction.

In fact it is almost inevitable that your objectives will change over time. Circumstances alter. New experiences stimulate new thinking and affect aspirations. This does not undermine the value of setting objectives but it reinforces the importance of building flexibility into your aims. Let your goals be a spur to action, not a strait-jacket.

A strategy for decision-making

Decision-making is about making choices when genuine options exist and where gaps in knowledge or information mean that responses are not automatic. Effective decision-making usually involves concentrating energy on real questions. There is little point worrying about issues that are out of your control. It is important to know what options exist and where to find out more about them. Gathering information to help decision-making is a continuing process. It is not, however, a mechanical process. No-one should be afraid to follow their instincts or to revise and reconsider as knowledge accumulates. 'Unswerving flexibility' is a useful decision-making rule.

Many people find it helpful to construct a flow chart or decision-tree to help with this type of cumulative and progressive decision-making. There are three core components:

- Identify your options
- Identify the issues that matter
- Gather enough information to make a choice

How can you use this approach to answer the first and most obvious question of all: 'Do I want to go to university?'.

Identify options Three options can easily be identified at once: 1) No, I want to get a job; 2) Yes, I've been working for years for this; 3) I want to take a year off to think about it.

The issues that matter These can range from a desire to keep in step with your contemporaries to the need to be sure that a mistake made now can be put right. For example, there are obvious risks in taking a year off if your first-choice university will not keep places open.

The information needed Once questions are identified the sources of help and information can be tracked down. Careers counsellors at school, university admissions staff and others have built up a vast body of expertise and experience in tackling these questions.

Once sufficient information is gathered, move on to the next issue. Always be willing to discuss decisions with others but avoid the twin threats of 'paralysis through analysis' and 'slow panic', the tendency to waste time on trivia and then panic.

In specifying the issues that matter, some people find it useful to introduce classifications or weightings. For example, in choosing a university it can be helpful to grade it under four headings

- Need to have
- Nice to have
- Irrelevant
- Downers

The need-to-haves are essentials – if they are not available, you do not want to go. The nice-to-haves are positive features that you take into account after the need-to-haves, though they may still make an important difference in choosing an institution or course. Irrelevancies have no effect on your choice. Downers are features that you want to avoid.

It can be useful to convert these classifications into weightings. Need-to-haves can be given 6–10 points, nice-to-haves 1–4 points. Don't be afraid to give negative marks to downers. It might, for example, be very important to you that your university offers sandwich courses. Give this a weighting of 10 points. Similarly, perhaps you like the idea of living in a big city with influential student political groups – but this is a nice-to-have, worth only 2 points. Perhaps, you have developed a hatred for examinations, meaning that a university which uses only examinations for assessing grades becomes a major downer, –8 points, say.

Some decisions need to be revised and reconsidered. Often, decisions about one issue are being made while information is being gathered to help with others. Keep control of this process. This can be done by keeping careful notes while making certain that the questions to be answered are kept to a minimum. A flow-chart backed up by simple checklists is invaluable at this stage.

An important decision-making skill involves sketching circumstances that will unfold if particular developments occur. Bear in mind not only the best case – you do even better in your exams than you hoped – but the worst case. The decisions you make should be able to cope with either scenario.

Always be willing to discuss your criteria, choices and decisions with others. Friends and parents – or their friends – can often help. Not only can they sometimes supply important information, they can be valuable sounding boards. And never be afraid to review or revise your thinking. It is better to admit a mistake now than three weeks into the first term of your first academic year.

2 CHOOSING A UNIVERSITY

Which universities you apply to is necessarily related closely to the course you want to take: the two are naturally complimentary (see chapter 3, Choosing a Course). Furthermore, the most popular courses are in any case offered by most universities. Nonetheless, which university to go to is a hugely important question. The ranking tables in chapters 8 and 9 highlight just some of the issues you may want to take into account. Remember, however, that the best university for you is the one that meets your needs, allows you to develop to your maximum potential and gives you the best learning and living experience.

At the heart of *The Times Guide* is the main ranking table of all universities in chapter 8, a detailed examination of 14 key aspects of university life. These range from the ease of entry to the proportion of foreign students. Each has been chosen to draw out a key feature which can be included in a personal checklist as part of your selection process. These are not the only aspects of university life that matter but they cover many of the most important areas in which all universities in the guide can be compared. Prospective entrants should link them with other information which matters to them.

This guide should be only one of the sources of information used. Discussions with other family members are essential. Staff at college, school or the local careers service have accumulated long experience of the issues to raise and the choices made. Local Training and Enterprise Councils (TECs) are increasingly important, especially when they have set up advice units such as Manchester's 'TEC Shop'. In areas such as Greenwich in London, the local authority has set up an Education and Training Shop. Although many universities have been forced to give up preliminary interviews, many still have open days or advisory interviews. These are important ways of getting a feel for the institution and whether you'll be happy and successful.

A personal checklist is useful. This should list all the features that you are looking for – ranging from details of the course to the social facilities on offer. *The Times Guide* gives the essential core information to fill in the checklist.

Among the factors you may want to consider are:

- The university's reputation
- The availability of desired subjects
- Academic reputation in that subject

- Course options, freedom of choice, etc
- Teaching systems (small tutorials, etc)
- Type of assessment (examination or continuous)
- Access to technology
- Environment (city, campus, etc)
- Sports and leisure facilities
- Flexibility: can you change subjects easily?
- Access courses available
- Transport and communications
- Special facilities (for the disabled, etc)

Draw up this checklist, be willing to change it, listen to others – but make up your own mind.

Other sources of information

Although *The Times Guide* is probably the most comprehesive guide to universities there are many other excellent and useful sources of information, among them the prospectuses of individual universities – and the alternative prospectuses put out by many student unions: these can give an invaluable insight into the trials, tribulations, pitfalls, pleasures and opportunities of a university. Learning to use sources such as these is one of the most useful skills a student can obtain.

Free guides *Grants to Students and Loans to Students* (Department for Education, Publications Dispatch Centre, Honeypot Lane, Canons Park, Stanmore, Middlesex HA7 1AZ; most local authorities and some schools make this available)
UCAS Handbook (Universities and Colleges Admissions System, PO Box 28, Cheltenham, Glos GL50 3SA)

Student guides *The Student Book*, Boehm, K and Lees-Spalding, J (Macmillan 1993)
PUSH '93, The Polytechnic and University Handbook, Rich, J (Black Box Publishing)

Reference books *University Entrance: The Official Guide* (Association of Commonwealth Universities for the Committee of Vice Chancellors and Principals)
Guide to the Colleges and Institutes of Higher Education (Standing Conference of Principals, Edge Hill College, Ormskirk, Lancs L39 4QP)
Degree Course Offers, Heap, B (Career Consultants Ltd)
Designated Courses (Department for Education, Sanctuary Buildings, Great Smith St., London SW1P 3BT)
Guide to Courses and Careers in Art, Craft and Design (National Society for Education in Art and design, The Gatehouse, Corsham, Wiltshire SN13 0ES)
Design Courses in Britain (Design Council, 28 Haymarket, London SW1Y 4SU)

Table 1

CIVICS OR REDBRICKS	CAMPUS	TECHNOLOGICAL	NEW OR METROPOLITAN	NEW OR COUNTY
Birmingham	East Anglia	Aston	West of England	Anglia Polytechnic
Bristol	Essex	Bath	Central England	Brighton
Hull	Exeter	Bradford	London Guildhall	Glamorgan
Leeds	Keele	Brunel	Coventry	Hertfordshire
Leicester	Kent	City	De Montfort	Humberside
Liverpool	Lancaster	Dundee	Derby	Kingston
Manchester	Reading	Loughborough	East London	Central Lancashire
Newcastle	Stirling	Heriot-Watt	Glasgow	Middlesex
Nottingham	Sussex	UMIST	Caledonian	Oxford Brookes
Queen's Belfast	Warwick	Salford	Greenwich	Paisley
Sheffield		Strathclyde	Huddersfield	Staffordshire
Southampton		Surrey	Leeds Metropolitan	Teesside
		Ulster	Liverpool JMU	Thames Valley

ANCIENTS	COLLEGIATE		NEW OR METROPOLITAN	
Aberdeen	Durham		Manchester Metropolitan	
Cambridge	London		Napier	
Edinburgh	Wales		Northumbria at Newcastle	
Glasgow	York		Nottingham Trent	
Oxford			Plymouth	
St. Andrews			Portsmouth	
			Robert Gordon	
			Sheffield Hallam	
			South Bank	
			Sunderland	
			Westminster	
			Wolverhampton	

Which type of university?

Be clear about the different types of university. Table 1 (above) breaks these down into seven basic categories. Any classification of this type is inevitably a little crude, not least because some institutions could, with justice, be placed in more than one category. For example, Oxford and Cambridge, though clearly ancient universities, are also collegiate. Similarly, York, though collegiate, is also a relatively new foundation. Changes in higher education also place some of these categorisations in doubt. The expansion of professional studies – business, pharmacy, and law, for example – suggests that an entirely new category of university –

professional studies universities – may well come to be as valid a categorisation as technological universities. Similarly, it seems likely that in time some institutions will shift from one category to another. This is especially true of the new universities. It could be argued that Reading is more of a 'county' university than, say, Teesside.

That said, the existing categories are a useful way to help answer the question of what type of university you want to attend. All have their strengths. These may be the traditions and historic standing of the ancients or the powerful local links and commitment to applied work of the metropolitan universities.

What should I look for? Where can I find out?

Most universities have developed their own distinct characters and ways of operating. As well as reading the advice here, don't be afraid to ask anyone you think can help. And take time to dig through the published material.

Location is often an important determining factor. For many students, the desire to get away from home, live in a big city or on a modern campus university with large numbers of people with similar interests is critical. There are distinct fashions in the choice of various locations. In recent years the large civic and metropolitan universities of the North and Midlands have enjoyed a surge in popularity. Two factors seem to have shaped this: the relatively low costs of living in these cities; and their lively and diverse local, cultural and leisure environments.

The popularity of campus universities has ebbed and flowed over the years, with students alternately valuing or rejecting the cohesion and sense of identity offered by a campus setting. London remains a major attraction for many students while the appeal of studying in Scotland, Wales or Northern Ireland can be very strong for some students. In other cases, fashion seems rarely to have been a factor. Universities such as St. Andrews, York, Durham, Bath and Bristol seem to have a permanent appeal. Likewise, the lure of the ancients, above all Oxford and Cambridge, is unchanging.

Access is not the problem it used to be. The mixture of bus deregulation and price offers by British Rail makes most universities on the UK mainland easily accessible. Even travel to Northern Ireland is easier and cheaper – in real terms – than in the past. Despite this, if you are determined to travel home a great deal, the journey from Manchester or Newcastle to London or the Southwest can soon make a hole in a grant or allowance. Hitching, the students' traditional stand-by, is no longer as easy or as safe as in the past. There are, however, often car pools operated in the university going to specific locations.

Facilities

The facilities offered by universities vary enormously. Some have long-established commitments to, say, the provision of residential accommodation to all first- or final-year students. Others recruit heavily from their local community and have a major commitment to creche or other relevant facilities. Elsewhere, there is both a commitment to and an investment in facilities for the physically disadvantaged or disabled.

In choosing your university, make up a comprehensive checklist of facilities that are important to you. It might include:

Residential accommodation How important is it to you that there is enough university-owned accommodation to guarantee a place for all first-and/or final-year students? Remember that the apparent convenience of university accommodation may diguise high costs and poor links with the local community.

Library facilities One way or another, you will spend a lot of of time in the library. Four aspects are especially important: 1) expenditure on books or periodicals; 2) staff support; 3) study space; 4) access. Often absolute expenditure on books can be less important than the quality of support given by library staff. Similarly, restrictions on the capital expenditure of universities over the last few years has placed a massive premium on study space especially during the periods just before examinations.

Leisure facilities Going to university is not just about getting a degree. It is about learning to live, work and enjoy yourself with others. Campus universities and those in small communities have often invested in excellent arts and leisure facilities while urban universities have built powerful links with their local communities.

Facilities for groups with special needs The increasingly heterogeneous nature of today's student population has highlighted the importance of providing special facilities for those who need them: the blind, the deaf, those with impaired sight or hearing, those in wheelchairs, student mothers (or fathers) who need child-care support. Some of the newer foundations were able to plan for the needs of these groups from the start. Others have invested heavily in alterations to existing buildings. In these latter cases there can be a significant lag between agreeing building plans and executing them. For example, if a university has bought existing buildings to accommodate new departments, they are unlikely to be designed for effective wheelchair access. Whatever its final intentions, the university in question may well find it takes some time before such access can be provided.

Many aspects of a university's response to special needs are reflected in investment in areas other than building and facilities.

Disabled students Support offered by some universities includes: readers for the blind and partially sighted; interpreters for the deaf; and counselling for those suffering from specific learning or personal difficulties.

Mature students often find that their needs change significantly at different stages in their university career. Before admission, the institution's commitment to their needs may be reflected in the nature of and support for its access courses. Immediately on admission, concerns often centre on likely changes in financial circumstances, lifestyle and domestic arrangements. Good quality financial advice backed by proper counselling may be crucial in tackling the 'entry' or 're-entry' problems.

Gender Women students in particular face a range of distinct problems. These range from sexual harassment to pregnancy advice. Alternative prospectuses are among the best sources of information and guidance on a university's response to these questions.

Sexual inclination The last few years have seen signs of increasing intolerance in this area at some universities and among some communities. If tolerance is important to you, check out the university's policies in advance, preferably through the institution's gay society – if there is one.

Ethnicity All universities have a formal commitment to equal opportunity. This will be codified in either their Charter or Articles of Association. In some cases, this commitment may go no further. National student organisations are pressing institutions to develop more clear-cut policies to tackle discrimination, harassment or abuse and to introduce programmes of affirmative action.

The universities with the clearest commitments in this area can generally be identified by the resources they devote to it and the identifiable programmes of action they have introduced.

Overseas students It is useful to sub-divide this group into those from within the European Community (EC) and those from outside the EC. For all institutional purposes, EC students are treated as 'home' students. This does not eliminate special needs or avoid tensions, for instance over accommodation, but it does provide a framework for producing policy responses.

Students from outside the EC have become increasingly important to the financing of many UK universities. This has had positive and negative effects. It has encouraged many institutions to recruit actively and thus to introduce greater cultural and social diversity. Unfortunately, some have not backed this up with investment in appropriate facilities, for example, in accommodation, support for spouses, help with transitional arrangements or finance. It is vital to be fully informed on these issues before choosing a university.

Other sources of information

Among the most useful guides and sources of information for these and other questions are:

Make a Fresh Start: The Mature Student's Handbook, Koving, M. Kogan Page, London

The Mature Student's Handbook, Rosier, I and Earnshaw, L. Trotman & Co., Surrey

Studying and Living in Britain, The British Council, Northcote House, Plymouth

or contact:

The British Council, 10 Spring Gardens, London SW1A 2BN
Campaign for Homosexual Equality, PO Box 342, London WC1X 0DU
Skill: National Bureau for Students with Disabilities, 336 Brixton Rd., London SW9 7A
UKCOSA (UK Council for Overseas Student Affairs), 60 Westbourne Grove, London W2 5SH
Union of Jewish Students, Hillel House, 1–2 Endsleigh St., London WC1H 0DS

Money

Cost is an increasingly important aspect of university choice. (for a more detailed review of students' finances, see chapter 6, Student Life: The Basics). Probably the best way to find out about costs is to ask friends who know the university or the area. The main things to check are accommodation, food and drink, energy (light and heat), travel and entertainment. Discounts for students and cheap food or drink in union, college or university restaurants or bars can make all the difference.

Bear in mind, too, the paradox that while the cost of living is higher in the south of England, particularly in London, the chances of finding work and thereby supplementing your income may also be higher. Similarly, though costs may be lower in other parts of the country, the likelihood of part-time work can be less. Find out which universities have set up agencies to find part-time or temporary work for students. Jobs are generally easier for women to find but worse paid.

3 CHOOSING A COURSE

Britain's universities offer a massive array of courses, programmes, combinations and options. *The Official Guide to University Entrance*, published on behalf of the Committee of Vice-Chancellors and Principals, lists almost 600, from accountancy to zoology.

Some courses are single honours, that is they concentrate on one subject. Others are joint honours, built around two subjects. Many are combined honours linking disciplines. It is also possible to study some subjects to general degree level. There are advantages to each model.

Single honours courses allow students to look into subjects in depth. Variety comes from within the subject. Combined honours are frequently designed to link cognate, or related, subjects. For example, English and history may be especially relevant to those interested in the fit between culture and history. There has also been a trend in recent years for universities to provide a vocational dimension to combined honours, for example chemistry and business studies, while the nature of some areas effectively means that they are 'combined' subjects, for example manufacturing engineering. In Scotland the 'general degree' tradition is much stronger than in the rest of the UK. The increased flexibility stemming from modularisation, credit transfer and other initiatives has also added greatly to the diversity of university offerings.

The organisation and structure of the course can make an enormous difference to the satisfaction obtained. For some, a sandwich course or a year abroad is an important part of the value of the degree, while others want the opportunity to concentrate uninterrupted with their studies. Some courses place a major emphasis on project work, sometimes on a group basis. Remember that courses can vary greatly between institutions, reflecting the approach of a given university and/or the interests of faculties. Always check the way a programme is organised at the university you are considering.

It is worth adapting the following check-list to fit your needs:

- Is it a single honours programme (if that is your preference)?
- Will I get a chance to spend a year abroad?
- Is continuous assessment used for more than 50 per cent of grades?
- Will I be able to do project work of my own choosing?
- Will I be expected to present my work to fellow students?
- Can I see my tutors frequently?

- Are practicals held frequently?
- Are the laboratories well equipped?
- Will I be expected to pay lab fees?
- Does the department have its own library or specialist material?
- Is free study time available? (and how much?)

New types of courses

The range of courses on offer in universities has widened significantly over the last few years. In part, this is because the pioneers and providers of these programmes were today's new universities. These courses include:

- BTEC and ScotVec Higher National Certificate or Diploma, General National Vocational Qualifications
- Professional studies, for example Institute of Chartered Secretaries & Adminstrators
- Special studies, such as Certificate in Industrial Relations & Trades Union Studies

Credits, transfers and exemptions For many, these are as valuable an educational experience as a conventional degree. Some also prize them as a route into a degree course. Some offer credits towards the final degree being followed. This means that a course or its equivalent which is part of a degree programme does not need to be taken again. The issue of credit accumulation and transfer has emerged as an increasingly important feature of university education in the UK. It means that a course credit obtained at one university (or elsewhere) can be transferred to a programme at another.

Credit Accumulation and Transfer Scheme (CATS) works by universities agreeing to recognise studies successfully completed elsewhere as equivalent to those undertaken at their university. A student who is forced to move will, therefore, be able to graduate. More and more companies are taking advantage of this type of scheme to link their in-company courses to university programmes by establishing a course equivalence. The qualifications of some professional bodies are being treated in much the same way. It also means that students who are obliged to break off their studies can return later with a minimum degree of disruption.

Modules The entire process of change toward credit accumulation and transfer is being made easier by the increased modularisation of degree courses: the breaking-down of courses into relatively free-standing units or modules. These can then be combined in ways which give far greater freedom and flexibility to institutions in course design and to students in programme choice. It is based on the system used extensively in the USA.

Typically, new students are expected to identify their main area of study, English, say. In the first three terms, they will be expected to complete a major in English by completing three modules: English 1, English 2 and English 3. This is a 'major'. They might also be required to complete an associated subsidiary of two or more linked courses and several electives or minors.

Some institutions have experimented with a virtual free choice in course combinations, the so-called supermarket system. Most, however, are stricter and insist on more tightly defined structures to courses. For example, you can't take English 3 until English 2 has been successfully completed.

Semesters The move to modules is closely associated with the re-organisation of the academic year at many universities into semesters. In some, this is largely a cosmetic change. Others have followed the example of pioneers such as the University of Stirling and introduced sweeping changes. At Stirling, for example, there are two 15-week semesters instead of the traditional three terms. The academic year starts in late August with the first semester, which lasts until Christmas. The second semester then starts in mid-February and goes straight through until June.

Distance, open and flexible learning The Open University was a pioneer of many of the above changes. It is, however, best known for its development of distance and open learning for degrees. This means that students do not follow their studies within the physical confines of the institution. They often work at a distance, supported by a system of course materials, local tuition and various forms of assessment and counselling. Many other institutions have introduced distance learning into their portfolios.

Flexible learning has also grown in importance. Flexible learning programmes are designed around the needs and circumstances of particular groups of students. In one form, a consortium of companies works with a university to develop a range of courses for their employees. In some cases, Ford for example, there is no need or expectation that this will lead to a formal qualification. In other cases, such as the flexible learning courses in information technology, a new degree programme may be developed.

Degree courses

These can usefully be classified into the following broad categories:

- Medicine
- Biological and physical sciences
- Engineering and technology
- Social studies

- Business and professional studies
- Humanities and languages
- Education
- Combined subjects

The faculties, schools and other internal structures of many universities mirror these broad categories. This generally means that it is easier to change degree programme or course within these categories than between them. Frequently, there are more combined degrees within these subgroups than between them.
The courses on offer include:

Medicine and related subjects Anatomy, Cellular Pathology, Chiropody, Dentistry, Forensic Science, Health Studies, Immunology, Medicine, Medicinal Chemistry, Medical Laboratory Science, Nursing, Opthalmic Optics, Pathology, Pharmacology, Pharmacy, Physiology, Physiotherapy, Speech Science, Speech Therapy, Toxicology, Veterinary Studies, Virology

Biological and physical sciences Agricultural Bacteriology, Agricultural Botany, Agricultural Chemistry, Agriculture, Agronomy, Aquaculture, Animal Science, Astronomy, Astrophysics, Bacteriology, Biochemistry, Biology, Biophysics, Biosocial Science, Botany, Cell Biology, Chemical Physics, Chemistry, Cognitive Science, Computer Science, Cosmetic Science, Dietetics, Earth Sciences, Ecology, Engineering Mathematics, Entomology, Equine Studies, Environmental Science, Fisheries Studies, Food Science, Forestry, Freshwater Biology, Forensic Science, Genetics, Geochemistry, Geology, Geophysics, Human Biology, Information Science, Life Sciences, Marine Biology, Materials Science, Mathematics, Microbiology, Mineralogy, Neurobiology, Neuroscience, Nuclear Science, Ornithology, Orthoptics, Parasitology, Pest Science, Physics, Planetary Physics, Plant Science, Psychology, Social Biology, Solid State Physics, Soil Science, Statistics, Topographical Science, Zoology

Engineering and technology Acoustic Engineering, Acoustics, Aerodynamics, Aeronautic Engineering, Agricultural Engineering, Aircraft Engineering, Air Transport Engineering, Aeronautics, Automotive Engineering, Avionics, Biochemical Engineering, Biomedical Electronics, Biotechnology, Brewing, Building and Construction, Building Studies, Building Surveying, Building Technology, Ceramics, Chemical Engineering, Civil Engineering, Communication Engineering, Computer Engineering, Computer Technology, Computing, Control Engineering, Crop Technology, Cybernetics, Data Processing, Digital Microelectronics, Electrical Engineering, Electromechanical Engineering, Electronic Engineering, Electronics, Energy Engineering, Energy Studies, Engineering, Environmental Engineering, Forestry, Fuel Science, Horticulture, Hydraulic Engineering,

Industrial Engineering, Information Technology, Instrumentation, Manufacturing Engineering, Marine Architecture, Marine Engineering, Maritime Studies, Materials Technolology, Mechanical Engineering, Media Production, Metallurgy, Meterology, Mineral Processing Technology, Music Technology, Microelectronics, Mining, Naval Architecture, Naval Engineering, Nautical Studies, Nuclear Technology, Oceanography, Offshore Engineering, Packaging Technology, Palaeontology, Petroleum Engineering, Pollution, Polymer Engineering, Production Engineering, Radiography, Seismology, Shipbuilding, Software Engineering, Solid State Electronics, Systems Analysis, Telecommunications Engineering, Textile Technology, Wood Technology, Water Resources

Social studies African Studies, Agricultural Economics, Akkadian, American Studies, Anthropology, Asian Studies, Behavioural Sciences, Communication Studies, Conservation Studies, Contemporary Studies, Cultural Studies, Demography, Development Studies, Econometrics, Economics, Economic History, Environmental Studies, Geography, Government, Human Communication, Human Sciences, Industrial Studies, Informatics, International Relations, Land Economics, Leisure Studies, Occupational Psychology, Peace Studies, Political Economy, Politics, Psychology, Religious Studies, Rural Environmental Studies, Social History, Social Psychology, Social Science, Social Statistics, Social Studies, Sociology, Sports Studies, Third World Studies, Transport Studies, Urban Studies, War Studies, Welfare Studies, Women's Studies

Business and professional studies Accountancy, Actuarial Studies, Administrative Studies, Advertising, Architecture, Banking, Business Administration, Business Economics, Business Management, Business Studies, Catering, Catering and Hotel Studies, Commerce, Consumer Studies, Decision Sciences, Ergonomics, Estate Management, Finance, Fisheries Management, Heritage Conservation, Home Economics, Housing Administration, Hotel and Catering Management, Information Studies, International Business, Journalism, Land Administration, Landscape Architecture, Landscape Studies, Law, Library Studies, Logistics, Management, Management Science, Marketing, Marketing Research, Nutrition, Occupational Therapy, Office Organisation, Operational Research, Organisational Behaviour, Organisational Studies, Personnel, Physical Education, Physiotherapy, Public Administration, Public Health, Public Relations, Publishing, Quality Control, Quantity Surveying, Recreational Studies, Retail Management, Social Adminstration, Social Work, Surveying, Tourism, Town and Country Planning, Urban Estate Management, Valuation, Wildlife Management, Youth and Community Work

Humanities, area studies and languages Aesthetics, American Studies, Amharic, Ancient History, Anglo-Saxon, Arabic, Area Studies, Archaelogy, Bantu, Bengali, Berber, Biblical Studies, Bulgarian, Burmese Studies, Byzantine Studies, Canadian Studies, Caribbean Studies, Catalan, Celtic Studies, Chinese, Classical Studies, Comparative Literature, Czech Studies, Danish, Divinity, Dutch, Egyptology, English, Ethics, European Studies, Film Studies, Film and Media Studies, Fine Arts, Finnish Studies, French, German, Greek (Ancient/Classical), Greek (Modern), Gujarati, Hebrew, Hellenic Studies, Hispanic Studies, Hindi, History, History of Art, History of Science, Humanities, Hungarian, Iberian Studies, Icelandic, Indian Studies, Indonesian Studies, Interpretation and Translation, Iranian Studies, Irish Studies, Islamic Studies, Italian, Japanese, Jewish Studies, Languages, Latin, Latin American Studies, Linguistics, Literature, Logic, Malay, Media Studies, Medieval Studies, Mediterranean Studies, Mesopotamia, Metaphysics, Middle East Studies, Modern Languages, Moral Philosophy, Music, Near East Studies, Norse, Norwegian, Oriental Studies, Philosophy, Phonetics, Polish, Portugese, Religious Studies, Renaissance Studies, Rumanian, Russian, Russian Studies, Sanskrit, Scandinavian Studies, Scottish Studies, Semitic Languages, Serbo-Croat, Slovak Studies, Slavonic Studies, Southeast Asian Studies, Spanish, Spanish Studies, Swahili, Swedish, Tamil, Thai Studies, Theology, Translation, Turkish, Urdu, Victorian Studies, Vietnamese Studies, Welsh Studies

Creative and performance studies Acting, Advertising Design, Animation, Architecture, Art and Design, Carpet Design, Ceramic Design, Community Arts, Crafts, Dance, Drama, Embroidery, Fashion, Footwear Design, Furniture Design, Glass Design, Graphics, Graphic Design, Illustration, Interior Design, Jewellery, Painting, Performance Arts, Photography, Printing and Typography, Printmaking, Product Design, Sculpture, Silversmithing, Stage Management, Technical Graphics, Textiles, Television, Theatre Design, Three Dimensional Design, Typography, Visual Communication

Education Education, Teaching

Combined subjects Among the most popular current combinations are: Business/Management/Professional Subjects and Social Studies; Business/Management/Social Studies and the Humanities or Languages; Business/Management/Social Studies and the Physical or Biological Sciences; Languages and the Humanities; Studies allied to Medicine with the Physical or Biological Sciences.

Which course?

Your choice from the bewildering variety of courses will largely be determined by the interaction of four different pressures. In brief, they are:

1. **Opportunity** Mix ambition with realism to eliminate those subjects you cannot follow. If in doubt, talk to your career or advisory staff.
2. **School studies** Recognise your strengths and weaknesses. Use this self-assessment to guide your choice.
3. **Career aspirations** Think long and hard about the type of career you hope to follow. Ask parents, friends and careers staff about the links between courses and the career you hope to have.
4. **Personal/life interest** Build interest, enjoyment and stimulation into your course. Taking a degree is rarely plain sailing and you will need self-motivation and commitment to get through your studies.

Opportunity In the UK, applications for courses generally exceed the number of places available. Choice is therefore immediately restricted by your realistic chances of getting an offer and meeting its requirements. The eight universities to which you can apply rapidly change from being too many choices to too few – especially if options are used up in unrealistic choices. The first step in the selection process is to eliminate those options for which you either do not have or are unlikely to obtain the entry requirements.

Many courses, for example economics, require A-level or Higher maths or a minimum grade at GCSE, O-level or HNC. Others demand A-levels or Highers in a related, cognate subject: for example, English for American studies, biology for medicine, and Greek for archaeology. There are subjects, too, that you will be able to take at university only if you have studied them for A-level or Highers.

These requirements may be waived for mature students, especially those entering through an access course. Other, directly relevant, experiences, especially work experience, may also be taken into account when you apply.

School studies There continues to be a strong link between what you study at school and what you study at university. But while an aptitude or liking for a particular subject at school can often be continued successfully at university, it is important to recognise that the nature of a subject and your response to it can change significantly between school and university. It may be rare to find someone who disliked a subject at school but enjoyed it at university, but the reverse is all too common.

Career aspirations These play an important role in the choice of university degree for many entrants. There are three important aspects of this issue to bear in mind in selecting a course:

1. Your views, attitudes and aspirations are very likely to change as you follow your studies. There are risks in making too firm a choice too early.
2. Examine the reality of the course and its genuine link with the career in question. Names can be deceptive, especially in fashionable areas. Environmental science courses, for example, often pay far more attention to geology and soil science than to Friends of the Earth.
3. The dynamics of the graduate job market have become increasingly volatile. A degree might get you an interview but getting the job probably depends on a host of other factors.

Personal/life interest Because most subjects offered at university are not part of the school curriculum, the scope for extending your interests and your personal development at university is immense. So don't limit your choice of subject to what you already know. Be imaginative – but be realistic, too.

To take an example at random, psychology provides new and exiting views of human behaviour. It is a powerful and well-structured body of knowledge and can lead to a wide range of career opportunities. Furthermore, it is a subject that requires careful attention to detail if it is to be most rewarding. Much of this detail may only be accessible through painstaking laboratory work. Sometimes the analysis of nervous systems requires dissection and other skills.

A sound choice depends on a proper understanding of:

● the subject
● the differences between courses at various institutions
● the style, strength and character of the departments offering the programme

Staying with the example of psychology, the experience offered by a department with a dominant commitment to research and a specialist interest in primatology will be different to that provided by a teaching-oriented unit with a major pre-occupation with child psychology.

The facilities on offer vary considerably between institutions. Resource shortages have hit laboratory subjects especially hard with the traditional notion of the well-founded laboratory under particular threat.

Other sources of information
Which Subject? Which Career?, edited by Jamieson, A. CRAC Publications, Cambridge
How to Choose Your Degree Course, Heap, B. Trotman & Co., Richmond
The Student Book 1994, Boehm, K. and Lees-Spalding, J. Macmillan.

4 STUDYING ABROAD

University education has always been international. In the Middle Ages, the travelling scholar and his students moved from country to country to pursue their work. In the 17th, 18th and 19th centuries European academics moved between countries with a greater ease than virtually anyone else. The second half of the 20th century has seen the process accelerate. It is common for university staff to spend long periods working in institutions outside their home country with either substantive appointments or on sabbaticals. Students, too, increasingly seek the chance to spend part of their studies in a foreign university.

This pattern is especially well established in North America. Most US and Canadian universities have 'study abroad' programmes which enable their students to follow courses at an overseas institution and gain credits towards their degree. There are three basic approaches:

1. Study for a time at another university, gaining credits from completing its courses
2. Study at university-owned facilities in Europe, Asia, etc.
3. Follow courses organised by the university in a foreign country and largely run by the university's own staff

The opportunities created by the first of these methods has stimulated British universities to establish extensive exchange programmes with collaborating institutions in North America and Europe. Many of these are well established and popular. In recent years some universities have extended these schemes to include exchanges with universities in other parts of the world, especially in Asia and Australia.

How do I set about going on one of these programmes?

Not all universities offer exchange programmes. Where they operate, they might be linked to specific departments, schools or faculties. Anyone keen to undertake an exchange must choose an institution offering such a programme. You should establish the terms and conditions – in advance. Most of the programmes are highly competitive. They may, for example, be restricted to students with a minimum average grade. Some host universities impose their own conditions, for example they may restrict their exchanges to UK students.

The European Community sees student mobility and exchanges as an important element in building a 'community of learning' and a greater sense among students of European citizenship. This view influenced the creation of the EC action programme, Erasmus, or EuRopean Community Action Scheme for the Mobility of University Students. The scheme is named after the Swiss-born 16th-century humanist and philosopher Desiderius Erasmus who spent his working life as a professor in universities in the Netherlands, France, England, Italy, and Switzerland. Erasmus helps students to spend at least three months at a university (or equivalent) in another EC country. The initial success of the programme has since encouraged universities to develop fully integrated common courses involving staff and students from several EC countries. A key feature of the Erasmus programme is the building up of a European system of credit transfer (ECTS). Initially, automatic credit transfer is being introduced in five subjects: mechanical engineering, chemistry, medicine, business studies and history.

Outside North America and Europe student exchanges and related programmes are far more patchy. Institutions such as London University's School of Oriental and African Studies that have direct links with other countries are the exception rather than the rule. The growing interest in Japan among UK academics has prompted some institutions to build up exchange and/or visits programmes. As ever, the main constraint on these and other international exchanges tends to be money.

The costs of these programmes vary a great deal. Formal exchanges with US universities will probably cost students next to nothing. The institutions concerned meet the bills, albeit only within strict guidelines. Under the Erasmus programme specific grants are provided to meet such expenses as language preparation, cost-of-living differentials and travel. Elsewhere, the pattern tends to be determined by local circumstances.

Always consult fully with the university's international links or liaison staff – they are often attached to the registrar's department – and the relevant departmental or faculty staff. They are in the best position to advise on what is available and the likely effect on you and your prospects. The best route into study overseas lies through programmes linked to UK universities. The links already exist and there is a wealth of institutional support if things go wrong.

You may see advertisements for the UK campus of American colleges. Although some of these are linked to institutions of high standing, you should take a great deal of care in dealing with them. Their links with their parent institutions should be scrutinised closely to ensure full and proper accreditation. Without this, it is very hard to win any recognition for the qualifications provided.

Can I opt to go to university overseas?

In theory, the answer is yes. In practice, it is very difficult without either links with the country/university in question or some compelling reason such as the fact that no British university offers the programme you want to study.

That said, studying at a university in Europe has become progressively easier with the introduction of the Single European Market in January 1993. Some barriers are already being dismantled, especially those linked to recognition of qualifications. Others, however, will take much longer to change, especially those to do with language, degree structure and student support. In North America, some of these barriers do not exist but others, notably cost, can be equally daunting. In 1992, the average cost of attending one of the top 10 US universities was over $50,000 pa, while the average across the top 100 US universities was over $20,000 pa.

The top 20 US universities

1 Harvard	7 Duke	14 Northwestern
2 Yale	8 Dartmouth College	15 Rice
3 Stanford	9 Columbia	16 University of
4 = Princeton	10 Chicago	California at Berkeley
4 = California Institute	11 Johns Hopkins	17 Brown
of Technology	12 Cornell	18 Washington
6 Massachusetts	13 University of	19 = Vanderbilt
Institute of	Pennsylvania	19 = Georgetown
Technology		

Source: US News 'America's Best Colleges' 1992

The top 20 European universities

1 Oxford	8 Bologna	15 King's College
2 Cambridge	9 Paris	London
3 Paris	10 London	16 Aix-Marseille
4 Leuven	11 Strasbourg	17 = Florence
5 Leiden	12 = Fribourg	17 = Frankfurt
6 Heidelberg	12 = LSE	20 = Kent
7 Munich	14 Tubingen	20 = Salamanca

Source: Les 100 Meilleures Universities en Europe, Libération 1989

If you are coming to Britain

ECCTIS 2000 is a database of information on the vast majority of certificated courses and programmes on offer in the UK and Ireland. Access to the ECCTIS 2000 can be obtained through British Council offices and libraries. For the nearest access point write to ECCTIS, Fulton House, Jessup Avenue, Cheltenham, Gloucestershire GL50 3SH.

Other sources of information

Information on Erasmus can be obtained from your university or from:
The Erasmus Bureau, rue Montoyer 70, B-1040 Bruxelles, Belgium or, for grant information:
UK Erasmus Students Grants Council, The University, Canterbury, CT2 7PD

General information on higher education in Europe, North America and elsewhere:

Higher Education in the European Community, Mohr, B, and Liebig I. Kogan Page, London

How to Study Abroad, Tinsley, T. How to Books, Plymouth

America's Best Colleges, US News and World Report, Washington DC, USA

Barron's Guide to US Universities and Colleges (annual)

Guide to American Colleges and Universities, ARCO, Prentice Hall, New York (annual)

How to Apply to American Colleges and Universities, Brennan, M and Briggs, S. VGM Career Horizons, Illinois, USA.

The International Student's Guide to the American University, National Student Textbook Co. Illinois, USA

A Guide to the Admission of Foreign Student, National Association for Foreign Student Affairs. Washington DC, USA

5 APPLYING TO UNIVERSITY

With the merger of polytechnics and universities in 1992, the application process for all British universities for the 1994–95 academic year onward has changed significantly. In place of the two former systems, one for universities, the other for polytechnics, handled respectively by UCCA (the Universities Central Council on Admissions) and PCAS (the Polytechnics Central Admissions System), there is now one – UCAS (Universities and Colleges Admissions Service). Instead of being asked to shortlist five choices by UCCA and four by PCAS, applicants are required to shortlist eight courses in any of the country's 96 universities.

Finding out
The first step is to get a copy of the UCAS Handbook. All schools, colleges and libraries will have one. They are also available direct from UCAS, PO Box 28, Cheltenham, Gloucestershire GL50 3SA.

Other valuable sources of information include:

- *University and College Entrance 1994*, available from the Association of Commonwealth Universities, Sheed and Ward, 2 Creechurch Lane, London EC3A 5AQ
- *The Scottish Universities Entrance Guide*, available from the Scottish Universities Council on Entrance, 12 The Links, St Andrews, Fife KY16 9JB
- The prospectuses of those universities you are interested in

Use them to draw up your shortlist of universities, programmes and courses. It is important to recognise that to gain entry you will need to:

- Meet the general requirements of the university
- Satisfy the specific demands of the course you chose
- Follow the correct admissions procedures

These are spelt out in the prospectuses of all universities.

The application process for 1994
The formal application process begins slightly more than one year before you want to go to university. In other words, if you're hoping to go to university in 1994, you need to apply from the beginning of September

1993. On the other hand, you should begin doing your homework a few months earlier. This is the timetable.

- **Between May and September 1993:** Find out all you can about the universities and courses you are interested in attending. Complete the selection processes described in the earlier chapters.
- **Between September 1 and October 15:** If you are hoping to go to Oxford or Cambridge, complete and submit your application.
- **Between September 1 and December 15:** Applicants for all other universities must complete and submit their applications.

There is no point submitting your application before September 1. All early applications will be held over until that date. Equally, there is no point delaying your application – a prompt application can work in your favour by allowing you more choice. Aim to have your application in by late October/early November. If for whatever reason you miss the December 15 deadline UCAS will still process your application but universities have complete discretion over whether to take them.

  Similarly, if you are applying for a grant, do so as early as possible. For most degree courses you will get a mandatory award from your local authority or from the Scottish Education Department (2 South Charlotte St., Edinburgh EH2 4AP). If you are not eligible for a mandatory award – because of the course you are following or because you have already had a grant – you may get a discretionary award. These are available from the same sources.

The next steps are:

- **From mid-September:** Applicants receive acknowledgements from UCAS that their applications have been received and are given a personal application number.
- **Late September and early October:** Early applicants to Cambridge who have left school may be invited for interview.
- **From mid-October:** universities and colleges review applications, send out invitations for interview or advisory visits and inform UCAS of their decisions.
- **From November:** UCAS informs candidates of the offers made to them – if any.

The application form

The application form lies at the heart of the entire process. For some, it is their only point of contact with the admissions tutor or selection staff at the universities of their choice. Making a mess of this can mean making a mess of the entire application. Put yourself in the shoes of the admissions staff. They may have to go through hundreds, even thousands, of application forms during a year. Make the application easy to read and understand by printing clearly in black ink.

The main categories of information are:

- **Name and address** Normally straightforward, but make sure you let UCAS and the university know – immediately – any change in address. Don't bank on the Post Office forwarding letters.
- **Choice of course** This, too, should be straightforward if you have followed the advice given in chapter 3, Choosing A Course. But before you complete this part of the form, take the opportunity to review your choices – and think again about the offers you are likely to receive and your chances of meeting their conditions. Be absolutely sure you know what you want to put on the form before you fill it in. Make a rough copy first. Then fill in the form.
- **Examinations you have passed** Honesty is the best policy here.
- **Examinations to be taken** Put everything down, even if it does not seem directly relevant.
- **Education and any employment** Be comprehensive but avoid minor details.
- **Further information** This can be the most important section. An interesting and informative set of comments can get the admissions officer on your side. But be wary of making yourself a hostage to fortune. In other words, be sensible. If you get asked to an interview, it's quite likely that you will be asked about the comments you have made in this section.

Check your form very carefully on completion. Make sure you have made clear if you want deferred entry. Ask someone you trust – a parent(?) – to look at it. Sign and date it. Hand it, with your fee and acknowledgement card, to your educational referee – in plenty of time.

The academic reference is crucial. Make sure that he/she knows why you are interested in the course or programme you have chosen. Encourage them to bring out your positive features, especially when the subject is new to you. Though you will rarely be in a position to influence directly what your academic referee puts on the form, avoid anyone you think may undermine your application with a casual comment. As admissions tutors in business studies, for example, will confirm, comments such as 'Jean is not very good academically – so she should do well in business studies' will not be relished.

Mature Students

Typically, these are defined as 21 years of age or older (23 in some cases). For those with conventional admissions qualifications, applications follow broadly the same route as for all other students. Candidates without these are still encouraged – some universities operate targets for the numbers or proportion of mature students. There is often a 'non-standard entry' route.

The University of Hertfordshire's prospectus, for example, comments

'Although [mature students] may not have standard entry requirements, we are happy to discuss and, whenever possible, accept alternative qualifications or work experience. We aim to give special support to mature students in several areas. For example, we run pre-entry workshops for those who need extra confidence and help in coping with a return to study.' These services are often backed by adult guidance services offered by the local authority or the local TEC (Training and Enterprise Council).

Overseas Students

The best source of advice in most cases is the British Council. Virtually all universities have appointed overseas student officers with specific responsibility to help you. You should, however, note that:

- You will probably need to provide evidence of the ability to speak and read good English. This can be through prior certification from an accredited agency or by way of a pre-entry language course offer by the university of your choice.
- UK universities are not well supplied with family accommodation or facilities.
- You may need to meet strict requirements for passports, visa, medical insurance and certification and probably provide evidence of financial support.

Some universities are better than others at providing hardship or other support for overseas students. Use your contacts, family or friends to find out about the institution before you apply. Don't turn up hoping things will easily and quickly fall into place if you have not made adequate preparations. All UK universities can be contacted by fax or telex. Use these whenever possible.

Entry requirements

The most common general requirements are for GCSE or Scottish O grade passes in one or more of English, maths, a modern language or a science. Some universities specify a minimum grade, for instance C or above in GCSE.

Some institutions reserve the right to waive these. The University of Westminster, for example, notes only that, 'A GCSE pass or its equivalent in English language and mathematics are required for entry to most of the first degree or diploma courses'. Elsewhere, universities have decided to dispense with general entry requirements. Brunel University prospectus comments that 'there are no general requirements beyond the minimum course requirements stated in the details of individual courses'.

It is, however, increasingly common to see standard minimum entry requirements for a first degree course being spelt out in the type of detail given by Nottingham Trent University as:

a. Passes in two subjects at GCE A-level with passes in three other subjects at GCSE or GCE O-level. You should note that General Studies is not always acceptable as an A-level pass
b. Passes in three subjects at GCE A-level with passes in one other subject at GCSE or GCE O-level
c. A Scottish Certificate of Education with five passes, of which three are at Higher grade
d. A Scottish Certificate of Education with passes in four subjects, all at Higher grade
e. A Leaving Certificate of the Department of Education, Republic of Ireland, with grade C or better in five approved subjects, including English, at Higher level (obtained at one sitting)
f. An Ordinary National Certificate or Diploma (ONC/OND) at a good standard
g. Business and Technical Council (BTEC) National Certificate or Diploma at Level III with appropriate levels of passes
h. Awards of the Scottish Vocational Education Council (SCOTVEC) with appropriate levels of passes
i. International Baccalaureate
j. European Baccalaureate

Normally, universities go on to point out that 'it is important to understand that possession of the minimum requirements does not, in itself, guarantee admission to the university'.

For BTEC HND courses you are likely to need some combination of:

● An appropriate BTEC National Certificate or Diploma
● An Ordinary National Certificate (ONC) or Ordinary National Diploma (OND)
● Passes at GCE A-level and GCSE or GCE O-Grades in appropriate subjects

How do UK universities deal with other qualifications?

The simple rule is, if in doubt ask – in advance. Universities are increasingly willing to offer places on the basis of US Scholastic Aptitude Tests (SATs), Achievement and Advanced Placement Tests (APTs) and other internationally recognised entry qualifications.

The exceptions Some institutions impose local conditions on entry. The most prominent are Cambridge, Oxford and some Scottish universities.

Cambridge requires applications to be submitted significantly earlier than other universities. The UCAS form and Preliminary Application Form (PAF) must be submitted by October 15 1993 for 1994 entry, to UCAS in Cheltenham and to Cambridge respectively. Interviews then take place in September, for those who have both left school and applied early, and in December for the majority. At the end of October, the first group will probably receive either a firm offer, a rejection or a notice of a deferral of decision to January. Those interviewed in December will be told in January whether they have been made a conditional offer or have been turned down. Some Cambridge colleges link conditional offers based on school-leaving examinations with grade requirements for either S-level papers or the Sixth Term Examination Papers.

Oxford organises its admissions on a college not a departmental basis. Candidates can either put forward an open application, that is without naming specific colleges, or list up to three colleges of their choice. The university has two entry routes:

1. Mode E, for pre-A-level candidates
2. Mode N, for post-A-level candidates

Mode E includes a written examination but offers are not conditional on any A-level, Higher or other examination results other than the university's matriculation requirements, which call for two A-level passes at grade E or better. For pre-A-level candidates, Mode N does not include a written examination but is based on a conditional offer. Post-A-level offers are based upon grades already achieved and are unconditional. All applications must be submitted by 15 October 1993 for October 1994 entry.

Scottish Universities are part of the UCAS system but have a number of distinct features, notably:

- The four-year degree structure. Some Scottish universities offer exemptions from the first year for candidates with A-levels or relevant technical qualifications.
- A more open degree structure. This is true especially in the first, foundation year where first-year classes are often open to students with a wide range of initial interests. Resource shortages in recent years have forced some institutions to restrict admission to the more popular subjects to those in closely related areas, usually in the same faculty.
- As far as possible, Scottish universities try to establish the same offer or 'going-rate' for the entire faculty or – in the case of Stirling University – the university. Again, this type of open and flexible approach is being adversely affected by resource shortages.
- Interviews are not normally required for entry, though several Scottish

universities offer 'advisory interviews'. These are designed to give a potential entrant an insight into the university and its way of life.

Meeting entry requirements

The next necessity is to meet the requirements for the courses on offer. These vary enormously between university and course. Universities such as Cambridge, Oxford, LSE, Bristol, Bath, Manchester and Imperial College can ask for very high A-level entry requirements. Some other universities eschew this approach and put a far greater emphasis on local links, specific skills or needs. Glasgow and Strathclyde, for example, have a tradition of drawing a high proportion of students from the west of Scotland. Aston and Sussex look for specific skill mixes in their students. The University of Central England in Birmingham and the University of East London have pioneered affirmative action programmes to encourage applications from a wide range of social classes and ethnic groups.

Entry requirements for courses vary between institutions and across departments in the same university. Admission standards are one of the few ways institutions can regulate entry and balance their portfolio of activities. Typically, the department, faculty or university will set its admissions standards to ensure that it gets the number of new entrants to the programme that it needs to ensure a proper balance of activities. There is always an element of risk in this. A department with requirements that are too restrictive may find that it has too few new students. On the other hand, too relaxed an approach can lead to a flood of students. There is a tendency to err on the side of caution – making relatively restrictive offers and, if necessary, going into 'clearing' to make up any shortfall. Universities are reluctant to increase 'offer' levels over the year. Resource shortages are making institutions acutely aware of the risks they run if departments make offers that are too low and they are obliged to admit students without having adequate finance to run courses properly.

Universities' income for students consists of two basic elements: a fee per student, normally paid by the local authority; and a recurrent grant from the Funding Councils. The fee will be paid almost regardless of student numbers, but to obtain the recurrent grant universities have to adhere to strictly defined quotas. In the past, it was possible to compensate for over-shooting in one area with short-falls elsewhere. This is no longer acceptable and universities are being penalised if their numbers are significantly out.

Interviews

These take two forms: 1) advisory interviews; 2) selection interviews. Advisory interviews give candidates a chance to see the university and get a feel for its distinct features. Selection interviews give the university information about you, so they can decide what, if any, offer to make.

The ground-rules are fairly straightforward. Anyone invited for interview should recognise that they cost the university time and money. They take place because the institution and the interviewers have decided that they matter and are worth the effort. Your approach should mirror this and be based on the five Ps.

- **Participate** If you are invited, go
- **Preparation** Make clear that you have chosen the university and course for positive reasons
- **Practice** Get a teacher, friend or family member to take you through a mock interview
- **Presentation** Play safe: dress smartly. You can make personal statements about appearance once you have been accepted
- **Punctuality** Most interviews are tightly scheduled. Being late without a good reason will work against you. If you are going to be late because of unavoidable delays, telephone and let the university know

Offers

Offers usually take three forms:

1. An unconditional offer. This means that your existing qualifications are good enough to win you admission.
2. A conditional offer. You will be given a place if you meet certain specified conditions, generally particular grades at A-level.
3. A rejection. The university is not willing to admit you.

After receiving offers, candidates must respond to UCAS and make clear whether they: 1) accept the offer; 2) accept the offer and one other as insurance, ie a university that will take you on the basis of significantly lower grades; 3) reject the offer.

There is no point replying to UCAS until all your offers are in: you gain nothing and risk missing out on an opportunity. Once you have heard from all the universities to which you applied, UCAS will anyway send you a further statement outlining all their decisions. You should reply to this final statement within 14 days, though extensions may be granted if you are attending open days at any of the universities or simply hoping to visit them. Either way, however, you must respond to UCAS by May 15. Failure to inform UCAS of which offers you want to accept, either firmly or as insurance, is taken as a rejection by you. UCAS will then inform the universities of this rejection on your behalf. Blank spaces on your form are also taken as rejections. Note that you cannot change your mind once you have accepted an offer. UCAS is adamant on this point.

What will the offer look like?

As mentioned above, offers are usually unconditional or conditional. In the former case, you have already been accepted. In the latter case, you will be required to achieve either certain grades at A-level, AS-level or Highers or a specified number of points in these exams.

A grade-based offer may be BBC, for example. In some cases, you will have to achieve these grades in specified subjects, for instance a B in maths, a B in chemistry and a C in physics. In others, the university will say only that you must get these grades without specifying in which subjects.

A points-based offer is similar and works by awarding points for particular grades on the following basis:

A-levels		AS-levels	
Grade	Points	Grade	Points
A	10	A	5
B	8	B	4
C	6	C	3
D	4	D	2
E	2	E	1

Note that the Scottish system is very different. These figures should be used only as the roughest guide.

When my results come out what should I do?

There are several golden rules.

- Be at home. You may need to take action or make decisions quickly. This is the time when Murphy's First Law – if anything can go wrong, it will – works with a vengeance.
- If in doubt – ask. Universities are under a lot of pressure at this time of the year but they are normally willing to help if possible. The people who cannot be helped are those who do not ask.
- Don't fret – act. If you have met the offer you should hear from the university within three or four days. If you don't, telephone the admissions tutor to confirm arrangements.

If I do better than expected what should I do?

Some applicants receive rejections from all the universities they applied to but then get higher grades than expected. They should contact UCAS about vacancies. At the same time get access to one of the electronic databases: ECCTIS, Prestel or Campus 2000. They are constantly updated. Check with the media, especially those that list vacancies. Get in touch with the universities you are interested in. Persistence and flexibility pay off at this stage.

If I do worse than expected what should I do?

Some candidates fall short by one or two points. Most universities think long and hard about whether to take them. As a first step, telephone the university to make sure they know about you. This is especially worth doing if there are particular reasons to explain your exam results, for example illness. If you do telephone, a follow-up letter making the same points is always advisable.

Assuming you have fallen short of the offer you most wanted but have met the conditions of your insurance offer and that, after getting in touch with them, your first-choice university isn't going to take you, this is the moment to take up your insurance offer. If you have also fallen short of your insurance offer by three or more points, however, don't despair. Though you will almost certainly receive a rejection letter from your second-choice university, there are still options open to you.

The most promising route is through 'clearing', when UCAS attempts to match students in your position with surplus places at other universities. UCAS will automatically send a Clearing Entry Form to you; it comes with full instructions. At the same time, talk to your school. It may well be able to help. And follow up any leads for vacancies such as those in the papers and on electronic databases.

Don't be afraid to contact universities direct. They are as keen to fill their places as you are to go to university. Universities adjust their numbers as late as the second week of term as students do not turn up or change their mind.

If you are determined to find a place, you almost certainly will.

Other sources of information

Besides those listed earlier try:

CRAC Degree Courses Guide, Hobsons Press, Cambridge

Getting into Oxford and Cambridge, Heap, B. Trotman & Co., Richmond

Getting into University, Heap, B and Lamely, S. Trotman & Co., Richmond

How to Complete Your UCCA Form, Higgins, T and Lamely, S. Trotman & Co., Richmond

Opportunities in Higher Education for Mature Students, CNAA, London

Grants to Students, Department for Education, London

Access to Higher Education Courses Directory, ECCTIS, Fulton House, Jessop Avenue, Cheltenham, Glos GL50 3SH

The British Council has a range of guides to courses in the UK.

6 STUDENT LIFE: THE BASICS

Money

This looms large from the start. If you have followed the timetable for applications spelled out in Chapter 5 you will already have been in touch with your local authority or the Scottish Education Department about your grant. No-one should be under the illusion that this is expected to see a normal, healthy person through an academic year, a fact the government acknowledged in setting up the student loans scheme (see page 47).

Grants have two components: fees and maintenance.

Fees These are paid to the university to meet the costs of your course. Everyone pays them, but in most cases the costs are met by the local authority or the Scottish Education Department. This is true for all full-time students following courses which attract mandatory awards. In some cases, students following courses which attract discretionary awards will get their fees paid but this is increasingly rare.

You will not get your fees paid if you have already had fees in the past for a full-time course or are an overseas student. In these cases, you should check what fees you will be expected to pay very carefully.

There is some talk of 'top-up' fees, a charge that students will have to pay themselves. Should these be introduced, they are unlikely to affect students already at university.

Maintenance All students who are ordinarily resident in the UK (and have been for three years) and who are taking a designated course are eligible for a mandatory maintenance grant.

Current rates (frozen since 1990–91) are:

- £1,795 for those living at home
- £2,265 for those studying outside London
- £2,845 for those studying in London

As it is assumed that your parents will contribute toward the cost of your university education, education authorities deduct from your grant an amount equivalent to what they assume your parents' contribution will be. The deduction is automatic and is made regardless of whether your parents contribute. The larger your parents' income, the larger the deduction. But even if your parents are millionaires, you should still get them to fill in the form as education authorities invariably err on the side of caution in awarding grants. If you don't fill in the form, you won't get a grant, however deserving.

Note that parents are not expected to make a contribution to your maintenance if your are: 1) over 25; 2) have been supporting yourself for three years or more; 3) have been married for two years or more.

Note also that those over 26 who are entitled to a mandatory award will receive larger sums than those listed above. These will be based on your earnings over the previous three years.

For those on discretionary awards, the grant, too, is discretionary.

Loans

The government has set up the Student Loans Company to fill the gap between the declining value of grants and the real costs facing students. All UK students on designated courses lasting at least one year can apply for loans at any time during the academic year. The maximum you will receive is the difference between what you actually received as your grant and what you would have received had grants not been frozen in 1990. Interest is charged at a rate broadly that of inflation. For more information contact the Student Loans Company, Student Helpline on 0345 300900.

Balancing the books

The odds are that whatever grant you end up with, money will be tight. Money management is an important skill. At its simplest, it means maximising income and minimising expenditure. How can you make your money go farther?

Increasing income ● **Savings** – try to build up your savings in the months before starting university, for instance summer earnings, money from relatives wanting to congratulate you on your exam successes (no-one minds if you ask for money: everyone understands how tight you are going to find life once at university)
● **Your grant** – don't forget to apply for it!
● **Scholarships and sponsorships** – chase these up by checking charities and, especially, small local funds or trusts operated by firms with which there are family connections. Check courses for the availability of company sponsorships or specialist scholarships, for instance sports scholarships.
● **Interest** – put all the money you can into bank, building society and other accounts that pay interest.
● **Parental contribution** – negotiate the best way for your parents to pay this.
● **Part-time work** – check at the university first to see what work is available that will have minimum effect on your studies, for example in the library or as a staff researcher.

● **Vacation earnings** – plan this holiday work as early as possible to get the best jobs.

● **Sales** – most people end up selling their second-hand text books, records, etc. But don't forget that it's always a buyers' market when you want to sell.

Expenditure ● Accommodation – rent, light, heat, breakages and any other costs: it will always cost more than you imagine.

● **Taxes** – council or other taxes

● **Food** – probably best to split into the need-to-have and the nice-to-have. Don't try to save on necessities as it can affect your health and ability to study. Use trips home to stock-up. Find the cheapest places locally to buy the things you need.

● **Drink** – same rules as food. Finding cheap sources pays.

● **Cigarettes** – give them up!

● **Daily travel** – walk or get a bike. Auctions are often the best bet, especially in cities. Share costs whenever possible: if you travel by car, take passengers and ask for a contribution.

● **Long-distance travel** – use long-haul buses or overnight trains.

● **Books** – keep to a minimum, share with friends and buy second-hand. Ask students from earlier years which recommended books are worth buying.

● **Stationery** – you can often buy in bulk if you get together with friends.

● **Clothes** – shop around. Don't blow your grant in the first few weeks.

● **Leisure** – movies, memberships, etc. Check facilities run by the union. Elsewhere, always ask for a student discount.

● **Credit cards** – avoid like the plague unless you know you can pay the monthly bill without incurring the interest charges. If you want a TV, buy it second-hand.

Insurance
It is surprising just how much money you have invested in that CD and stack system, Walkman, camera, guitar, PC, Gameboy, bike, etc. You won't find out yourself until they go missing or are ruined. Insurance is a must if you want to have some peace of mind. Endsleigh Insurance Services offers a special Possessions Insurance for Students.

Accommodation
Accommodation is going to be one of your largest costs. It can vary from £50 a week in London, the Southeast and some other cities to £30 in the Northeast, Scotland and Northern Ireland. Furthermore, lighting, heating, water and other charges are often extra. No wonder halls of residence are so popular.

All universities offer some help in finding accommodation, especially for first-years. This varies from the guarantee of a place in a hall of residence to no more than assistance in finding accommodation in designated residences.

Start thinking about accommodation early on. It is the type of question that can be discussed at interviews, open days and advisory visits. If possible, have a look at the facilities on offer. As soon as you are clear which university you will be going to, take active steps to confirm your accommodation. This is especially important if you are entering late or through clearing. Persistence pays. Last-minute vacancies are common and it is surprising how often those who stick at it get what they want.

If you can't get a place in a hall of residence, it's even more important to start looking early. If you leave it late, the best places will have gone. It is a good idea to call into the university at the end of the previous term to check on student notice-boards for offers of accommodation. At the same time, if the university has an accommodation office, visit it. And don't be shy about putting notices up yourself, especially if you want to share or have a special need, say for family accommodation.

Once you have found somewhere, avoid deposits and other advance payments if at all possible. Somewhere better may turn up. The chances of a refund from anyone but the university are negligible.

Buying is an option for a tiny minority. If you are considering it, check the offers that some building societies are making to students.

Arriving, enrolling and registering

The first few days of your first year are a mixture of enjoyment, worry, terror, anticipation and annoyance in liberal doses. How you cope will influence the next few weeks at the very minimum, possibly the whole year and conceivably your entire university career. The golden rules are: don't be intimidated; and remember that almost everyone you meet will be enduring the same anxieties and making the same discoveries – even the staff.

- Find out where you will be living and eating as early as possible. It is good to have somewhere to escape to and relax in.
- Don't be afraid to strike up conversations, especially with fellow first-years.
- Keep an open mind. Try everything. Visit the Freshers Fair and attend the public lectures or briefing sessions.
- Don't worry if you get lost, go to the wrong building, lecture hall, etc. It happens to everyone.
- Remember the three As: ask, ask and ask.

Some of the best places to meet people are in the queues to register for courses or modules. These can seem interminable, especially for the most popular courses. If you have to register for each course separately, go to the one that is most important first.

Check your enrolment and registration instructions before you arrive.

Some institutions allow you to pre-register or indicate any restrictions. Check these off in advance and pre-register if possible. It is usually easier to withdraw from a popular course than to get on to one.

Bring half-a-dozen recent passport photos. You'll need them for IDs, library cards, student union membership card, registration forms, etc.

Health

You are as likely to get ill during your student life as at any time. Some ailments are more common in large populations of young people, others quite rare. It pays to plan in advance.

Register with the student health service or a local doctor as soon as possible after you arrive. There are some advantages in using the Student Health Service, especially its experience in dealing with the particular needs of students; most bear no resemblence to 'A Peculiar Practice'.

Sex

In any population of young and lively people, sex is bound to be a recurrent issue. Perhaps the best rule is that 'no' is always as good an answer as 'yes'.

Aids can be a concern. Everyone knows the precautions. Take them.

Fear and ignorance are the biggest barriers to the effective treatment of most other sexually transmitted diseases. No-one is cured by worrying or fretting. At the first signs, go to the student health service or the local Sexually Transmitted Diseases (STD) clinic. In most cases, the problems turn out to be minor and easily treated.

Other sources of information

NUS Information Sheets can be obtained from National Union of Students, 461 Holloway Rd., London N7 6JL, and from your local student union.
Money to Study, Family Welfare Association, Dalston, London E8 4AU.
Grants to Students, Department for Education, London.
Discretionary Awards Survey, National Union of Students, London.
Sponsorships, Careers and Occupational Information Centre TEED, Moorfoot, Sheffield S1 4PQ.
Directory of Summer Jobs in Britain, Vacation Work Publications, 9 Park End St., Oxford OX1 1HJ.
The Student Survival Guide, Cox, E. and Hodge, P. Trotman and Co., Richmond.
The Student Cookbook, Baker, J. Faber, London.

7 THE TIME OF YOUR LIFE?

University is going to present you with challenges that school will have done little to prepare you for. Virtually anyone who gets into university has the ability to cope successfully with the demands of the subject they are studying. Staffing levels and facilities are organised to provide the backing needed.

But though the freedom you will find can be exhilarating, it will demand discipline and work to bring the best from it and you. You will be expected to take the initiative and to think seriously for yourself. There will be new skills to learn and to refine in analysis, criticism and presentation. The key is self-management. As usual, a few simple rules go a long way.

Time management

Time-management skills are the most basic. Most people at university have similar physical and mental attributes. Some, however, seem to be able to get things done, produce assignments on time and go out and enjoy themselves while others are constantly under pressure and stress. The answer to this conundrum often lies in the way time is managed.

The choice is fairly simple. Introduce a few simple time-management skills and take control – or don't and hope for the best. The principles are straightforward.

- Keep interruptions to a minimum
- Organise your time into blocks
- Create space
- Organise your working environment so that you can find things easily
- Plan for contingencies – the book you need won't be in the library when you want it at the last minute
- Schedule activities
- Do the hard things first
- Avoid the temptation to rush from one crisis to the next in the hope that something will turn up.

Time is a resource like any other. You can use it profitably or waste it. We all have the same 24-hour day and seven-day week. The smart move is to get the way you use time under your control. Do a simple audit. It shows immediately where you may be going wrong. All you need is something like this:

Date .... Day ....

Time	Activity	Control	Notes
0800			
0830			
0900			
0930			
1000			
1030			
1100			
1130			
1200			

and so on

Do the audit regulary and on different days. It will rapidly show you what you are spending too much or too little time on.

Action lists

The second step is the creation of action lists. Itemise each task. This will soon give a picture of the scale and feasibility of your work programme. Again, for the best results, do it regularly. This will only work if you understand exactly what you are being asked to do: so always make sure you know what is expected of you. If you are working with others, be clear about who's doing what. Put in the completion date. This should be realistic and assume some need to spend time on final polishing.

Set priorities. Dintinguish between important and urgent tasks – and don't confuse them. The latter should always take priority. Absolute preference is given to important *and* urgent work.

Remember Murphy's Fourth Law: If there is a possibility of several things going wrong, the one that will cause the most damage will be the one to go wrong.

Faced with several tasks, scheduling events for the greatest effectiveness is essential. The first step involves the allocation of sufficient time for each piece of work. The sequence has a marked influence on performance. Often the hardest and most onerous work is put off until last. This is probably a mistake. It means that the most daunting job is undertaken when reserves of energy are at their lowest and fatigue is beginning to affect performance.

A disciplined approach to the work undertaken can be based on the mnenomic AID. Activities can be categorised as: Action; Information; Dump.

Stress

Time pressures and the accompanying sense of lack of control are major sources of stress. This is not necessarily a bad thing. Stress is a natural part of life. The human body has evolved to cope with certain levels of anxiety. The trick is to recognise that stress is a good servant but a terrible master. Use it to enhance performance but never let it get control.

Student life is closely linked with some of the most common causes of stress:

● Change
● Too much/too little time
● Poor physical conditions
● Ambiguity or confusion about roles and responsibilities
● Complex and changing personal relationships
● Insecurity
● Frustration
● Conflict, especially with family or close friends
● New or changing responsibilities

The effects of a failure to manage stress increase over time. These can include:

● Lack of concentration
● Memory failures
● Slower responses
● Aversion to planning
● Hypochondria
● Irritability
● Sense of powerlessness
● Absenteeism
● Insomnia
● Lack of energy

Recognition of the problem is the precondition for successful action. Some symptoms are easier to recognise in others than in ourselves. The more obvious early warnings are moodiness, an inability to concentrate and a lack of satisfaction or enjoyment in leisure pursuits.

Stress Management

This is built around three stages: 1) pre-stress schooling; 2) stress management; 3) post-stress adjustment.

Pre-stress schooling means avoiding stress. Learn to identify what causes stress in you and avoid these situations wherever possible. Learning to say 'no' is perhaps the most important lesson. Some students take on extra work that they can't manage because they feel undervalued and seek reassurance about their worth. The consequent sense that they have too much to do and too little time in which to do it is a potent source of stress. Frustration is another. Don't fight battles that can't be won.

Stress management takes many forms. Rest is probably the best cure: fatigue and stress are common partners. The other obvious cure is to do something completely different. Give yourself a break. Take the day off. Visit friends. Go to a museum. See a movie. Have lunch. Go shopping. The problems that have been worrying you will almost always seem easier to deal with if you can put some distance between yourself and them. There are risks in this approach, the main one being that you must be careful not to allow these diversions to get out of hand. Displacement activities – doing anything other than the task in hand and convincing yourself that it is as important – must be watched carefully. There comes a point when you must return to what you are really supposed to be doing. So a positive approach is essential. Self-discipline is vital. The more you put in, the more you get out.

'Comfort' eating should be avoided. It produces no lasting comfort and will in the end cause stress itself. Drink is even worse. Stress produces dehydration – and so does alcohol. The net result is that you end up feeling worse. Swimming, long baths, showers or soft drinks, even the famous cup of tea, reduce dehydration. Meditation and relaxation exercises are also effective at reducing tension and overcoming the physical consequences of stress. Sport helps, too, the more energetic the better. It shifts attention from the problem while using up the energy released by stress.

Post-stress adjustment of behaviour and response is important to avoid long-term dangers. Physical fitness is valuable. Many of the worst symptoms of stress are physical. The less able the body is to cope, the greater the risk. Other changes in behaviour are equally important. Problems of role ambiguity and conflict can only be resolved through discussion and clarification of tasks. See the lecturer, talk to your tutors, tackle the professor. 'Stability zones' are invaluable for those facing regular and considerable stress. These are places or situations in which you feel secure. Regular reviews of work and behaviour are parts of this process of adjustment. This is especially important in handling those newer tasks and responsibilities that will face you at university.

Communication

Success at university depends at least as much on how effectively you can communicate as on what you know. Developing your ability to put ideas across effectively, whether orally or on paper, is crucial. A powerful case can lose almost all impact if it is put across badly.

Unreadable, messy scripts have probably cost students more marks in assignments, tests and exams than ignorance, lack of understanding and error. If your handwriting is poor, you can always use a typewriter or word-processor for assignments. Exams are another matter. Ultimately, the onus is on you to do what you can to make your writing clear. Think of it from the examiner's point view. He or she may be faced with upwards of 50 scripts, each about 4,000 words long and all probably answering the same five or six questions. Remember that it is not what you write but what the examiner reads that decides your mark.

Communication may be a two-way process, involving sender and receiver, but the crucial point is that the receiver is much the more important partner. As sender, you know what you are trying to get across. The receiver doesn't. If the receiver is still in the dark when you have finished, you have failed. The rules which guide formal presentation illustrate many of the principles underlying all effective communication.

By far the most important is to be clear in your own mind what you want to say. This is much easier said than done. There will be moments when, however hard you have struggled with a subject, you either can't get it fixed in your mind or find an effective way to put it on paper. Don't panic. Talk to your lecturer. Talk to your friends. Above all, when you come to write it up, make it as simple as possible. Draw up a list in note form of the points you want to make. Each point should be no more than 12 words. If you have thought it through effectively, the bare bones of the essay will be there. Resist the temptation to over-elaborate in writing it up. Style is far less important than content. If the content is right, the style will take care of itself.

- Decide what you want to say
- Think about your audience – how can you make your presentation memorable for them?
- Adjust the message to the capabilities of the audience
- Think about the way you are going to put your message forward
- Design presentation for clarity
- Reinforce verbal with visual signals
- Provide opportunities for feedback

Preparation is vital. In essays or assignments, this means allowing time to read your work after it is finished – don't forget this in exams. Nothing has ever been written that cannot be improved by judicious editing. In seminars or tutorials, don't forget to summarise – the longer the presentation, the more frequent the summaries.

Attention spans decline rapidly after a fairly short time. Visuals aids are an excellent way to extend them. Use feedback or discussion to reinforce, clarify and redirect messages. Always try to put yourself in the shoes of those listening.

Managing projects and long assignments

A fundamental difference between school and university is that at university you will be asked to take on long and often complex projects. Not only will these involve something very like original research, in many cases you will have to set the subject matter, too. It's obvious that projects such as these provide scope for stimulating and fulfilling work. Equally, the lack of clear guidelines, the fact that it is you setting the agenda, can be daunting. Research-based theses and project reports are complex and information-hungry tasks that place significant demands on your ability to manage yourself.

The heart of any project is the definition of the task or work to be done. The GIGO principle – Garbage In, Garbage Out – is fundamental. You need to be clear in your own mind:

- What you are trying to achieve
- What you need to complete the task
- How you are going to set about it

This means preparing a summary statement of the question and the hypothesis to be tested and/or tackled. Ask yourself:

- Why is the project interesting?
- What do I, or those I can ask, know about it?
- Is success dependent on forces outside my control?
- How much help do I need?
- Is the help readily available?

It is worth preparing a time-based action plan. Always work backwards from the deadline. If you have several months in which to do the work, it's easy to think that the deadline is so far away that it will take care of itself, that time stretches forward indefinitely. A last-minute rush can destroy much of the good work you did at the start of the project. The reader's irritation at poor grammar, bad spelling and shoddy presentation can obscure whatever other merits your work may have. Thus:

15 May	Hand in project
10 May	Proofread and correct
7 May	Revise and edit final draft
23 April	Start final draft
17 April	Collate information
6 April	Send out reminders to respondents
23 Mar	Mail survey
19 Mar	Type final questionnaires
12 Mar	Review pilot survey
7 Mar	Start pilot survey
1 Mar	Draft questionnaire
26 Feb	Complete initial literature review
2 Feb	Agree project with tutor

Build in recycling time. Drafts will not be right first time. Questionnaires, for example, take several efforts to get right. Remember Murphy's Laws.

PART 2

THE LISTINGS

8 UNIVERSITY RANKINGS

The league table in this chapter is a new and unique method of measuring the performance of British universities. Since its first appearance in *The Times* in October 1992, it has been the subject of continued and heated debate among academics.

There are those who believe that all attempts to measure the performance both of individual institutions and of the system as a whole are wrong in principle. Institutions are unique and autonomous. They serve distinct communities and have diverse missions. In the eyes of critics, any attempt to rank universities can be misleading, may be spurious and might be dangerous. This is despite the success and the contribution of comparable guides elsewhere. Since the early '80s, for example, *US News and World Report* has produced similar rankings of American colleges and universities every year. Despite initial misgivings, the publication is now backed by the American Association of University Professors and the Council of Aid to Education. Increasingly, US academics and commentators have come to see analayses of this type as legitimate aids to students, staff and institutions alike.

For details of how *The Times* tables were constructed, see Appendix 1.

How the table works

The table uses 14 key aspects of university life as its yardsticks (in every case, the most recent complete year's figures have been used). These range from entry standards to the proportion of foreign students. Each has been chosen to highlight the performance of every university in these areas and to allow potential students to build them into their own selection processes. They are:

1 Entry points This is probably the indicator most familiar to the largest number of applicants. It is a measure of the number of A-level, Higher or equivalent points required for entry. (For an explanation of how these are arrived at, see chapter 5, Applying To University). In most institutions, the points required vary significantly between subjects. The 'average' pointage for each university was calculated by weighting the pointage for a subject area by the number of entrants. Figures are for 1989-90.

Care should be taken in interpreting these figures. Among the most important provisos are:

- The commitment of some institutions to 'access' initiatives designed to create opportunities for entrants with non-conventional or no qualifications. Inevitably, an institution with this laudable goal will find its measure depressed in the table.
- The tendency for the value of Scottish Highers, HNC, BTEC or professional qualifications to be undervalued in assigning points to them.

2 Student/staff ratios Staff are defined as full-time teaching or equivalent staff. This excluded research staff and academic-related administrative staff but included part-time staff calculated by their equivalence as full-time staff. The same assumption is made about students. Hence a staff/student ratio of 1:12 means that there is the equivalent of 12 students per member of staff across the institution. The university figure was calculated, where it was not included in the institution's own data such as an annual report, by weighting ratios by subject across the institution. Figures are for 1989–90.

Inevitably, there are several problems with this approach, not least that there are wide variations in staff/student ratios between subjects. Where laboratory science subjects operate on relatively low staff/student ratios, for example, professional subjects have high ratios. An institution with a strong bias in either direction will do relatively well or badly in this tabulation.

A more pervasive bias comes from the increased use in some institutions of large numbers of part-time staff. The conventional measures of staff equivalence tend to understate their contribution. A similar problem occurs with part-time students. There may, however, be some degree of cancelling out in these relationships in some institutions.

Despite these concerns, staffing levels are central to the nature of the student's learning experience.

3 Research and consultancy income A frequent criticism of the table when it appeared in *The Times* was the emphasis given to research. Few denied the importance of research to the quality and value of the university experience, but questions were asked about its relative importance. It was therefore decided to cut the weighting from 22 per cent to 18 per cent. The points were redistributed to other areas. Figures are for 1989–90.

The research income measure is constructed on two basic measures:

1. Funds from research councils and medical charities, largely using peer review, ie assessment by other academics on research quality
2. Funds from government, industry and public bodies, and largely allocated by the likely users of the research on the basis of likely direct value or useability

The figures were then linked to the number of staff to derive a figure for research income per capita member of full-time academic staff (excluding academic-related administrative staff).

4 Staff qualifications: PhDs The principal measure was the number of PhDs among staff. Despite its role having changed recently, and in some areas declined, a PhD is the traditional entry qualification for academic positions in universities. Gathering this material involved some of the most laborious and time-consuming work of the table. An initial detailed analysis of the Directory of the Association of Commonwealth Universities was followed up by scrutiny of the Calendars' and staff lists of individual institutions and other staff listings. Figures are for 1989–90.

5 Staff qualifications: professional The same detailed research employed for the examination of PhDs was employed for professional qualifications. A liberal approach was employed in gathering these. This meant that non-Chartered professional bodies or institutions were included as well as the Royal and Chartered Societies. Figures are for 1989–90.

6 Library spending Libraries have been described as the 'heart and soul' of a university. Even if this exaggerates their importance in a world of quick and easy communication and expanded use of on-line data, it remains the case that libraries are at the centre of the student's working life. The data on library expenditure includes books, periodicals, other documents (audio-visual material, for example) and staffing. Capital costs are not included. Figures are for 1989–90.

7 Student accommodation For many prospective students, the availability, cost and quality of student accommodation is a matter of prime concern. That said, its importance often declines as students progress through their university life. The appeal of a city-centre flat can soon outweigh the appeal of a Hall in the suburbs. The table measures the proportion of all full-time students who can be accommodated by the university in facilities it owns or controls. It does not include accommodation 'recommended' by the institution.

It should be stressed that the nature of accommodation can be more important than its volume. Few universities have significant amounts of accommodation for married students or those with significant disabilities, for example. Figures are for 1991–92.

8 Completion rates This figure attempts to measure the proportion of those going to university who undertake a first degree or its equivalent and graduate successfully. No distinction is made between the character of qualifications. Figures are for 1989–90.

9 Firsts If completion rates are a measure of quantity, the number of first-class degrees obtained is one of several possible measures of quality. Nonetheless, the use of the figure has been criticised on the grounds that it is too easily controlled by universities. While some institutions may aim to award a pre-set proportion of firsts every year, say 5 per cent, others award firsts purely on merit. Thus while the former will have more or less the same number of firsts every year, the latter will see the number vary from year to year. Furthermore, universities that place a premium on academic achievement will always score more highly than those that value more pragmatic virtues, largely by virtue of attracting more obvious academic high-fliers in the first place. The figure is thus potentially biased toward the hot-house universities – even if their hot-house plants cannot survive outside. That said, all these arguments suggest more that the system by which firsts are awarded is in need of reform rather than that their use as an indicator of quality is flawed. Figures are for 1989–90.

10 Research ratings The continuing importance of research as an indicator of some aspects of the quality of a university was well illustrated by the decision of all but one of the new universities to participate in the research assessment exercise undertaken by the Universities Funding Council in 1992. This measure is derived from the analysis of the overall performance of universities published in *The Times* in December 1992.

11 Value added Perhaps the most common demand placed on universities is to demonstrate the degree to which they can be said to add 'value' to their students by having accepted them in the first place and then overseen their university careers. Many questions can be raised about this. For example, how much 'value' is added to someone's life by a well-funded and high-achieving university such as Cambridge? Is a student at Cambridge because they are going to be successful anyway, or do they become successful because they were at Cambridge? Either way, how can you measure the performance of Cambridge graduates against those of an institution such as Paisley University which commits itself to an innovative access programme targeted on those without traditional qualifications?

The Times table tackles these issues by relating the entry qualifications of the entrants to a measure constructed from completion rates, firsts and employment figures. The employment figure is built up from the proportion of all students who are in permanent employment within six months of their graduation, the numbers who are registered unemployed and those going on to research and further study. Those in temporary work are not included. The figures for permanent employment are given greater weighting than the other indicators. In part, this is a subjective decision by the authors, though it also reflects changing priorities within universities and increased concern about career prospects among students.

The figures in the table are a first stab at this issue, and are for 1989–90. It is expected that future editions of the guide will return to the question.

12 Graduate students Graduate students add a distinctive set of interests and values to a university. Their presence often marks particular areas of strength or competence. The table measures the proportion of the student population involved in graduate studies.

The nature of this guide has led to the exclusion of certain institutions that are entirely or largely graduate schools. These include institutions such as the Royal College of Art, London Business School and Cranfield Institute of Technology. These exclusions have probably had a more marked effect on the subject analysis than the institutional analysis. The figures are for 1989–90.

13 Employment This is a composite measure built up from:

- The percentage of graduates in permanent employment within six months of graduation
- The proportion of graduates unemployed within six months of graduation
- The percentage of graduates going on to research or further study within six months of graduation

As mentioned above, the proportion in permanent employment is given the greatest weighting. The figures are for 1989–90.

14 International students The university community is almost by definition an international community. Overseas students – here defined as those from outside the European Community – bring different and diverse insights and values. This indicator is derived from the percentage of all students who are classified as overseas. Figures are for 1989–90.

Conclusions

Overall, the analysis highlights the strength in depth of the UK's universities. They offer a range and diversity to meet most needs. Among individual institutions some issues emerge. The most obvious is the continuing strength and success of Oxbridge. This should, however, be related to the strength of London. The high costs of their capital-city base allied to generally unsympathetic attitudes among some policy makers have not undermined the quality of London and its colleges.

It is remarkable that a higher education system with a reputation for rigidity has seen so many relatively new institutions reach the highest standards. Warwick, York and Sussex epitomise the success of the foundations of the 1960s, while Bath and Loughborough illustrate the achievements of the technological universities. Institutions with distinctive missions or strengths also emerge well. This is especially noticeable in the achievements of Imperial College and the London School of Economics.

These accomplishments have been built on an ability to generate resources to achieve goals and the determination to deploy these effectively. This raises wider questions. It is clear that major changes and net new resources are needed. The resource base of the former Polytechnics shows major disparities with the older universities. In the face of these handicaps, their achievements have been, and continue to be, remarkable.

The data illustrates other inherent biases and imbalances. Size of institution and discipline-mix affects outcomes. A university with a large medical school will look very different from one without. There also seems to be a regional bias in resource allocation which influences outcomes. An institution in an economically distressed area will find many resources harder to obtain. The existence of these distortions reinforces the case for additional resources, greater awareness and debate on the development of higher education and a greater degree of strategic academic planning across the system and through the national funding councils. These efforts should be designed to maximise the contribution of all the universities rather than minimise their costs. Universities, in turn, will need to mobilise these resources with increasing skill to ensure that new entrants gain the maximum benefit from their university experience.

Universities are listed in rank order. Where two or more universities are given equal points this is because scores have been rounded up or down to eliminate decimal points.

The following abbreviations are used in the table:
Glasgow Cal: Glasgow Caledonian University
Kings: Kings College London
Lampeter: St David's University College
Liverpool JMU: Liverpool John Moores University
LSE: London School of Economics
Queen Mary: Queen Mary and Westfield College, London
Royal Holloway: Royal Holloway and Bedford New College
UCL: University College London
UMIST: University of Manchester Institute of Science and Technology

	Entry points	Student/staff ratio	Research income	Staff qualifications PhDs	Staff qualifications professional	Library spending	Student accommodation	Completion rates	Firsts	Research rating	Value added	Graduates	Employment	International students	TOTAL
WEIGHTING	120	110	110	35	25	85	55	85	65	80	100	20	100	20	*1000*
1 Cambridge	119	108	92	31	8	83	53	83	64	79	52	18	34	18	*843*
1 Oxford	118	103	91	30	8	84	51	80	64	78	63	16	42	15	*843*
3 Imperial	112	102	93	35	16	70	33	76	55	76	53	18	44	19	*801*
4 UCL	99	96	96	33	7	70	26	45	60	78	90	19	44	18	*779*
5 LSE	116	78	82	34	9	82	36	38	59	78	63	20	51	20	*765*
5 Edinburgh	112	106	85	26	10	77	39	66	42	73	59	17	40	13	*765*
5 London	99	102	95	34	7	80	34	43	57	68	78	17	33	19	*765*
8 Warwick	112	79	85	29	12	51	45	75	50	75	70	19	41	15	*758*
8 York	112	95	80	32	10	57	48	70	43	68	73	14	50	6	*758*
10 Bath	113	89	68	21	8	65	46	45	63	71	51	10	76	13	*738*
11 Durham	117	71	68	31	9	79	53	78	46	68	52	10	46	7	*734*
11 Bristol	116	80	74	27	9	76	45	78	53	63	54	8	45	6	*734*
11 Manchester	112	96	83	32	12	70	41	65	43	70	53	11	41	8	*734*
11 Southampton	105	88	87	27	9	77	31	75	58	62	54	14	37	10	*734*
15 Kings	99	101	89	16	13	70	29	50	62	67	66	16	37	15	*730*
16 Birmingham	105	78	75	30	10	60	42	75	41	68	86	14	36	7	*728*
17 Glasgow	105	99	87	32	10	69	31	40	40	53	93	12	41	12	*724*
18 Loughborough	99	90	66	29	13	63	51	73	60	53	52	15	48	10	*722*
19 Sussex	71	46	86	25	13	80	43	66	44	69	68	15	74	17	*715*
19 St Andrews	112	83	62	31	10	63	46	70	56	67	45	11	45	14	*715*
19 Liverpool	99	86	82	33	9	50	36	65	44	56	79	15	48	10	*715*
19 Sheffield	105	93	70	32	10	60	36	75	39	63	59	13	46	13	*715*
23 Newcastle	99	97	73	29	5	77	39	50	42	63	57	11	45	11	*698*
23 Surrey	73	70	87	19	12	40	51	65	58	60	60	18	68	17	*698*

	Entry points	Student/staff ratio	Research income	Staff qualifications PhDs	Staff qualifications professional	Library spending	Student accommodation	Completion rates	Firsts	Research rating	Value added	Graduates	Employment	International students	TOTAL
WEIGHTING	120	110	110	35	25	85	55	85	65	80	100	20	100	20	*1000*
23 Nottingham	105	83	75	24	7	65	41	73	45	68	41	12	46	11	698
26 Leeds	99	91	79	33	6	48	37	69	45	58	43	10	41	9	666
26 UMIST	99	42	99	32	12	24	65	59	59	74	63	15	28	19	666
28 Royal Holloway	73	84	70	27	7	65	43	50	54	66	57	6	48	9	660
29 Swansea	73	94	52	28	11	40	36	78	31	49	98	12	38	13	652
29 Brunel	86	51	77	20	5	74	39	45	46	47	64	19	68	10	652
29 Aberdeen	73	58	77	18	14	70	34	80	60	44	51	13	46	12	652
32 Kent	86	51	63	22	5	69	42	75	33	44	97	13	30	18	647
32 East Anglia	105	67	68	18	5	57	38	69	27	58	58	16	45	16	647
32 Bradford	65	64	65	18	15	40	29	69	48	38	94	14	75	11	647
32 Reading	75	77	68	32	6	52	40	50	29	54	99	19	30	15	647
36 Exeter	97	83	45	16	5	48	47	69	37	58	58	15	53	7	638
37 Leicester	86	43	77	29	5	77	38	78	20	53	71	16	25	12	632
37 Lancaster	86	41	55	16	5	48	47	78	36	72	85	18	29	16	632
39 Queen Mary	73	98	45	26	8	50	24	42	53	61	80	13	33	18	627
40 Stirling	73	32	57	22	11	45	53	75	57	51	57	14	53	18	620
40 Strathclyde	73	52	74	24	14	44	27	65	59	52	51	13	56	16	620
40 Aston	86	20	61	23	7	70	49	50	62	48	56	18	64	6	620
43 Heriot-Watt	73	63	84	13	8	29	28	40	55	47	86	13	55	14	609
43 Cardiff	86	61	56	24	14	70	30	69	43	44	48	17	33	14	609
43 Dundee	73	67	89	18	13	60	37	42	41	44	52	11	51	9	609
46 Essex	73	40	65	25	5	76	44	65	31	73	48	13	22	19	600
46 Goldsmiths'	73	57	47	11	5	60	25	70	51	36	91	9	55	9	600
48 City	82	53	54	20	5	57	21	42	48	47	52	19	58	18	578

	Entry points	Student/staff ratio	Research income	Staff qualifications PhDs	Staff qualifications professional	Library spending	Student accommodation	Completion rates	Firsts	Research rating	Value added	Graduates	Employment	International students	TOTAL
WEIGHTING	120	110	110	35	25	85	55	85	65	80	100	20	100	20	*1000*
48 Belfast	86	99	45	25	11	41	22	69	19	35	54	11	52	8	*578*
50 Salford	64	39	59	21	15	41	52	65	61	34	55	7	42	18	*574*
51 Lampeter	56	62	34	21	9	79	46	75	14	33	81	5	49	5	*570*
52 Aberystwyth	65	72	51	17	9	76	41	45	7	40	92	14	18	14	*562*
53 Keele	66	62	54	15	9	52	55	62	18	37	59	18	28	16	*551*
54 Hull	81	25	52	19	10	37	53	78	18	34	52	16	46	18	*538*
55 Bangor	51	23	73	19	11	68	33	62	33	38	74	11	25	12	*532*
56 Buckingham	36	88	23	9	9	41	45	70	20	24	55	5	82	20	*526*
57 Leeds Metro	43	86	36	16	21	30	8	50	40	18	80	9	79	6	*521*
58 Ulster	56	69	41	15	16	39	15	65	10	39	56	7	59	15	*503*
59 Portsmouth	43	58	39	9	20	37	11	59	22	18	89	7	62	5	*479*
60 Middlesex	48	18	39	13	22	25	5	38	40	26	94	9	83	5	*468*
61 Manch'r Metro	44	54	31	10	23	35	7	38	35	22	82	8	66	5	*460*
61 Kingston	39	41	27	15	24	16	20	37	33	33	77	8	82	7	*460*
61 West of England	45	51	31	15	24	25	11	45	10	29	64	9	86	13	*460*
61 Hertfordshire	28	46	37	13	24	29	28	50	32	17	63	7	76	7	*460*
61 Coventry	24	78	35	13	21	18	19	73	14	29	58	5	62	9	*460*
66 Oxford Brookes	51	23	33	17	22	20	16	50	26	23	52	8	81	13	*437*
66 Sheffield Hallam	42	21	31	10	17	34	17	44	30	31	72	6	76	5	*437*
66 Brighton	41	69	19	14	20	20	13	44	12	26	76	6	66	9	*437*
66 Central England	46	64	46	10	23	20	18	40	27	10	56	10	60	6	*437*
70 De Montfort	31	64	21	10	16	30	15	42	24	13	59	5	67	5	*403*
71 Liverpool JMU	32	22	22	12	22	33	9	45	28	10	91	5	53	6	*391*
71 L'don Guildhall	24	22	41	16	24	17	9	40	12	16	69	5	80	12	*391*

	Entry points	Student/staff ratio	Research income	Staff qualifications PhDs	Staff qualifications professional	Library spending	Student accommodation	Completion rates	Firsts	Research rating	Value added	Graduates	Employment	International students	TOTAL
WEIGHTING	120	110	110	35	25	85	55	85	65	80	100	20	100	20	*1000*
71 Northumbria	34	39	23	9	19	35	18	36	31	26	63	5	46	5	*391*
74 Wolverhampton	18	23	26	11	23	37	19	42	8	16	84	7	59	10	*384*
75 Westminster	15	61	11	6	21	21	5	36	11	27	69	5	74	18	*380*
76 Central Lancs	40	51	18	10	18	15	17	45	33	10	60	5	47	5	*375*
76 Napier	27	60	21	10	23	41	5	42	15	10	57	5	53	5	*375*
76 Anglia	23	36	25	7	25	18	26	36	9	10	75	6	72	5	*375*
79 Greenwich	20	32	21	12	20	23	21	40	10	21	63	6	73	5	*367*
79 Plymouth	26	56	10	5	20	23	16	45	16	32	60	5	46	5	*367*
81 Notts Trent	35	34	22	10	18	27	7	40	22	10	57	5	63	5	*355*
81 South Bank	10	44	6	6	19	30	9	40	6	30	70	8	69	6	*355*
83 Robert Gordon	10	22	24	6	21	14	14	65	24	14	61	5	61	5	*346*
84 North London	17	43	9	6	17	24	8	40	28	28	54	6	47	7	*336*
85 Thames Valley	13	37	14	5	19	20	5	43	13	13	66	6	59	16	*329*
85 Sunderland	10	34	31	5	19	14	26	38	17	19	61	8	39	6	*329*
87 Huddersfield	13	24	20	8	18	24	17	42	14	20	67	6	41	6	*319*
87 Glamorgan	13	47	14	7	18	14	10	43	28	10	61	5	39	8	*319*
87 Paisley	10	25	35	5	19	18	17	34	30	10	63	5	43	5	*319*
90 Bournemouth	38	37	22	5	16	12	5	36	10	12	65	5	39	5	*307*
91 Staffordshire	16	25	13	5	23	13	22	38	12	10	61	7	49	5	*300*
91 Humberside	10	17	30	5	16	14	11	50	23	10	63	5	39	6	*300*
93 East London	10	15	9	5	24	14	20	35	12	10	64	17	30	10	*276*
94 Glasgow Cal	21	19	18	5	17	14	5	33	10	10	65	5	30	5	*258*
94 Teesside	10	21	8	5	15	18	12	36	10	26	63	5	22	5	*258*
96 Derby	10	20	5	5	14	15	14	32	10	10	61	5	23	5	*230*

Some universities are shown with equal points; their positions in the table depend on decimal place differences too small to be entered here

9 THE TOP UNIVERSITIES BY SUBJECT

Ranking universities by subject is both more useful to prospective students and more problematic than establishing their overall standings. There can be pockets of excellence in the most mediocre institutions – and blackspots in the best. Aggregate scores may determine positions in the larger pecking order but reputations will vary between subject groupings.

Universities of all types are being encouraged to concentrate on their strengths, making it even more likely that unexpected institutions will appear at the head of these subject rankings. Published statistics make such gems hard to unearth, however. Although the funding councils' ratings for research are based on subject areas, many of the other key indicators are not broken down in this way.

The tables have been calculated on the basis of five elements: 1) entry standards; 2) staff/student ratios; 3) completion rates; 4) employment prospects; and 5) academic reputation, this last having been derived from the results of the research assessment exercise carried out in December 1992.

As fewer criteria have been used than in the main ranking table in chapter 8, scores are bunched more closely. One result is that it is harder to separate the performances of universities of broadly similar strength. In order to minimise what might otherwise be the risk of misrepresentation, more universities have been bracketed together than in the main table.

The most extreme example is medicine, where four universities share top spot and no less than five share the next position, fourth. The sciences are another area where competition for top place was tight, though a similar bunching is obvious throughout the tables.

Perhaps the biggest surprise in all the tables is the appearance of University College London in joint first place in the medicine table. The college set its sights on producing Britain's top medical school when the Middlesex and University College hospitals merged, and the rankings suggest that it has succeeded. The faculties of life and clinical sciences, which make up the school, have expanded recently and gained strength as a result.

Generally, the traditional universities emerge extremely strongly from all the tables, with Oxford and Cambridge the most consistent scorers. Oxford appears in first or second place in every table bar one, Cambridge in first or second place in every table bar two. In medicine, sciences and languages they share top place. Imperial College underlines its strengths in sciences and engineering with joint first place and undisputed first place respectively, LSE its consistent strength in social sciences with first place. Essex, in third place in social sciences, makes clear the advantages of specialisation and shows, too, how smaller universities can overcome the handicap of size.

But if the new universities generally have difficulty breaking into the higher reaches of most of the rankings, in one area they scored consistently well: business and management. Business subjects have been the new universities' boom subject for several years. Though most of the top places are occupied by older universities, Sheffield Hallam and Manchester Metropolitan both appear in the top 10, the only new universities to figure in the top 10 in any subjects. Middlesex, Greenwich, Hertfordshire, Kingston, Leeds Metropolitan, Plymouth, London Guildhall, Thames Valley and Liverpool JMU complete an exceptionally strong showing among the new universities in the subject. As the table focuses on undergraduate studies, it does not include the best-known business schools, which concentrate on postgraduate studies.

Business and Management

1 Bradford	10 Aston	16 Greenwich
Lancaster	Manchester	Hertfordshire
Warwick	Metropolitan	Heriot-Watt
4 Bath	Sheffield Hallam	Kingston
Cardiff	13 Middlesex	20 Leeds Metropolitan
Strathclyde	Stirling	Plymouth
UMIST	Ulster	22 London Guildhall
8 City		Thames Valley
Imperial College		24 Liverpool JMU

Engineering

1 Imperial	8 Leeds	15 Bath
2 Cambridge	Manchester	Cardiff
Oxford	Southampton	Heriot-Watt
4 UMIST	Strathclyde	Nottingham
5 Birmingham	Surrey	Queen's, Belfast
Durham	Swansea	Sheffield
7 Loughborough	University College	21 Newcastle
	London	22 Leeds Metropolitan
		Plymouth
		25 Salford

Humanities

1 Oxford
2 Cambridge
3 Edinburgh
  St Andrews
5 LSE
  Manchester
7 Glasgow
  University College London
  King's College London

10 Royal Holloway
   Warwick
   East Anglia
12 Birmingham
   Bristol
   Durham
   Essex
   Exeter
   Nottingham

18 Swansea
19 Bradford
   Leeds
   Reading
   Sheffield
23 Brighton
   Oxford Brookes
25 Sheffield Hallam

Languages

1 Cambridge
  Oxford
3 Edinburgh
4 Leeds
  Manchester
  Queen Mary
7 Bristol
  Glasgow
  Reading
  St Andrews
  Sussex

12 Birmingham
   Durham
14 East Anglia
   Exeter
   Swansea
17 Lancaster
   University College London

19 Nottingham
   Sheffield
   Swansea
   York
23 Hull
24 Coventry
   Napier
   East London

Medicine

1 Cambridge
  Oxford
  University College London
  London
4 Edinburgh
  Glasgow
  King's College London
  Manchester
  Newcastle

10 Liverpool
11 Birmingham
   Bristol
   Nottingham
   Southampton
16 Leeds
   Sheffield

17 Queen's, Belfast
   University of Wales College of Medicine
18 Aberdeen
   Leicester
   Sheffield

Sciences

1 Cambridge
  Imperial College
  Oxford
4 Birmingham
  Bristol
  Manchester
  Nottingham
8 Durham
  Edinburgh
  Glasgow

11 Leeds
   Leicester
   Liverpool
   St Andrews
   University College London
   Warwick

17 Cardiff
   Dundee
   King's College London
   Reading
   Sheffield
   Southampton
   Sussex
25 Nottingham Trent
   Plymouth
   Westminster

Social sciences

1 LSE
2 Oxford
3 Essex
4 Birmingham
  Warwick
6 Bristol
  Cambridge
  Lancaster
  York

10 Edinburgh
   Glasgow
   Manchester
   Sussex
14 Bristol
   Hull
   Leicester
   Liverpool
   Nottingham

19 East Anglia
   Plymouth
   Stirling
   Swansea
   Ulster
24 Manchester
   Metropolitan
   Middlesex

10 UNIVERSITY PROFILES

Some famous names are missing from our university listings: the Open University, the separate business and medical schools, Birkbeck College and Cranfield Institute of Technology among them. Their omission is no reflection on their quality, simply a function of their particular roles, which in most cases make them unsuitable for comparisons and descriptions of the sort given in this chapter. The guide is based on provision for full-time undergraduates and the factors judged to influence this.

The Open University, though Britain's biggest university, with 75,000 students, could not be included because most of the measures used in our listings do not apply to it. As a non-residential, largely part-time institution, Birkbeck College, London, could also not be compared in many key areas.

Several universities have been omitted because they are mostly postgraduate institutions. Although Cranfield, for example, offers undergraduate degrees in two of its campuses, the institute is primarily for graduate students. The Manchester and London business schools were excluded for the same reason.

Similarly, specialist institutions such as the Royal College of Art and the medical schools could not fairly be compared with generalist universities. A number of colleges with degree-awarding powers also do not appear because they have yet to be granted university status. Likewise, the Joint University College in Stockton on Tees is too new for valid comparisons to be drawn between it and other universities.

Student numbers in the profiles are those supplied by the universities themselves for 1991–92. Although some have published figures for 1992–93, which in almost every case show an increase in numbers, for the sake of consistency and in the interests of comparing like with like, we have thought it best to use the last complete set of statistics. Where the numbers of arts and science students do not coincide with the male/female totals, this is because some universities use additional subject categories or have included postgraduate students in the larger figures.

The entry requirements for individual degrees, given in brackets after subjects, are the traditional universities' published estimates of A-level grades required for entry in the 1993–94 academic year. Many are likely to be higher for 1994–95, especially in the arts and social sciences. The new universities do not publish A-level entry requirements.

UNIVERSITY OF ABERDEEN

Regent Walk, Aberdeen AB9 1FX (tel. 0224 272000)

Founded 1495

Times ranking: 29

Enquiries: academic registrar

Full-time students: 3,051 (f), 3,527 (m)
2,932 **arts**, 2,968 **sciences**

Main Subject Areas: arts and social sciences (4-year MA); divinity (BD); engineering (BEng, BSc Eng); law (LLB); medicine (MB, BSc); science (BSc, BTechnol).

Aberdeen has overcome its funding difficulties of the 1980s and strengthened its senior academic staff. New chairs have been established in subjects as diverse as Celtic and Spanish, international relations, and environmental and occupational medicine.

The university's modular courses are so flexible that almost 75 per cent of students change their intended degree before graduation. The compact prospectus includes entry requirments for 1993.

Theology (BBC), medicine and law (both three Bs) are among the university's traditional strengths. Biological sciences are second only to social sciences in size. Plant and soil science and zoology are aslo highly rated, as are geography, geology and land economy.

The original King's College buildings are the focal point of an appealing and quiet campus, complete with cobbled main street with some sturdily handsome Georgian buildings, about a mile from the city centre. A bus service links the two main sites with the Hillhead residential complex. The students' union runs free late-night buses.

The university finds accommodation for about half its students and guarantees a hall place for all first-years. The oil industry has left the city with notorious accommodation problems. As a result, the university is committed to add 500 residential places every year. New entrants will have the unique opportunity of celebrating the university's 400th anniversary in 1993 and, curiously, its 500th anniversary in 1995. The reason, simply, is that today's university is a fusion of two ancient institutions which came together in 1860. Indeed Aberdeen likes to boast that for 250 years it had as many universities as the whole of England.

The students' union has good facilities and is also one of the cheapest places in the city to eat and drink. A separate students' representative council carries out the political functions. Students seem to like Aberdeen on the whole, despite its remoteness (to the sizeable English contingent at least) and the long and often bitter winters.

ANGLIA POLYTECHNIC UNIVERSITY
Victoria Road South, Chelmsford, Essex CM1 1LL (tel. 0245 493131)

Royal charter 1992, formerly Anglia Polytechnic
Times ranking: 76

Enquiries: student administration
Full-time students: 2,486 (f), 1,744 (m)
2,820 **arts**, 1,410 **sciences**

Main subject areas: humanities and arts combined and single subjects (BA); graphic arts and music (BA); business studies, accountancy, economics and law (BA); technology, building management, software engineering (BSc). Also a range of diploma courses.

Two well-established colleges, the Chelmer Institute and Cambridgeshire College of Arts and Technology, came together in 1989 to form the first regional polytechnic. Even as one of the growth areas of the last decade, East Anglia always lagged behind other parts of England for the number of students going into higher education.

The new university now boasts of teaching across four counties through a network of associated colleges in Suffolk and Norfolk. The two main campuses are at Chelmsford and Cambridge, but there are also sites at Brentwood and at a country house management centre near Chelmsford.

Anglia has a strongly European outlook, encouraging students to take a language option and providing opportunities to take part of many courses abroad. Employers play an active role in course planning, contributing to a healthy employment rate for graduates.

As a polytechnic, Anglia received only one quality award in 1992, for courses in art, design and the performing arts. The European business administration degree (twinned with Berlin Fachhochschule) is well regarded, giving students two years in Germany and one with a company, as well as two university years.

Other unusual courses include a combination of European business and music, and one of five women's studies degrees in the new universities. Law and computing courses are also popular, as is European social policy, which gives students six months in Holland. A new campus is on the way in Chelmsford to ease overcrowding. Until it has been completed, residential accommodation and student facilities will remain no more than moderate. The two main sites have only 317 hall places, and houses leased by the university do not yet fill the gap in provision. Priority for places goes to those with special needs or who live more than 80 miles from the university.

Students say that, being so far apart, the separate sites have their own atmospheres and that as a result the university lacks a distinct identity.

ASTON UNIVERSITY

Aston Triangle, Birmingham B4 7ET (tel. 021-359 3611)

Founded 1895, royal charter 1966
Times ranking: 40

Enquiries: admissions office
Full-time students: 1,724 (f), 2,203 (m)
1,576 **arts**, 1,983 **sciences**

Main subject areas: engineering and applied science (BEng and SSc); life and health sciences (BSc); management and modern languages (BA and BSc). Three-year degrees or four-year sandwich programmes.

Sir Frederick Crawford, Aston's thrusting vice-chancellor, has tried to raise the university's standing by introducing a shift to high entry grades and high-calibre staff. But having run into opposition from the funding council, the policy has so far had limited success. December 1992's research assessment ratings showed improvement, but still left Aston below most of the traditional universities.

Aston was given one of the lowest allocations for both teaching and research in 1992–93, while in 1991–92 only the council's safety net provided the university with an acceptable level of support. Staffing levels have suffered as a result.

As a former college of advanced technology, Aston's strength is on the science side, although the proportion of arts students has been growing in recent years. There is a wide range of combined honours programmes for those who want to avoid excessive specialisation.

Pharmacy (BBC) and opthalmology (BCC) are among the top-rated degrees. Two-thirds of the undergraduates take sandwich courses, with beneficial effects on graduate employment prospects. European engineering degrees are especially popular, and both management and modern languages are growing fast.

The 40-acre landscaped campus is a 10-minute walk from the centre of Birmingham. Conveniently placed halls have room for two-thirds of the undergraduates, and all first-years from outside the West Midlands are offered a place. In addition to the campus residences, there is a student village four miles away at Handsworth Wood, bringing the total number of residential places to more than 2,000. A small number of rooms cater specifically for the disabled.

Modernisation has left all departments occupying purpose-built accommodation, as well as providing modern and extensive computer facilities, especially in the library.

Students describe the university as lively, and welcome its proximity to the city centre. They complain that teaching groups are getting larger, but the students' guild (the union) says that lecturing standards are generally high.

UNIVERSITY OF BATH

Claverton Down, Bath BA2 7AY (tel. 0225 826826)

Founded 1894 (in Bristol), royal charter 1966
Times ranking: 10

Enquiries: registrar
Full-time students: 1,649 (f), 2,773 (m)
1,229 arts, 2,516 sciences

Main subject areas: architecture and building engineering (BArch, B Eng, BSc); materials science, electronic and electrical, chemical and mechanical engineering (BEng, MEng); biological sciences, chemistry, management, mathematical sciences, pharmacy, physics, physiotherapy and social sciences (BSc); modern languages (BA and BSc); education (joint honours).

Still a small technological university, Bath's high placing in *The Times* table reflects all-round strength in its field. Last year the university passed up the opportunity to grow substantially and change character by merging with the city's college of higher education.

Although expansion is under way, the accent is still on quality. The universities' Academic Audit Unit gave Bath a clean bill of health in the summer of 1992, complimenting the university particularly on its sandwich programmes. The majority of undergraduates choose this route to a degree, helping to produce the best graduate employment record among the traditional universities.

Research is Bath's greatest strength, however. Mathematics, statistics and computer science (all ACC), social policy and administration (BCC), chemical engineering (BBC) and materials science (CCD) are all highly rated. The schools of pharmacy and education both won important national projects in 1992.

A new American vice-chancellor, David VandeLinde, is expected to make changes, possibly including student assessment of lecturers. His initial priorities are to raise Bath's international profile and to make its courses more flexible.

First-years can normally expect one of the 1,600 residential places on campus, some of which are reserved for disabled students. The university occupies modern buildings on an exposed site overlooking one of Britain's prime tourist cities.

A £5-million expansion of teaching accommodation is under way. The extra space will be needed, since the size of the intake has increased by 20 per cent in each of the last two years. More than 20 new professors have arrived since 1989.

Students find the campus quiet at weekends and struggle to afford some of Bath's attractions, but most like its location. There is a strong tradition in competitive sports.

QUEEN'S UNIVERSITY, BELFAST

Belfast BT7 1NN (tel. 0232 245133)

Founded 1845, royal charter 1908
Times ranking: 48

Enquiries: admissions officer
Full-time students: 4,354 (f), 5,170 (m)
3,124 **arts,** 4,349 **sciences**

Main subject areas: arts, economics and social sciences (BA, BSSc); law (LlB); science (BSc); agriculture and food science (BAgr, BSc); engineering (BEng); medicine (MB); theology (BD); education (BEd).

Queen's remains Northern Ireland's leading university, despite the popularity of the University of Ulster (see page 196). Queen's was one of three university colleges for the whole of Ireland in the 19th century, and still draws students from all over the island. However, the numbers coming from mainland Britain have declined as the troubles have dragged on. Fewer than three per cent come from 'over the water' now.

The emphasis is on research, although the funding council has been trying to steer the university more in the direction of teaching. It was one of three traditional universities to suffer a cut in research funds in 1992–93. Only two departments are judged internationally outstanding.

Engineering (three Bs for civil, BBC for electrical and electronic), physics, sociology and history (all three Cs) are well regarded, demonstrating the university's breadth. In some faculties, specialisation can be delayed until the end of the first year.

Applicants are generally interviewed, but those who receive offers are invited to visit the university. The high proportion of home-based students means that most are familiar with the surroundings already.

The majority of students live within a mile of the main campus, which is in turn a mile from the centre of Belfast. The university's 1,700 residential places accommodate 90 per cent of first-years, and private sector rents are relatively low.

The university area, one of the most attractive in Belfast, is also one of the city's main cultural and recreational centres. Queen's runs an international arts festival each November, and its film theatre is one of the best in the province.

Most students have become used to the impact of the troubles, which have never spilled over into university life, although a small number of staff and students inevitably have been victims over the years. Not surprisingly, given conditions in the city centre, social life is concentrated on the students' union and the surrounding area.

UNIVERSITY OF BIRMINGHAM

Edgbaston, Birmingham B15 2TT (tel 021-414 3344)

Founded 1828, royal charter 1900
Times ranking: 16

Enquiries: academic secretary (admissions)
Full-time students: 4,416 (f), 6,007 (m)
4,471 **arts,** 4,680 **sciences**

Main subject areas: full range of disciplines in seven faculties: arts; commerce and social science; education; engineering; law; medicine and dentistry; science.

One of the big civic universities, Birmingham offers an unusually wide range of courses, but still achieves high research ratings. It has seldom been out of the top five research council earners in the last 20 years.

Psychology and history (three Bs), metallurgy (three Cs), theology and African studies (BCC) and modern languages (BDD for German) are all rated internationally outstanding for research. Chemical engineering, physics, sociology and English are also well regarded.

The 230-acre campus in leafy Edgbaston includes one of the top university libraries in Britain and extensive facilities run by the guild of students. The University Centre adds to the catering facilities.

Five of the seven halls of residence are conveniently placed in an attractive parkland setting nearby. They are self-catering and include family units. First-years are guaranteed accommodation, although they may have to share rooms.

More than 1,000 of the 10,500 students are from overseas. The university boasts 100 different nationalities, divided into small groups throughout the campus.

Home students are either interviewed or invited to one of the open days the university holds each spring, the largest of their kind in Britain. There is also an admissions forum in September.

Sports facilities have improved considerably in recent years, and include the Raymond Priestley Centre 170 miles away in the Lake District for water sports and outward-bound activities. The main playing fields are five miles from the university, served by coaches and minibuses.

Birmingham's students have never gone in for the political extremism that has often been common on other campuses. They tend to identify with the city, and speak highly of both the quality and cost of university accommodation.

UNIVERSITY OF CENTRAL ENGLAND IN BIRMINGHAM

Perry Barr, Birmingham B15 2TT (tel. 021-414 3344)

Royal charter 1992, formerly Birmingham Polytechnic
Times ranking: 66

Enquiries: external affairs unit
Full-time students: 4,341 (f), 4,406 (m)
5,035 **arts,** 3,712 **sciences**

Main subject areas: art and design (BA); built environment (BA, BSc); business and management (BA); computing and information studies (BSc); education (BEd); engineering and computer technology (BEng, BSc); health and social sciences (BSc, BA, LlB); music (BA). Also a wide range of diploma courses.

The new university made its intentions clear by opting out of the funding council's latest research assessment exercise, the first to include the new universities. A change of title has not changed the institution's view of itself as primarily a teaching establishment.

In fact, Central England enjoys a healthy income from research and consultancy, but most activities are in the applied fields, where the university expects to compete successfully with its longer established rivals. Such a highly focused approach is typical of the style of Peter Knight, a former union activist turned vice-chancellor, who has had a number of disputes with his staff.

In another initiative in 1992, the university waived tuition fees for part-time students to prevent an exodus as a result of the recession. Almost half of the 15,500 students are part-timers, and UCE was inundated with enquiries when the policy was announced.

The university's best-known feature is its conservatoire, which forms part of Birmingham's new convention centre and has Simon Rattle as its president. Courses from opera to world music give it a reputation for innovation.

Other sites are spread around the city, from teacher training in Edgbaston to art and design in Bourneville, where the faculty is the largest in Britain and includes a school of jewellery. The modern main campus is two miles from the city centre.

The emphasis is on the vocational. The built environment faculty, for example, runs interprofessional courses that promote teamwork between students of architecture, surveying and planning. The business school has more students than some colleges, and is able to offer a wide menu of courses as a result.

Only education received a quality rating in 1992, but music courses are well regarded. Nonetheless, the appointment of a pro-vice-chancellor in 1993 with a brief to concentrate on questions of quality underlines the university's commitment to excellence.

The university controls almost 2,000 residential places in halls of residence and student houses. Students complain that sports facilities are poor and university social life limited.

UNIVERSITY OF BOURNEMOUTH
Talbot Campus, Fern Barrow, Poole, Dorset BH12 5BB (tel. 0202 524111)

Royal charter 1992, formerly Bournemouth Polytechnic, originally Dorset Institute of Higher Education
Times ranking: 90

Enquiries: academic secretary
Full-time students: 3,141 (f), 3,542 (m)
4,053 arts, 2,630 sciences

Main subject areas: business information systems (BA, BSc); computing and cognition (BSc); electronic engineering (BEng); finance and law (LLB); food and hospitality management (BA, BSc); human resources and safety management, marketing, advertising and public relations, media production (BA); nursing, health and community studies (BSc); product design and manufacture, tourism and heritage studies (BA).

When its only degree (a BEd) closed in the early '80s, the future looked bleak for the Dorset Institute. Now there are 44 undergraduate and 24 postgraduate programmes, although there has been no attempt to restart courses in education since the Weymouth campus closed.

University status came only two years after success was achieved in a long battle to become a polytechnic. In two years, student numbers have grown from 4,600 to more than 7,000. By 1995–96, there should be 9,300 students taking a wider range of subjects.

In 1992–93 alone, three full-time and six part-time postgraduate courses have been added to the curriculum, together with eight new degrees. New teaching accommodation both on campus and in the centre of Bournemouth should be ready for use in September 1993.

The university's forte is identifying gaps in the higher education market, and filling them with innovative courses, usually with a strongly vocational slant. Degrees in retail management, public relations, tourism and heritage management are all examples.

Art, design and performing arts courses were judged outstanding in the polytechnics' last quality assessments. Sandwich courses in business and management also received awards. A high proportion of all undergraduates take sandwich courses, and most three-year degrees include work placements.

The town and the subject mix attract mainly middle class students from the Midlands and the south of England, although Bournemouth's familiarity to European language students also helps to establish a regular intake from across the Channel.

Student accommodation is relatively cheap and plentiful on the private market. The university itself has little of its own. An increase on the 250 residential places available in 1992–93 is planned, and first-years will be given priority in their allocation.

UNIVERSITY OF BRADFORD
Richmond Road, Bradford BD7 1DP (tel. 0274 733466)

Royal charter 1966, college of advanced technology 1957–66
Times ranking: 32

Enquiries: admissions office
Full-time students: 2,058 (f), 3,310 (m)
1,682 arts, 2,886 sciences

Main subject areas: chemical, civil, electrical and mechanical engineering (BEng); chemistry, electronic imaging, technology and management science, archaeological, biomedical and environmental sciences, computing, mathematics, optometry, psychology (BSc); pharmacy (BPharm); applied social studies, business and management, human, European and peace studies, modern languages and social sciences (BA).

Ravaged by cuts in the early 1980s, Bradford began to grow again before many of the traditional universities. Student numbers had increased by more than a third at the end of the decade, and have gone on rising.

In particular, Bradford has carved out a niche for itself with mature students, who account for almost one in five of the undergraduates.

Admissions tutors let it be known that they are less obsessed with A-level grades than many of their rivals in other universities. The relatively small, lively campus is close to the city centre. Only the 400 business and management students are taught elsewhere. The management centre is three miles away.

More than two-thirds of the undergraduates take sandwich courses, a legacy of the university's previous existence as a college of advanced technology and one which regularly places Bradford near the top of the graduate employment league.

An interdisciplinary human studies course broadens the horizons of the scientists and technologists who form the majority of the students. This includes philosophy, psychology, literature and sociology. Civil (CCD) and mechanical (CDD) engineering, European studies (BCC) and business and management (three Bs) are all top rated.

Students have access to an advanced computer network with 1,000 workstations and 2,800 possible connection points throughout the campus, an unusually large number for the number of students. Having upgraded the facilities, the university is now increasing the use of computer-assisted learning.

First-years are guaranteed accommodation either on campus or in halls only a short walk away. Others tend to live out in the cheap and plentiful flats and houses available in the private sector.

Town and gown relations are good, and students generally become attached to Bradford. More southerners are being attracted by the low cost of living.

UNIVERSITY OF BRIGHTON
Mithras House, Lewes Road, Brighton BN2 4AT (tel. 0273 600900)

Royal charter 1992, formerly Brighton Polytechnic
Times ranking: 66

Enquiries: admissions office
Full-time students: 3,568 (f), 3,694 (m)
3,817 **arts**, 3,445 **sciences**

Main subject areas: art, design and humanities (BA); business and management (BA, BSc); education, sport and leisure (BEd, BSc); engineering and environmental studies (BEng, BA); health (BA, BSc); and information technology (BSc, BA). Also many certificate and diploma courses.

Three sites in Brighton and one in Eastbourne house the six faculties. An innovative credit ratings system recognises prior learning and allows for easy transfer between the university and other institutions in Britain and Europe.

Numerous European links give most courses an international flavour, often involving a period of study on the Continent. The university has a cosmopolitan air, with more overseas students than most of the former polytechnics.

There is also close collaboration with neighbouring Sussex University (see page 192). A joint degree in engineering was the first such venture between a university and a polytechnic, and there are plans for a Sussex Technology Institute.

Brighton has a strong faculty structure, each occupying its own building. But a fully modular academic system will soon allow students to construct their own degrees from the entire menu of courses. Most undergraduates are allocated a personal tutor, who will advise on combinations.

Courses in science, business and management, art and design, and health are all top-rated. In particular, the four-year sandwich degree in fashion textiles design has acquired an international reputation. Work placements are organised in the United States, France and Italy, as well as Britain.

Most of the 900 hall places in Brighton and Eastbourne are allocated to new students. The university also manages 1,500 units of accommodation, as well as offering access to a network of 3,000 landlords and landladies, so all first-years are given the option of organised places.

Students like raffish Brighton, although the cost of living can be high. They warn that the different sites each have their own character. Student union facilities are limited, but provision for sport is good, especially at Eastbourne, where the university has an Olympic-sized swimming pool.

UNIVERSITY OF BRISTOL
Senate House, Bristol BS8 1TH (tel. 0272 303030)

Founded 1876, royal charter 1909
Times ranking: 11

Enquiries: admissions officer
Full-time students: 4,034 (f), 5,231 (m)
3,669 **arts,** 4,185 **sciences**

Main subject areas: full range of disciplines in six faculties: arts, science, medicine (including dentistry and veterinary science), engineering, law and social science.

Bristol is a traditional alternative to Oxbridge, emerging apparently unscathed from brief but serious financial difficulties at the start of the decade. But if the university is still recovering its financial strength, peer review suggests few academic problems.

A moderately successful funding appeal forms the basis for a new phase of expansion in a variety of fields. The university is aiming to increase student numbers gradually, while maintaining a position near the top of the research league.

Seven areas were considered internationally outstanding in the 1989 research rankings, demonstrating Bristol's strength in depth. Classics (BBC), Russian, Spanish and geography (three Bs), civil engineering, physics and chemistry (BCC), pharmacology and law (ABB) were all given top billing. A similar haul in 1992 included physiology (BCD), economics (AAB) and ancient history (ABC).

The main library has more than one-million volumes, and 12 others serve individual departments and faculties. The computer centre is open 24 hours a day.

Departments are spread close to the city centre, with the halls three miles away in the traditional student areas of Clifton and Stoke Bishop. The university has more than 3,000 residential places, so can accommodate most first-years.

Bristol was one of the original members of the European Credit Transfer System, enabling students to take part of a degree abroad, and is committed to a more European outlook. Links are being established with universities in Eastern Europe as well as within the EC.

Preview days are held in May. The university is popular with independent schools, and has among the highest entry standards in Britain. The 130 degree courses are constructed on traditional lines, creating a highly academic environment.

Students like the way the university merges into the city, although private sector rents and other living costs are high. But sports facilities are good, while the largest students' union in the country is the focal point of social and political activity.

UNIVERSITY OF THE WEST OF ENGLAND, BRISTOL

Coldharbour Lane, Frenchay, Bristol BS16 1QY (tel. 0272 656261)

Royal charter 1992, formerly Bristol Polytechnic
Times ranking: 61

Enquiries: admissions officer
Full-time students: 4,212 (f), 4,747 (m)
6,286 arts, 2,673 sciences

Main subject areas: applied sciences (BSc); art, media and design, business and management (BA); built environment, computer studies and mathematics (BSc); economics and social science (BA); education (BEd); engineering (BEng); health and community studies (BSc); humanities, languages and European studies (BA); and law (LLB). More than 5,000 students also take certificate or diploma courses.

One of the top new universities in *The Times* table, the University of the West of England (UWE) chose a regional title from more than 100 suggestions in order to reflect the institution's ambitions. More than half the students live within an hour's travelling distance, and the university hopes to be 'an engine for economic recovery' in the Southwest.

A high ratio of applications to places confirms the university's standing in a wide range of subjects. Information technology, business, social science and education courses have all won quality awards. A strong vocational bias, which the new university is committed to retaining, has also helped the institution to the top employment rating in our table.

UWE expects Bristol University to be the research leader for the region, and is positioning itself to be one of a new generation of 'comprehensive' universities, validating further and higher education programmes in colleges. The franchising of courses has already begun in a number of centres.

At the same time, a new entrance system will credit vocational qualifications and practical experience equally with traditional examination results. The effect should be to add substantially to the 16,000 full- and part-time students now at the university.

There are three sites in Bristol itself, as well as the main campus at Frenchay, close to Bristol Parkway station, which also houses England's higher education funding council. Extensions and improvements are planned on all sites.

With only 870 residential places controlled by the university, most students have to fend for themselves in a relatively expensive housing market. There are complaints that Frenchay is isolated, but sports facilities are reasonable and the students' union well organised.

BRUNEL UNIVERSITY

Uxbridge, Middlesex UB8 3PH (tel. 0895 274000)

Royal charter 1966
Times ranking: 29

Enquiries: admissions officer
Full-time students: 1,166 (f), 2,709 (m)
952 **arts,** 2,259 **sciences**

Main subject areas: pure and applied sciences, design, psychology (BSc); engineering and technology (BEng, BSc); education (BEd); law (LLB); economics, sociology, government and business management (BA).

The vast majority of Brunel's undergraduates are on four-year sandwich courses, although three-year degrees are creeping in. The university operates the 'thin sandwich' system, in which students spend six months in each of the first three years at work.

The course structure and technological emphasis serves graduates well in the employment market. The system also can leave Brunel's students in a healthier financial state than some others, since most of the placements are paid.

All students have the option of including language or business programmes in their courses. The university has a link with Henley Management College, which provides some teaching on undergraduate courses, as well as collaborating in research.

Only 3,000 students share the spacious, if uninspiring, campus on the edge of west London. A former college of higher education provides a smaller, more picturesque site on the Thames, at Runnymede.

Poor research ratings in the 1980s have pushed Brunel in the direction of a predominantly teaching university, although as the 1992 research assessments demonstrated a determination to revive research perform-ance has begun to pay off. The funding council made its intentions clear by limiting Brunel to the lowest research budget among England's traditional universities, and compensating with a big increase for teaching. Art and design were the top-rated areas for research.

Law (three Bs), sociology (BCC) and electronic and electrical engineering (BBC) are all well regarded. There is also a special four-year engineering programme (AAB) designed to train future managers.

Unusually, most applicants in all subjects are interviewed. Brunel was also among the first of the traditional universities to establish access courses, run in further education colleges, to bring underqualified appli-cants up to the necessary standards for entry.

Most first-years are offered one of the university's 1,900 residential places. Student union facilities are good, and students like Brunel's intimacy, although some feel cut off at Runnymede.

UNIVERSITY OF BUCKINGHAM
Buckingham MK18 1EG (tel. 0280 814080)

Founded 1974, royal charter 1983
Times ranking: 56

Enquiries: admissions office
Full-time students: 337 (f), 486 (m)
712 **arts,** 73 **sciences**

Main subject areas: European studies, English, history, politics, dance (BA); law (LLB); accounting, business studies, hotel management and economics, biological sciences, psychology and computer science (BSc).

By far the smallest of the universities, Buckingham has now lost the distinction of being the youngest. Britain's only private university was a Conservative experiment of the 1970s, which had to wait almost a decade for its royal charter.

Although in 1992 Buckingham installed Baroness Thatcher as its chancellor and her former minister, Sir Richard Luce, as vice-chancellor, the university now sees itself as a non-partisan institution. As indicated by a solid position in our league table, academic respectability has now been achieved.

Law, accounting (both three Cs) and biology (DDE) are all popular. There are also innovative combinations, such as law, biology and the environment, in this case targeted on the growing field of pollution litigation.

Buckingham runs on calendar years, rather than the traditional academic variety. Between October and December, before enrolling, all students have the opportunity to attend specially designed language courses at a French, German or Japanese university.

Degree courses run for two 42-week years, minimising the length of career breaks for the university's many mature students. Most undergraduates are from overseas, but the proportion from Britain is growing, even with fees set at £7,460 in 1993.

All students take at least one foreign language as part of a programme of supporting courses during their time at Buckingham. Some are designed for non-specialists, others tailored for particular groups, but all are intended to broaden the curriculum.

Campus facilities are improving, although they do not yet compare with those available at the traditional universities. The students' union is still developing both socially and politically, and sports facilities are being expanded. First-years are guaranteed one of the 495 residential places.

As its rivals become ever larger and more impersonal, Buckingham hopes to make a virtue of its size and become more selective. A new academic centre, containing an expanded library, lecture theatres and a language centre, should give the university the focal point that it has lacked so far.

UNIVERSITY OF CAMBRIDGE

University Registry, The Old Schools, Cambridge CB2 1TN (tel. 0223 337733)

Founded 1209
Times ranking: 1

Enquiries: Administrative secretary, Intercollegiate applications office, Kellet Lodge, Tennis Court Road, Cambridge CB2 1QJ (tel. 0223 333308).
Full-time students: 5,600 (f), 8,400 (m)
5,400 **arts,** 5,100 **sciences**

Main subject areas: full range of disciplines divided into five faculties: arts, engineering, medicine and veterinary science, science and mathematics, and social sciences.

Top of the first *The Times* league by a whisker from Oxford and joint top with its ancient rival in the second, Cambridge remains at the pinnacle of the university system in many subjects. Traditionally supreme in the sciences, the university has added strength in the arts and social sciences, as well as opening a management school.

More students now come from state schools than the independent sector, and several colleges are trying hard to attract more applicants from comprehensives. The tripos system was a forerunner of the currently fashionable modular degree, allowing students to change subjects (within limits) mid-way through their degrees.

The students, in a lively alternative prospectus, say there is no such thing as Cambridge University, just a collection of colleges. However, teaching is university-based while a shift of emphasis towards the centre is taking place with the aid of a successful £250-million funding appeal.

CHRIST'S
Christ's College, Cambridge CB2 3BU (tel. 0223 334900)

Undergraduates: 370

Christ's prides itself on its academic strength. It is also one of the few colleges still to offer places on two E grades at A-level, meaning not that entry standards are low but that the college is sufficiently confident of its ability to identify potential high-flyers at interview that it is in effect prepared to circumvent A-levels as the principal criteria for entry. The college has a 50/50 state-to-independent ratio. Women make up 40% of the students. Though the college has a reputation for being dominated by hard-working natural scientists and mathematicians, it maintains a broad subject range.

The atmosphere is supposedly so cosy that one student described Christ's as 'a cup of Horlicks', but some complain of short bar opening hours and a poor relationship between undergraduates and fellows.

Accommodation in college is guaranteed for all first- and third-year students, some of whom will be allocated rooms in the infamous New Court 'Typewriter', probably the least attractive building in the city. The Typewriter houses the excellent New Court theatre, home to Christ's Amateur Dramatics Society and Christ's Films, one of the most adventurous student film societies. College sport has flourished in recent years, with teams competing to a good standard in most sports. The playing fields (shared with Sidney Sussex) are just over a mile away.

CHURCHILL
Churchill College, Cambridge CB3 0DS (tel. 0223 336000)

Undergraduates: 390

Founded in 1960 to help meet 'the national need for scientists and engineers and to forge links with industry', Churchill consistently finishes high in the academic league tables. Maths, natural science, engineering and computer science are traditional strengths. The college also has some of the university's best computer facilities. Deferred entry is encouraged in all subjects.

Churchill has the joint highest ratio of state to independent pupils (75/25) but one of the lowest proportions of women undergraduates, only one in four.

Some are put off by Churchill's unassuming modern architecture and the college's distance from the city centre; others argue that the distance offers much-needed breathing space. One undeniable advantage is Churchill's ability to provide every undergraduate with a room in college for all three years.

✓ There are extensive on-site playing fields, and the college does well in rugby, hockey and rowing. The university's only student radio station (broadcasting to Churchill and New Hall) is based here.

CLARE
Clare College, Cambridge CB2 1TL (tel. 0223 333246)

Undergraduates: 390

Though for many Clare's outstanding features are its gardens and harmonious buildings, hard-pressed undergraduates are just as likely to praise the rent and food charges, among the lowest in the university. Accommodation is guaranteed for all three years, either in college or nearby hostels.

One of the few colleges which openly encourages applications from 'candidates of a good academic standard who have special talents in non-academic fields', Clare tends to feature near the top of the academic tables. Languages, natural science and music are especially strong.

The ratio of male to female students is largely balanced at 57/43, while that between private and state school pupils is almost exactly 50/50.

Music thrives. The choir records and tours regularly, and Clare Cellars (comprising the bar and JCR) is rapidly becoming *the* Cambridge jazz venue. Sporting emphasis is as much on enjoyment as competition. The women's teams have had outstanding success in recent years. The playing fields are little more than a mile away.

CORPUS CHRISTI
Corpus Christi College, Cambridge CB2 1RH (tel. 0223 338000)

Undergraduates: 247

The only college to have been founded by town residents, Corpus's size inevitably makes it one of the more intimate colleges. It prides itself on being a cohesive community, but some find the focus on college rather than university life excessive. No one academic area is particularly favoured and deferred entry is encouraged in all subjects.

The kitchen fixed charge is above average at just under £100, and self-catering is limited. All undergraduates are allocated a room in college or neighbouring hostels.

There is a fairly even sexual and social balance. The male-to-female ratio is 65/35, the independent-to-state school ratio 50/50. The college bar has an enviable atmosphere.

The sporting facilities, at Leckhampton Court (just over a mile away), are among the best in the university and include a swimming pool. Corpus's sporting reputation nonetheless owes more to enthusiasm than success. Drama is also well catered for, and the college owns The Playroom, the university's best small theatre.

DOWNING
Downing College, Cambridge CB2 1DQ (tel. 0223 334800)

Undergraduates: 383

Downing's imposing neo-Classical quadrangle may look more like a military academy than a Cambridge college but the atmosphere here is anything but martial. Founded in 1800 for the study of law, medicine and natural sciences, these are still the college's strong subjects. Indeed Downing is often called 'the law college'.

A reputation for hard-playing, hard-drinking rugby players and oarsmen is proving hard to shake off. But while sport undoubtedly enjoys a high profile, pressure to conform to the sporty stereotype is never excessive.

First-years are allocated rooms in college, but only half of all other undergraduates are guaranteed rooms in college or college hostels. The completion of a new college accommodation block in 1994 will increase the figure to 94 per cent.

There is a two-to-one male-to-female ratio and a good balance between state and independent school backgrounds. The new student-run bar/party room has improved college social life.

EMMANUEL
Emmanuel College, Cambridge CB2 3AP (tel. 0223 334200)

Undergraduates: 400

Thanks in no small part to its huge and reasonably priced bar, Emmanuel has something of an insular reputation, for all that Emma students are also active in university clubs and societies. Academically, Emmanuel is a midtable college, with no particular subject bias. Deferred entry is greatly encouraged.

A 50/50 state-to-independent ratio contributes to college's unpretentious atmosphere. One in three undergraduates are women.

Accommodation in college is virtually guaranteed for all first- and third-year students. Second-years are housed in college hostels. With self-catering facilities limited, most students eat in Hall. The college offers 30 travel grants to undergraduates every year.

In the summer, the college tennis courts and open-air swimming pool offer a welcome haven from exam pressures. The duck pond is one of the most picturesque spots in Cambridge.

The sports grounds are excellent, if some distance away, and in a fairly strong sporting college the hockey elevens have enjoyed recent success.

FITZWILLIAM
Fitzwilliam College, Cambridge CB3 oDG (tel. 0223 332000)

Undergraduates: 380

Based in the city centre until 1963, the college now occupies a large, modern site on the Huntingdon Road. What it may lack in architectural splendour, Fitzwilliam makes up in friendly informality. Around 70 per cent of its undergraduates come from the state sector, and slightly under one third are women, though the college hopes 'significantly to raise this proportion in the coming years'.

Approximately 75 per cent of undergraduates are allocated rooms in college (first- and third-years guaranteed) but many second-years are obliged to fend for themselves in the city's relatively expensive private housing market. A new accommodation block is planned.

Fitzwilliam's academic record is improving, with languages and natural sciences the strongest subjects. Applications are also encouraged in archaeology and anthropology, classics, social and political sciences and history of art. As at Christs', offers of places on the basis of two Es only at A level are sometimes made.

On the extra-curricular front, the badminton, hockey and football teams are among the best in the university. The playing fields are a few hundred yards away. The twice termly 'Ents' (college entertainments) are exceptionally popular. Music and drama thrive.

GIRTON
Girton College, Cambridge CB3 oJG (tel. 0223 338999)

Undergraduates: 495

The joke about needing a passport to travel to Girton refuses to die. In fact, with the city centre a 10-minute cycle-ride away, the college is closer than many hostels at other universities. But if comparative isolation inevitably encourages a strong community spirit, Girtonians still manage to participate in university life at least as much as students at more central colleges.

Only Homerton, Trinity and St John's have more undergraduates. On the other hand, since Girton stands on a 50-acre site and the majority of second-year students live in Wolfson Court (near the University Library), there is no question of over-crowding.

Since going co-educational in 1979, the college has maintained a balanced admissions policy and currently has a 57/43 male-female ratio. Almost 60 per cent of undergraduates are from state schools. Girton also has the highest proportion of women fellows in any mixed college (50 per cent).

The on-site sporting facilities, which include a swimming pool, are excellent. The college is active in most sports, with athletics and, appropriately, water polo particularly strong.

Philip Brett, Head Gardener

GONVILLE AND CAIUS *West Rd CB3 9DS*
Gonville and Caius College, Cambridge CB2 1TA (tel. 0223 332400)

Undergraduates: 454

Caius, universally known as 'keys', is among the most beautiful of Cambridge's colleges, as well as one of the most central. It has an excellent academic reputation, especially in medicine and history, though the humanities, law in particular, are also highly rated. Book grants are available to all undergraduates.

Accommodation is split between the central site on Trinity Street and Harvey Court, a five-minute walk away. Rooms are guaranteed for all first- and third-years. The majority of second-years live in hostels, none of which is more than a mile away. Undergraduates are obliged to eat in Hall at least 45 times a term, a ruling some find restrictive but which at least ensures that students meet regularly.

The college has something of a Home Counties/public school reputation. At 65/35, for example, the independent-to-state school ratio is below average while only one-third of Caians are women. However, Caius is 'eager to extend the range of its intake'.

Caius tends to do well in rowing and hockey, but most sports are fairly relaxed. A lively social scene is helped by the student-run Late Night Bar.

HOMERTON
Homerton College, Cambridge CB2 2PH (tel. 0223 411141)

Undergraduates: 600

Designated 'an Approved Society of the University', Homerton is a teacher-training college offering four-year BEd courses.

All first-years have rooms in or around the college, but thereafter may have to take their chance in the open market. There is a 50/50 state-independent split, but with men making up no more than 10 per cent of those on the BEd course it's no surprise that the first-year atmosphere has been likened to that of a girls' boarding school.

Recent speculation over the possible sale of the college's 25-acre site to a supermarket chain has died down. Homerton looks set to stay in its present location about a mile from the city centre.

The college's position and specialized nature mean that the onus is very much on Homerton students to take the initiative if they wish to get involved in university activities. In most respects, however, Homerton is no different from the other undergraduate colleges and students can take advantage of Formal Hall, sport (there are on-site playing fields), music and drama.

JESUS
Jesus College, Cambridge CB5 8BL (tel. 0223 68611)

Undergraduates: 460

For those of a sporting inclination Jesus is perhaps the ideal college. Within its spacious grounds there are football, rugby and cricket pitches as well as three squash courts and no less than 10 tennis courts, while the Cam is just a few hundred yards away. With these facilities, it is hardly surprising that sports, in particular rowing, rugby and hockey, rate high on many students' agendas. That said, sporting prowess is far from the whole story.

The music society thrives, and has extensive practice facilities. And though Jesus lacks a theatre of its own, the college is active in university drama. On the academic front, the Fellows-to-undergraduates ratio is generous, and, while English and history are among the college's strong suits, the balance between arts and sciences is fairly even.

Rooms in college are guaranteed for all first- and most third-year students. The majority of second-years live in houses directly opposite the college. State-to-independent and male-to-female ratios are close to 50/50.

KING'S
King's College, Cambridge CB2 1ST (tel. 0223 350411)

Undergraduates: 389

The reputation of King's as the most right-on place in the university has become something of an in-joke. It is true that the college has a three-to-one state-to-independent ratio and that it has banned Formal Hall and abandoned May Balls in favour of politically correct June Events. But you do not have to be devoted to every liberal cause either to gain admission or to have a rewarding three years.

The college has fewer undergraduates than the grandeur of its buildings might suggest, one result being that accommodation is guaranteed, either in college or in hostels a few hundred yards away. With the highest ratio of Fellows to undergraduates in Cambridge, it is not surprising that King's is one of the most academically successful colleges. No subjects are especially favoured. Applications are not accepted in law and veterinary medicine.

Sport at King's is anything but competitive. An extremely large bar/JCR is the social focal point, while the world-famous chapel and choir form the heart of an outstanding music scene.

LUCY CAVENDISH
Lucy Cavendish College, Cambridge CB3 0BU (tel. 0223 332190)

Undergraduates: 60   *Vince Lucas Head Gardens*

Since its creation in 1965, Lucy Cavendish has given hundreds of women over the age of 21 the opportunity to read for Tripos subjects. A number of its students had already started careers and/or families when they decided to enter higher education. The college seeks to offer financial support to those with family responsibilities, though as yet it has no child care facilities or married quarters

Accommodation is provided for all who request it, either in the college's four Victorian houses or in its modern residential block. The college's small size enables all students to get to know one another. Plans to increase the intake are unlikely to alter the intimate and informal atmosphere.

Law is still the dominant subject in terms of numbers of students, but the college welcomes applications in the sciences and other disciplines. All the Fellows are women. For subjects not covered by the Fellowship, there is a well-established network of university teachers.

Coloum Shepherd   CS428@cam.ac.uk

MAGDALENE
01223 332111
Magdalene College, Cambridge CB3 0AG (tel. 0223 332100)

Undergraduates: 317

As the last college to admit women (1988), Magdalene has still to throw off a lingering image as home to hordes of public school hearties. In fact, just over half its undergraduates are from the state sector while 35 per cent are women. That said, the sporty emphasis, on rugby and rowing in particular, is undeniable. The nearby playing fields are shared with St John's.

Despite finishing closer to the foot of the academic league tables than its Fellows would wish, Magdalene is strong in architecture, law, social and political science and medicine. The college is currently encouraging applications in maths and natural sciences.

Accommodation is provided for all undergraduates, either in college or in one of 23 houses and hostels, 'mostly on our doorstep'. Living in is more expensive than in most colleges. Magdalene is justly proud of its river frontage, the longest in the university, which is especially memorable in the summer.

NEW HALL
New Hall, Huntingdon Road, Cambridge CB3 0DF (tel. 0223 352941)

Undergraduates: 314

One of three remaining all-women colleges, New Hall enjoys a largely erroneous reputation for feminism and academic underachievement. Founded in 1954 to increase the number of women in the university, it occupies a modern grey-brick site next door to Fitzwilliam. Students are split 50/50 between state and independent schools.

The college lays claim to certain paradoxes. While a rent strike in November 1992 attested to a degree of political activism, tradition is far from rejected. June 1993, for example, will see New Hall's first-ever May Ball, an event to be hosted jointly with Sidney Sussex.

If its results place the college near the bottom of the academic league, they are not unfavourable compared with those obtained by women throughout the university. Natural sciences, medicine, languages, English and history are New Hall's strongest areas. Applications are also particularly encouraged in maths, computer science and engineering.

The college has all the usual bar and cafeteria facilities, but many students choose to socialise elsewhere. Sport is a good mixture of high-fliers and enthusiasts, with grounds, shared with Fitzwilliam, half a mile away.

NEWNHAM
Newnham College, Cambridge CB3 9DF (tel. 0223 335700)

Undergraduates: 390

Newnham has long had to battle with a blue-stocking image. Its entry in the university prospectus insists that it 'is not a nunnery' and that the atmosphere in this all-women college is no stricter than elsewhere. With a one-to-one state-independent ratio, the college has also successfully cast off a reputation for public-school dominance.

Newnham is in the perfect location for humanities students, with the lecture halls and libraries of the Sidgwick Site just across the road. The college is, however, keen to encourage applications in engineering, maths and the sciences. All of the Fellows are women.

Around 95 per cent of students live in for all three years. This is not to say that ventures into the social, sporting and artistic life of the university are the exception rather than the rule. Newnham students are anything but insular.

As well as being blessed with the largest and most beautiful lawns in Cambridge, Newnham has its playing fields on site. The boat club has been notably successful, while college teams compete to a high standard in tennis, cricket and a number of minority sports.

nick.firmanepem.com.a
.u

PEMBROKE
Pembroke College, Cambridge CB2 1RF (tel. 0223 338100)

Undergraduates: 350

0223 339858

Another college with a reputation for public-school dominance (the current state-to-independent ratio is around 40/60), Pembroke's image is changing. Rowing and rugby still feature prominently, but with a female population of about 40 per cent the heartiness is giving way to a more relaxed if still somewhat insular atmosphere.

Around 50 per cent of undergraduates live in college, including all first-years. The rest are housed in fairly central college hostels, though standards of these are variable. Academically, Pembroke is considered solid rather than spectacular. Engineering and natural sciences have the largest number of undergraduates, but the subject range is wide.

The bar is inevitably the social focal point, but a restriction on advertising means that Pembroke bops attract few students from other colleges. The Pembroke Players generally stage one play a term in the Old Reader, which also doubles as the college cinema, and many Pembroke students are involved in university dramatics. The Old Library is a popular venue for classical concerts. Indeed music is a Pembroke strength.

In a city of memorable college gardens, Pembroke's are among the most memorable. *Head Gardens*

Peterhouse College etc.

PETERHOUSE
Peterhouse College, Cambridge CB2 1RD (tel. 0223 338200)

Undergraduates: 220

The oldest and smallest of the colleges, Peterhouse is another college that has had to contend with an image problem. But while by no means as reactionary as its critics would have it, Peterhouse is certainly not overly progressive. There is a two-to-one male-to-female split, while the state school-independent ratio is 'the university average'.

The college's diminutive size – its entire student population is the same as one year's intake at Trinity – inevitably makes for an intimate atmosphere. But this does not mean that its undergraduates never venture beyond the college bar.

Peterhouse is known above all as 'the history college'. But while history is indeed a traditional strength, there are in fact no more history students than there are natural science students or engineering students. Academically, the college is a consistent mid-table performer.

The 13th-century candle-lit dining hall provides a fitting setting for what by common consent is the best food in the university. Rents are below the university average, and undergraduates live in for at least two years, with the remainder choosing rooms in college hostels, most within one or two minutes' walk.

The sports grounds are shared with Clare and are about a mile away. The college teams have a less than glittering reputation.

Steve Tyrell - Head Gardener

QUEENS'

Queens' College, Cambridge CB3 9ET (tel 0223 335511)

Undergraduates: 451   *01223 335560*

There is a strong case for claiming that Queens' is the most tightly knit college in the university. With all undergraduates housed in college for the full three years, a large and popular bar and outstanding facilities, it is easy to see why. Queens' also has the distinction of attracting an above-average number of applicants. The male-to-female (57/43) and state-to-independent (56/44) ratios are good.

Though not to all tastes, the mix of architectural styles, ranging from the medieval Old Court to the '80s Cripps Complex, is as great as any in the university. In addition to three excellent squash courts, the Cripps Complex is also home to Fitzpatrick Hall, a multi-purpose venue containing Cambridge's best-equipped college theatre. Partly as a result, Queens' has perhaps the foremost college drama society. The hall is also used for films and discos.

Law, maths, engineering and natural sciences are the leading subjects in a college with an enviable academic record. Queens' is not especially sporty. The playing fields (one mile away) are shared with Robinson.

ROBINSON

Robinson College, Cambridge CB3 9AN (tel. 0223 311431)

Undergraduates: 390

Robinson is the youngest college in Cambridge and admitted its first students in 1979. Its unspectacular architecture has earned it the nickname 'the car park'. On the other hand, having been built with one eye on the conference trade, rooms are more comfortable than most and many have their own bathrooms. About 90 per cent of students, including all first- and third-years, live in college or in houses in the attractive gardens.

Robinson has been close to the bottom of the academic tables recently. There is no particular subject bias and one in four fellows are women, the second highest proportion in any mixed college.

Its youth and balanced admissions policy (one-to-one schools ratio, 44 per cent female intake) ensure that Robinson has one of the more unpretentious atmospheres. The auditorium is the largest of any college and is a popular venue for films, plays and concerts. The college fields (shared with Queens') are home to excellent rugby and hockey sides, and the boat club is also successful.

FAo the garden

ST CATHARINE'S
St Catharine's College, Cambridge CB2 1RL (tel. 0223 338300)

Undergraduates: 405 *Fax 01223 330819*

Known to everyone as Catz, this is a medium-sized, 17th-century college standing opposite Corpus Christi on King's Parade. The principal college site, with its distinctive three-sided main court, though small, provides accommodation for all first- and third-year students. The majority of second-years live in flats at St Chad's Court about a 10-minute walk away. The rest seek rooms on the open market.

Catz is not one of the leading colleges academically. Geography and law are usually the strongest subjects. Forty per cent of the students are women, while the split between independent and state school pupils is about even.

College social life centres on the large bar, which has been likened, among other things, to a ski chalet or sauna. With a reputation for being sporting rather than sporty, Catz is one of the few colleges that regularly puts out three rugby XVs, and also has a good record in football and hockey. The playing fields are about a 10-minute walk away.

Adam Magee   a. mageejoh.cam.ac

ST JOHN'S
St John's College, Cambridge CB2 1TP (tel. 0223 338600)

Undergraduates: 531 *01223 33871*

Second only to Trinity in size and wealth, St John's has an enviable reputation in most fields. The wealth translates into excellent accommodation in college for almost all undergraduates throughout their three years as well as book grants – and a full-time bicycle repair man.

There is no particular subject bias and John's has a formidable academic record. A reputation for heartiness persists, and the female intake is slightly below average at 30 per cent. The state school-independent split is about 50/50.

The boat club's performance is not always as lofty as its reputation, but rugby, hockey and cricket are all traditionally powerful. In such a large community, however, all should be able to find their own level. Extensive playing fields shared with Magdalene are a few hundred yards away and the boathouse is extremely good.

The college film society organises popular screenings in the Fisher Building, which also contains an art studio and drawing office for architecture and engineering students. Music is dominated by the world-famous choir.

Paul Gallant

gardens@sel.cam.ac.uk

SELWYN
Selwyn College, Cambridge CB3 9DQ (tel. 0223 335846)

01223 331868

Undergraduates: 319

Described by one undergraduate as 'the least overtly intellectual college', Selwyn has a down-to-earth and relatively unpressured atmosphere. Located behind the Sidgwick Site, it is in an ideal position for humanities students, and its academic strength has traditionally been on the arts side.

One of the first colleges to go mixed (1976), Selwyn now has a 40 per cent female population. The state-to-independent ratio is one to one. Accommodation is provided for all students, either in the college itself or in hostels, all of which are close by.

As well as the usual college groups, the Music Society is especially well supported. The bar is popular if a little 'hotel-like'. In sport, the novice boat crews have done well in recent years, as have the hockey and badminton sides, but the emphasis is as much on enjoyment as achievement. The grounds are shared with King's and are three quarters of a mile away.

SIDNEY SUSSEX
Sidney Sussex College, Cambridge CB2 3HU (tel. 0223 338800)

Undergraduates: 307

Students at this small, central college are forever the butt of jokes about Sidney being mistaken for the branch of Sainsbury's over the road. Two other, more serious aspects of life at Sidney stand out: almost every year its undergraduates raise more for the Rag Appeal than any others; while rents are comfortably the lowest in the university (all students are housed either in college or one of 11 nearby hostels).

Exam results generally place the college in the middle of the academic leagues. Engineering, geography and Medieval and modern languages are the strongest subjects.

Sidney has a good social balance, with a one-to-one state to independent ratio, while 33 per cent of the undergraduates are women. There is a large student-run bar which is the venue for fortnightly bops, an active drama society (SADCO) and plenty of involvement in university activities.

The sports grounds are shared with Christ's and are a 10-minute cycle ride away. Sidneyites are enthusiastic competitors, but the college does not have a reputation for excellence in any individual sports.

Dennis Sutton Scotman
(Hd. Gravelener)

TRINITY
Trinity College, Cambridge CB2 1TQ (tel. 0223 338400)

Undergraduates: 648

338530

The legend that you can walk from Oxford to Cambridge without ever leaving Trinity land typifies Cambridge undergraduates' views about the college. Indeed, the college is almost synonymous with size and wealth. However, the view that every Trinity student is an arrogant public schoolboy is less easily sustained. That said, it is true that only about a quarter of Trinity undergraduates are women, the lowest proportion in any of the mixed colleges. On the other hand, there is little obvious bias towards independent schools in the admissions policy.

Being rich, Trinity offers book grants to every student as well as generous travel grants and spacious, reasonably priced rooms in college for all first- and third-year students as well as many second-years. The college generally features in the top 10 academically. The strongest subjects are English, maths and natural sciences.

Trinity rarely fails to do well in most sports, with cricket in the forefront. The playing fields are half a mile away.

For such a large college, the bar is unbelievably small. The Trinity Sweatys attract students from all over the university.

Andrew Myson   adm57@cam.ac.uk

TRINITY HALL
Trinity Hall, Cambridge CB2 1TJ (tel. 0223 332535)

Undergraduates: 322   *Porters Lodge 01223 332500*

The outstanding performance of its oarsmen has ensured the prevailing view of Trinity Hall as a 'boaty' college, but it is also known for its drama, music and bar. The Preston Society is one of the better college drama groups and stages regular productions both in the college theatre and at other venues. Weekly recitals keep the Music Society busy. The small bar is invariably packed. Not surprisingly, many undergraduates' rarely feel the need to go elsewhere for their entertainment.

The college is strong academically. Law is a traditional speciality, though the natural sciences are also well represented. About one-third of the undergraduates are women and around 60 per cent are from public schools.

All first-years and approximately half the third year live in the college, which is situated on the Backs behind Caius. The remainder take rooms either in two large hostels close to the sports ground (a mile from college), or in college accommodation about five minutes' walk away.

CITY UNIVERSITY
Northampton Square, London EC1V 0HB (tel. 071-477 8000)

Founded 1894, royal charter 1966
Times ranking: 48

Enquiries: undergraduate admissions office
Full-time students: 1,443 (f), 2,481 (m)

Main subject areas: engineering (BEng, MEng); mathematics, studies related to medicine, business and management (BSc, LLB); social science and music (BA).

Almost half of the university's students are on postgraduate courses, mainly in the large schools of engineering and journalism or in the Barbican-based business school. The rest are in a cluster of buildings on the borders of the City of London.

In spite of its history as a college of advanced technology, City now has nearly as many students taking arts and social science subjects as on the science side. It has acquired a strong reputation for music (BBC) in association with the Guildhall School of Music and Drama, and for business studies (also BBC).

The university is also practising what it preaches in the management field, through a manufacturing company with a turnover of £7.5 million a year. Most courses have a vocational slant and many, such as air transport engineering and clinical communication studies (both BCC), are highly specialised.

A number of degrees can be taken either as four-year sandwich programmes or on a three-year, full-time basis. The university is another to feature regularly at the head of graduate employment lists.

City should be comparatively well off in 1993, having received above average budget increases for both teaching and research. Recent expansion has also provided a healthy income from fees. Almost one in five of the students are from overseas.

First-years who accept a place by the middle of May are guaranteed accommodation in one of the four modern halls, which are all within easy reach of the campus. All the halls have workstations linked to the university's mainframe computer.

Students find the cost of living high, both in and out of the university, and complain about the food. However, they speak highly of the staff, who are considered unusually supportive. In spite of this, drop-out rates are relatively high.

Sports facilities are good, but those for outdoor games are inconveniently placed south of the river. The students' union is cramped, but due for replacement in 1995.

COVENTRY UNIVERSITY

Priory Street, Coventry CV1 5FB (tel. 0203 631313)

Royal charter 1992, formerly Coventry (originally Lanchester) Polytechnic

Times ranking: 61

Enquiries: academic registry (tel. 0203 838482)
Full-time students: 2,432 (f), 2,908 (m)
2,480 **arts,** 2,860 **sciences**

Main subject areas: engineering (BEng); applied science (BSc); art and design, social, biological and health sciences, business (BA, BSc). About a third of students on certificate or diploma courses.

Coventry is behind only Leeds Metropolitan, Portsmouth and Middlesex among the new universities in *The Times* table. As a polytechnic, it scored consistently in the funding council's quality ratings for teaching, and has built up a thriving research and consultancy base.

A rough balance is maintained between arts and science students in order to preserve an all-round educational environment. Quality awards in seven out of the nine academic areas in 1992 suggest that the generalist approach is paying off. Engineering, social sciences and art and design all fared particularly well.

Coventry specialises in practical and socially oriented activities, linking higher education with business and industry. Its reputation has attracted hundreds of managers from the former Soviet Union, learning everything from how to privatise Lada cars to selling baked potatoes on the streets of Moscow.

The university's priorities are closer to home, however. One project has seen an old welfare building converted into a self-help centre for local people with business ambitions. But the main contribution to the area comes in the shape of 11,000 full- and part-time students, many of whom begin courses at further education colleges.

Most full-time and sandwich students construct their own degree programme within faculty limits. They are encouraged to take a foreign language and develop computer skills. Each module is assessed separately and credited towards the final degree classification.

A disused factory is being refurbished to add teaching room to the city-centre campus. The 18-hectare site is beginning to feel the strain of considerable expansion in recent years. Further growth is planned over the remainder of the decade.

The university has 1,500 residential places, but many first-years still have to rely on the private sector, where rents are generally low and accommodation relatively easy to find. Students say that town and gown relations are not always good, but the union provides a good social base.

DE MONTFORT UNIVERSITY

The Gateway, Leicester LE1 9BH (tel. 0533 551551)

Royal charter 1992, formerly Leicester Polytechnic

Times ranking: 70

Enquiries: academic registrar

Full-time students: 4,060 (f), 6,104 (m)

1,269 arts, 1,475 sciences

Main subject areas: applied physical sciences (BSc); arts (BA); built environment, business, combined studies, health and life sciences, design and manufacture (BA, BSc); computing and mathematical sciences (BSc); engineering (BEng, BSc); and law (LLB, BA). Also more than 20 certificate and diploma courses.

Like the 13th-century Earl of Leicester, after whom the university is named, De Montfort University has a fiefdom of sorts: it is made up of a network of campuses in a 50-mile radius. Based on what was Leicester Polytechnic, the new university has been spreading ever outwards in pursuit of a target of 30,000 students by the year 2000.

Two campuses in Leicester itself will soon become three with the addition of a nursing and midwifery college, and there is a substantial outpost at Milton Keynes. Now, Bedford College of Higher Education and the Lincolnshire Colleges of Art and Design, and Agriculture and Horticulture have also agreed to join the fold.

The latest additions will bring teacher training, sports science, craft-related art and design, conservation, restoration, agriculture and horticulture into the curriculum. The number of students will reach 18,500, strengthening the university's further education provision, as well as extending the range of higher education subjects.

Professor Ken Barker makes no bones about De Montfort's academic ambitions. 'Higher education has been too busy chasing Nobel prizes, instead of giving industry and the community the service they really need,' he said in welcoming the new arrivals.

Law, mathematics, business studies and art and design are already strong at degree level in the new university. The limited range of postgraduate programmes has also been growing steadily.

Before the new colleges joined, De Montfort had 1,256 hall places (766 for men and 490 for women) and room for another 392 students in a head tenancy scheme. Priority is given to younger first-years, most of whom are found accommodation.

The new, energy-efficient School of Engineering and Manufacture, which opens in September, has already won architectural awards. Other buildings inherited from the local authority are less than beautiful, but are being renovated gradually.

There are purpose-built student unions on all sites, and a health service shared with Leicester University. Students find the main campus by far the most lively. Inevitably, conditions will become more variable as extra sites are added.

UNIVERSITY OF DERBY

Keddleston Road, Derby DE3 1GB (tel. 0332 47181)

Royal charter 1992, formerly Derbyshire College of Higher Education
Times ranking: 96

Enquiries: registry
Full- and part-time students: 4,518 (f), 4,059 (m)
6,514 arts, 2,043 sciences

Main subject areas: technology and science (BSc); humanities, business, art and design (BA); law (LLB); health (BSc); education (BEd). Certificate and diploma courses, as well as degrees.

The newest of the new universities, Derby was the only higher education college to acquire a university title with the former polytechnics. Ministers took an extra three months to come to a decision, but were convinced that, alone of the college candidates, Derby met both the academic and physical criteria for promotion.

The city had long claimed to be the largest in Europe without a major higher education institution. The college, itself a product of several mergers, had been expanding rapidly to be ready for a change of status, and is still growing.

Having missed out on the advantages enjoyed by the polytechnics, Derby has some leeway to make up in *The Times* table, but developments already under way should improve its position in years to come. Applications for places doubled in 1992. Having increased the size of its intake by one-third in a single year, the university is set to meet its target of 12,000 students by 1996.

A high proportion of the 8,000 students now at the university are local, 2,500 of them taking part-time courses. The academic programme is in the process of transition to a modular system and, as host to the Trans-European Exchange and Transfer System, Derby offers more opportunities than most to take part of a course abroad.

Photography, film and television studies are highly rated, and are underpinned by a £1-million research centre. Engineering is also strong, and a new materials research group is ranked fourth in the country by the Science and Engineering Research Council. Health and community studies, too, are supported by a new research unit.

A new city-centre site, financed partly from the council's City

Challenge, will soon join the main campus, which overlooks rolling countryside. The new premises will rehouse the school of art and design, while an engineering research centre is being planned in partnership with Rolls Royce and British Rail, two local employers with whom the former college of higher education had a long relationship.

The university is adding to a limited stock of residential accommodation, but many first-years will still have to rely on the private housing market. In the main, students are fiercely proud of the university's achievements, although some complain that the facilities do not match up to other campuses.

UNIVERSITY OF DUNDEE
Dundee DD1 4HN (tel. 0382 23181)

Founded 1882, part of St Andrews University until 1967
Times ranking: 43

Enquiries: admissions office
Full-time students: 2,545 (f), 3,054 (m)
3,018 **arts,** 1,951 **sciences**

Main subject areas: medicine and dentistry (MB, BDS); science and engineering (BSc, BEng); law (LLB); arts and social science (BA); and environmental studies (BArch, BSc).

Though a merger with neighbouring Duncan of Jordanstone College of Art, whose students already share facilities, will add another 1,200 students, the university is still relatively small. Only the medical school, set in 20 acres of parkland, lies outside the compact campus near the centre of Dundee.

The medical school and Centre for Medical Education, at nearby Ninewells Hospital, rate as world leaders in a number of fields, including nursing studies and the treatment of wounds. Professor Ronald Harden's system of assessing medical trainees is used in many countries.

Biotechnology (CDD) is the other flagship department, and is recognised as one of Europe's top centres for the subject. Its academics hold research grants worth more than £10 million, and were among the first in Britain to be invited to participate in Japan's Human Frontier science programme.

Psychology (BCC), electronic engineering (two Ds) and biological sciences (CDD) are also strong. The law department is the only one in Scotland to offer an English LLB, as well as Scottish and Northern Irish qualifications.

Vocational degrees predominate, but a number of combinations, such as American or European studies, are now available. Transfers between courses are relatively easy.

Interviews are usual only in medicine, dentistry, architecture and town planning. However, others offered a place are invited to visit Dundee before committing themselves.

First-years who need accommodation are guaranteed one of the 850 residential places provided they accept by the end of August. One student in five lives at home. Private rented accommodation is reasonably priced.

The student association has spacious premises for the size of university, and sports facilities are good. The Royal and Ancient Club, at St Andrews, offers £1,000 bursaries to the most promising golfers.

Students find the city unattractive, if welcoming, but there are compensations in the magnificent countryside and coastline, both within easy reach. The campus is the focal point of social activity.

UNIVERSITY OF DURHAM
Old Shire Hall, Durham DH1 3HP (tel. 091-374 2000)

Founded 1832
Times ranking: 11

Enquiries: academic registrar
Full-time students: 2,924 (f), 3,163 (m)
3,227 arts, 2,054 sciences

Main subject areas: full range of disciplines apart from art, medicine, dentistry and veterinary science. Faculties of arts and social sciences (BA), and of science (BSc).

Long established as a leading alternative to Oxbridge, Durham even delays selection to accommodate those applying to the ancient universities. A collegiate structure and picturesque setting are further attractions for a predominantly middle-class student body.

An insistence on interviews gives candidates the chance to see if Durham is the university for them – and vice versa. Since 90 per cent of undergraduates come from outside the Northeast, most are seeing the small cathedral town for the first time.

Applications have to be made to one of the 12 colleges, all but one of which are mixed. The colleges range in size from 200 to 600 students and form the focus of social life, though all teaching is done in central departments.

Chemistry (CCD), geography (BBC), music and physics (both BCC) are among the top departments. Only Oxford and Cambridge have higher entry standards.

Durham is determinedly traditional. Whenever possible, teaching takes place in small groups, and most assessment is by written examination. Resits are permitted only in the first year, although the dropout rate is the lowest in the country.

The university has broken out of its traditional mould with two recent projects, however. The first saw the establishment in the city of the Teikyo University of Japan. The second was the opening of a college at Stockton in partnership with Teesside University.

In addition to the facilities available in colleges, there is a large central students' union overlooking the river. The university dominates the town, but Newcastle is only a short train journey away for those looking for a change of scene.

Sport occupies an important place in university life. Representative teams have outdone Oxford and Cambridge in some of the most prestigious pursuits, including rugby, cricket and rowing.

The university finds accommodation for more than 4,000 of its 6,000 students, and guarantees places for first-years. Students stress the importance of finding the right college, since they all have their own character. Some feel uncomfortable with the high proportion of colleagues from independent schools.

UNIVERSITY OF EAST ANGLIA
Norwich NR4 7TJ (tel. 0603 56161)

Royal charter 1963
Times ranking: 32

Enquiries: registrar and secretary
Full-time students: 2,417 (f), 2,708 (m)
2,786 **arts,** 1,377 **sciences**

Main subject areas: natural sciences (including mathematics, computing and electronic engineering) BA; arts and social sciences (including law and accountancy) BA and LLB.

The University of East Anglia (UEA) is in the midst of an ambitious building programme to house the extra students it plans to take over the next few years. Over £18.5 million is being spent to provide another 1,100 residential places. At present, the campus, two miles from the centre of Norwich, has 1,400 study bedrooms, while the university controls enough accommodation elsewhere to guarantee all first-years a place. But despite occupying 270 acres of parkland, UEA only recently passed the 5,000 student mark.

With most students coming from outside the region, including 16 per cent from overseas, the university feels obliged to make its own provision for growth. The construction projects will also include a building, paid for by the regional health authority, for academic developments in physiotherapy (BBC) and occupational therapy (BCC), as well as a drama studio. Health-related studies are among UEA's fastest-developing areas. Although there is no medical school, the university validates courses in nursing, and several of the highly rated research teams are involved in the field.

Environmental sciences (AAB for a four-year degree, including a year in the United States) is particularly highly regarded. The climatic research centre is one of the leaders in the investigation of global warming.

Schools of studies encourage broad combinations of subjects. The biggest are economic and social studies, and English and American studies. Malcolm Bradbury's association with the creative writing course has attracted a string of big names, and made English degrees (three Bs) particularly popular.

Art history (BBC) is another strong subject, aided by the presence of the Sainsbury Centre for the Visual Arts, perhaps the greatest resource of its type on any British campus. The centre, which acquired a new wing two years ago, houses a priceless collection of modern and tribal art.

Social and sporting facilities are good. Most students enjoy the campus life, even if some find communications from Norwich frustratingly slow.

UNIVERSITY OF EAST LONDON
Romford Road, London E15 4LZ (tel. 081-590 7722)

Royal charter 1992, formerly Polytechnic of East London, originally North East London Polytechnic
Times ranking: 93

Enquiries: precinct registrar
Full-time students: 3,560 (f), 3,550 (m)
3,500 **arts,** 3,600 **sciences**

Main subject areas: built environment (BSc); business (BA); health and rehabilitation, science (BSc); social sciences (BA, LLB); technology (BSc, BEng). Certificate and diploma courses are also offered.

Once known as a pathfinding polytechnic, some of East London's more innovative features, such as the School for Independent Study, have been fading recently. In fact, the institution came in for considerable criticism from the Council for National Academic Awards before university status arrived in 1992.

Only the sandwich courses in art and design were rated in the polytechnics' last quality awards. Otherwise, inspectors found fault with the systems and computing, business studies and manufacturing systems courses.

The institution has never been far from controversy in its 20-year history. Dogged by student unrest in the '70s, in the '80s it was plagued by disputes with staff and continuing financial uncertainty. The difficulties continued in 1991 when the director, and former Labour education minister, Gerry Fowler, resigned suddenly. His successor, fully intent on putting the university's turbulent past behind it, faces the daunting task of welding together a university sprawling over six sites in some of the most deprived areas of London.

More than half of the students are over 21 on entry, and a third take part-time courses. The university caters particularly for the ethnic minorities in its locality, drawing almost half its students from them. Classes in English as a second language, designed mainly for overseas students, are provided free of charge.

Most degrees are vocational, one in seven students taking sandwich courses. UEL has regained architecture and teacher education, ensuring that it offers one of the widest ranges of subjects in the new universities.

Libraries are divided between the sites according to subject. But if spending on books has generally been low, there is an unusual science fiction collection.

UEL has more residential accommodation than many of the former polytechnics. Two new halls have added 500 places to the 1,300 already owned or controlled by the university. Although the students' union is active, its members complain that the university lacks a focal point.

UNIVERSITY OF EDINBURGH

Old College, South Bridge, Edinburgh EH8 9YL (tel. 031-650 1000)

Founded 1583
Times ranking: 5

Enquiries: schools liaison office
Full-time students: 5,748 (f), 6,766 (m)
5,274 arts, 4,891 sciences

Main subject areas: complete range of traditional disciplines in eight faculties: arts (BA); divinity (BD); law (LLB); medicine (MBChB, BSc Med Sci, BDS); music (BMus); science and engineering (BSc, BEng); social sciences (BSc Soc Sci); veterinary medicine (BVMS).

Despite a cash crisis that prompted a freeze on staff appointments in 1991, Edinburgh remains Scotland's leading university. The £5-million deficit has been brought under control. New developments are in train.

Chief among them is an expansion in student numbers to 15,500 in

1993–94. As part of this ambitious programme, the university aims to add 1,000 residential places by 1995 at a cost of £30 million. The university already has accommodation for 5,000 students, half of them in halls of residence, meaning that all first-years who live outside the city are guaranteed a place.

The university has long had a cosmopolitan flavour, in part the result of being in the Scottish capital, in part the result of the mix of students. The proportion of Scottish students, for example, still the single largest group, has dropped lately to little more than half the student body. Much of the slack has been taken up by English students, with whom the university has always been popular. In addition, 15 per cent of places are taken up by overseas students.

The university buildings are scattered around the city, but most of the faculties border the historic Old Town. There is also a new science campus two miles to the south.

Notable among the large number of subjects in which Edinburgh enjoys a high reputation are medicine (ABB), biology (CCD), microelectronics (three Cs) and languages (BBC for Chinese, but all EC languages are taught, as well as Japanese, Russian, Persian and Turkish). The law faculty is the largest in Scotland. Computer science, geology and geophysics (all three Cs) are all also strong.

Sir David Smith, the principal, has introduced a number of radical policies, including a green initiative, which covers teaching, research and even student behaviour. The university is also collaborating with district and regional authorities in the development of a 'science city' on its 230-acre Bush Estate near the airport.

Library facilities are outstanding, the students' association extensive and well organised. Scientists can feel isolated, but there are few complaints from most of Edinburgh's students – except about the weather.

UNIVERSITY OF ESSEX
Wivenhoe Park, Colchester CO4 3SQ (tel. 0206 873333)

Royal charter 1965
Times ranking: 46

Enquiries: admissions officer
Full-time students: 1,694 (f), 2,374 (m)
2,096 **arts**, 1,019 **sciences**

Main subject areas: arts (BA); engineering and technology (BEng, MEng, BSc); sciences and mathematics (BSc); social sciences (BA, LLB).

Essex is only now living down its reputation as a hotbed of student unrest in the '60s and '70s. A reputation for high-quality research, especially but by no means exclusively in the social sciences, is ousting what was once an all-pervading image of Essex as a byword for political activism.

As the only university to feature in the top ten allocations for both teaching and research, Essex plainly does not need to convince the funding council of its excellence. Only its size and arts bias prevented its finishing higher in *The Times* table.

Sociology (BCC) is especially strong, attracting a series of prestigious research projects as well as favourable ratings for teaching. Electronic engineering, linguistics and computer science (all BCC) are also highly rated.

But improvements in the university's real function have been unable to disguise that the university's glass-and-concrete campus outside Colchester is showing distinct signs of a quarter of a century of wear. Teaching and administration blocks cluster around a network of squares; most residential accommodation is in six less than lovely tower blocks nearby.

Essex was originally expected to grow rapidly to become a medium to large university, but government cuts intervened and it has remained among the smallest. Now expansion is under way again, thanks to a £5-million development plan, which will add 1,200 residential places in a new student village. The first 234 places, together with a day nursery and extra teaching accommodation, should be ready for the 1993–94 academic year. The university already has 2,500 places, enabling it to guarantee accommodation to all first-years.

Many of the lecturing staff are graduates of the high-flying academics attracted to Essex by its pioneering broad approach to subjects. In most schools, undergraduates still follow a common first year before specialising.

Almost a quarter of the students are over 21 on entry, an unusually high proportion for a traditional university. Essex has been more flexible than most of its rivals about entry qualifications, and has encouraged applications from comprehensive schools in deprived areas of east London and its own county.

Social and sporting facilities are good, partly because they were designed for a larger student population. Town and gown relations in the garrison base of Colchester have not always been smooth, and the campus can be bleak in winter, but students do not doubt the academic quality.

UNIVERSITY OF EXETER

Northcote House, Queen's Drive, Exeter EX4 4QJ (tel. 0392 263263)

Royal charter 1955
Times ranking: 36

Enquiries: admissions officer
Full-time students: 3,201 (f), 3,118 (m)
3,633 **arts,** 1,533 **sciences**

Main subject areas: arts, social sciences (BA); engineering and technology (BEng, BSc); science and mathematics (BSc); law (LLB); education (BA Ed, BSc Ed, BEd).

Judged in terms of applications per place, Exeter is one of the country's most popular universities, especially on the arts side. For some, its principal handicap is its image as an alternative to Oxbridge for undergraduates from the private sector. So seriously did the university take this apparent problem that at one point in the '80s it established a quota of places for state-school pupils.

The main campus, close to the centre of Exeter, is one of the most attractive in Britain. The highly rated school of education (three Cs with physical education) is a mile away in the former St Luke's College. The university has also established a foothold in Cornwall by taking on the Camborne School of Mines.

There is a long tradition of European integration, exemplified by the European Law degree (AAB). All students are offered tuition in European languages, and a number of degrees now include the option of study abroad.

Modular degrees are arriving. They are already established in arts, law and social studies, allowing students to construct a programme from a wide range of courses at the end of their second year.

Unlike many of its rivals, Exeter is satisfied to remain relatively small. The intake of 2,000 undergraduates in October 1992 was less than 10 per cent up on the previous year's. Future expansion will be equally gradual.

Although Exeter's greatest strength is in the arts, psychology (AAB) and geography (three Bs) are highly rated, while engineering (three Cs for mechanical) will benefit from its additional base at Camborne. History, English literature (both three Bs) and drama (BBC) have long been among the most heavily subscribed courses in their fields. French (BBC) is also strong.

The Northcott Theatre, on the main campus, is one of the cultural centres of the region, and sporting facilities are excellent. The guild of students, which was rated among the most right-wing in a new student guide, has a prize-winning radio station.

Students resent the 'green welly' image, but value the easy access to beautiful countryside and beaches. Exeter may be less lively than larger city universities, but its academic standing is high.

UNIVERSITY OF GLAMORGAN

Pontypridd, Mid Glamorgan CF37 1DL (tel. 0443 480480)

Royal charter 1992, formerly Polytechnic of Wales
Times ranking: 87

Enquiries: admissions officer
Full-time students: 1,995 (f), 3,781 (m)
2,631 **arts,** 3,145 **sciences**

Main subject areas: 13 departments in three faculties: environment studies (BSc); technology studies (BEng, MEng, BSc); and professional studies (BA, BSc, LLB). Also certificate and diploma courses in all three areas.

Wales's second university used to be the smallest of the polytechnics. Although still not large, Glamorgan is expanding rapidly, largely by franchising its courses to colleges at home and abroad.

Twinning programmes operate in five overseas centres, while in Wales a growing number of further education colleges are also offering the university's certificate, diploma or degree courses. More than 1,000 part-time and 200 full-time students are registered in 1993.

Glamorgan has also made Pembrokeshire College an associate college, providing an outpost in West Wales, and is experimenting with the Principality's first compact at Afan College. Students will be guaranteed places on diploma or degree courses if they fulfil set conditions.

The university's own campus is a 12-mile train ride out of Cardiff, overlooking the market town of Pontypridd. Originally based in a large country house, the university now has purpose-built premises for the science and technology departments.

The best-known degrees are in engineering and professional studies, but the separate Welsh higher education system has prevented their being judged against their English equivalents. Electrical and electronic engineering are also strong, and have been at the forefront of the university's thriving teaching company business.

Glamorgan is committed to retaining its vocational slant. A diploma in management has been tailored to the needs of the Driver and Vehicle Licensing Agency, for example. A new degree in theatre and media drama, produced in collaboration with the Welsh College of Music and Drama, caters for would-be production staff as well as actors.

Many of the students choose to live in Cardiff, which is both livelier than Pontypridd and a better source of accommodation. The university has only 500 hall places, though hopes to build more if funds can be raised. Recent spending has been on a three-storey recreation centre to capitalise on a fine sporting tradition, especially in rugby. The students' union is the focus of social life. Its bars are the only areas in the university excluded from an otherwise blanket no-smoking policy.

UNIVERSITY OF GLASGOW
Glasgow G12 8QQ (tel. 041-339 8855)

Founded 1451
Times ranking: 17

Enquiries: academic registrar
Full-time students: 5,861 (f), 6,915 (m)
5,048 **arts,** 6,323 **sciences**

Main subject areas: 120 departments in eight faculties: arts, social sciences (BA, BEd, BMus); divinity (BD); engineering (BEng, MEng); law and financial studies (LLB, BAcc); medicine (MB, BDS); science (BSc); veterinary medicine (BVMS).

Glasgow is Scotland's largest university as well as one of its oldest. The university has the rare distinction of having been established by Papal Bull, and began its existence in the Chapter House of Glasgow Cathedral. It is also the most obviously Scottish: 80 per cent of students are from north of the border. Glasgow was also the first university to have a school of engineering.

Strengths today include medicine (three Bs), electrical engineering (two Cs), genetics (CCD) and veterinary science (AAB). The numbers of students taking science courses are the largest such concentration outside London.

The impressive, compact campus is in the city's lively West End, with the vets on a greenfield site four miles away. Most of the 3,000 residential places are within easy walking distance of the main campus. First-years are guaranteed a place if they live outside daily commuting distance.

Interviews are usual only in medicine, dentistry, veterinary science and nursing. Good A-level passes should secure admission to the second of four years in some science, engineering and arts degrees. Among some innovative degrees are Scottish language and literature, law with modern languages, and literary and linguistic computing. The Cities in Change programme is intended to develop into an urban studies degree in the autumn of 1993.

The library is large, with 2,500 workstations as well as a number of valuable collections. The Hunterian musuem and art gallery are similarly noteworthy.

Students can choose between two independent student unions, until recently segregated by sex. The Queen Margaret Union and the more rumbustious Glasgow University Union both run bars and leisure facilities, while the students' representative council has responsibility for student political activities. It also has its own shops and a travel agent.

Most students like the combination of campus and city life offered by the university and appreciate what seems generally agreed to be the city's stimulating and gutsy atmosphere, although the relatively high drop-out rate remains something of a worry. Sports facilities are reasonable, though a separate membership fee for the athletic union reduces participation.

GLASGOW CALEDONIAN UNIVERSITY
Cowcaddens Road, Glasgow G4 oBA (tel. 041-331 3000)

Royal charter 1992, formerly Queen's College (founded 1875) and Glasgow Polytechnic (founded 1972)
Times ranking: 94

Enquiries: academic registrar
Full-time students: 1,869 (f), 2,397 (m)
2,097 **arts,** 2,169 **sciences**

Main subject areas: health, science, engineering and construction (BSc, BEng); business, management and social sciences (BA, BSc). Diploma courses are also offered.

The proposal to call Glasgow's new, merged university The Queen's University, Glasgow, brought objections from Queen's in Belfast and a consequent long hiatus over a title. In the end, the institution became the only university to have its name determined by the students and staff. A ballot in December 1992 produced the name Caledonian from four possibilities acceptable to the authorities.

The new university is one of Scotland's largest with almost 10,000 students, including part-timers. There are three sites: City, adjoining Glasgow's Queen Street and central bus stations; Park, in the tree-lined West End; and the more outlying Southbrae, which houses the health faculty opened by the Princess of Wales in 1991 and where the health facilities are among the most extensive in Britain.

Ian Lang, the Scottish Secretary, has enthused about the potential unleashed by marrying the polytechnic's science and management strengths with the health care and business studies expertise of Queen's. Laboratories costing £11 million for health, science, engineering and construction, which were opened by the polytechnic in 1992, will assist the process.

Degrees are strongly vocational, and are complemented by a range of professional courses. A high proportion of the students are on part-time or sandwich courses. Among the full-time programmes, the unique BA in risk management is especially popular.

The polytechnic pioneered credit accumulation and transfer in Scotland, and the scheme is still the country's largest, covering the full range of courses.

Links with Europe are developing from a strong base in the two partner institutions, both of which offered courses taught partly abroad. A quarter of the polytechnic's undergraduates took language courses, while at Queen's business and management students learnt French or German.

Queen's had a strong majority of women among its students, evening up the balance of the sexes in the new institution. The college has also provided most of the 200 residential places available to students. Priority is given to overseas students, English, Welsh and Irish students, and those from the Scottish islands. Most of the students come from the west of Scotland, however, and either live at home or in lodgings, taking advantage of the private housing market. Sports facilities are not good, but the students' union is active on all sites.

UNIVERSITY OF GREENWICH
Wellington Street, Woolwich, London SE18 6PF (tel. 081-316 8000)

Royal charter 1992, formerly Thames Polytechnic
Times ranking: 79

Enquiries: registry
Full-time students: 3,487 (f), 4,906 (m)
2,839 **arts,** 3,088 **sciences**

Main subject areas: built environment, business (BSc, BA); social sciences and humanities (BA); education (BEd); science and technology (BSc, BEng). Also a wide range of certificate and diploma courses.

The former Thames Polytechnic grew over the years by absorbing a number of colleges of art and education. As a result, Greenwich has a wider range of courses and more accommodation than many of the new universities.

Though there are seven sites in all, with outposts in Docklands and Dartford, in Kent, an imaginative deal with Greenwich council has ensured that the university remains firmly rooted on the south bank of the Thames. The sites may be rationalised over time.

The university has strong links with European institutions, a legacy of its polytechnic days. (At one point the polytechnic considered relocating in Kent to exploit these links.) Today, there are formal exchange arrangements with universities or colleges in France, Germany, Greece, Ireland and Spain.

Five of the eight academic areas in which degrees are offered won quality awards in the last assessment by the Polytechnics and Colleges Funding Council. Engineering and technology, and science and education both fared particularly well. Architecture and some business and management courses were also rated highly. The education faculty, based on the old Avery Hill College, is one of the few in Britain to train teachers for primary, secondary and further education.

There are libraries and bars on all seven sites. The students' union operates on four. Sports facilities are widely spread, but comprehensive. The Dartford campus used to house a physical education college. At Woolwich there is access to a dry ski slope.

Greenwich's legacy also means that it is one of the few new universities to guarantee accommodation for first-years who apply before the end of August. There are more than 1,200 hall places; accommodation officers are available on 081-316 8115 to advise on availability.

With none of the sites in Greenwich proper, some students consider the university's new title misleading. The point has also been made that, like many multi-site institutions, conditions are variable according to the subject chosen.

HERIOT-WATT UNIVERSITY
Riccarton, Edinburgh EH14 4AS (tel. 031-449 5111)

Founded 1921, royal charter 1966
Times ranking: 43

Enquiries: admissions officer
Full-time students: 3,619 (f), 4,096 (m)
3,114 arts, 2,565 sciences

Main subject areas: science (BSc); engineering (BSc, MEng); economic and social studies (BA); environmental studies (BArch, BSc); art and design (BA); textiles (BSc); education (BEd).

Although best known for its degree in brewing and distilling (three Ds), Heriot-Watt has a variety of such programmes, as well as more conventional degrees, offshore engineering (three Ds), actuarial mathematics and statistics, and microwave and optoelectronics (CDD) among them. Physics (CCD) and civil engineering (CDD) are the top-rated departments for research.

The range of subjects has been extended by the addition of nearby Moray House College of Education, Edinburgh College of Art and the Galashiels-based Scottish College of Textiles. Science, engineering, economic and social studies are located on a single parkland campus at Riccarton, in west Edinburgh.

The Riccarton campus contains half of the 2,300 residential places, including a 250-bed hall with en suite facilities in every room. Accommodation is virtually guaranteed to all first-years from outside Edinburgh as long as they apply by early September.

Heriot-Watt is technologically based, with business and language courses complementing its strengths in science and engineering. The university is moving to modular degrees over the next few years, and already offers highly flexible combined studies programmes.

More than a third of the students come from outside Scotland, including 14 per cent from overseas. The university has been expanding, despite some financial difficulties, and was given a substantial increase in its teaching budget for 1992–93.

Research income has been healthy, both from research councils and industrial partners. In 1989–90, only Oxford and London had a better record when adjustments were made for size. The large and growing commercial research park at Riccarton was the first of its type in Europe.

Heriot-Watt has also been a leader in the use of information technology for teaching, harnessing the most advanced computing facilities to allow students to work at their own pace. A huge research and development programme with the computer giant Digital has smoothed the way.

Students praise the extensive sports facilities and the modern union at Riccarton. The campus is far enough from the city centre (seven miles) to be the inevitable centre of social life.

UNIVERSITY OF HERTFORDSHIRE

College Lane, Hatfield, Herts (tel. 0707 28400)

Royal charter 1992, formerly Hatfield Polytechnic
Times ranking: 61

Enquiries: admissions office
Full-time students: 3,978 (f), 5,286 (m)
4,313 **arts**, 4,951 **sciences**

Main subject areas: business (BA); engineeering (BEng); health and human sciences (BSc, LLB, BA); humanities and education (BA, BEd); information sciences, natural sciences (BSc). Certificate and diploma courses also offered in most areas.

One of the few genuinely rural universities, Hertfordshire has three spacious sites, as well as an observatory and biology field-station. Though the main campus is in Hatfield, there is a business school at Hertford, while humanities and education are based at Wall Hall, near the M1.

As a result, many students have to commute from the surrounding towns and villages. The accommodation office considers 15 miles a reasonable distance, although most of those living away from home can have at least one year in residence. Three-quarters of the 1,600 hall places are reserved for first-years. Most are at Hatfield, and are arranged in self-catering units with some rooms adapted for the disabled. All sites have wheelchair facilities.

Hatfield Polytechnic's reputation was built on engineering, science and computing, which account for a large slice of the new university's work. However, health, arts and humanities are all growing fast. European links are a speciality. Exchange programmes operate with 40 universities and colleges.

Courses are modular, giving a degree of flexibility that especially suits those students over 25 (almost a third of the student body), many of whom are taking a career break. Nearly half the undergraduates take a language option, and they are encouraged to take 'free choice' courses in subjects outside their degree programmes, which can contribute to their final results.

The university also has a well-developed sandwich course system. A high proportion of the 11,000 students include work placements in their degrees, and the close links with employers have brought in valuable research and consultancy contracts.

Hertfordshire's academics have always been strong on research, particularly in areas such as medical electronics. They took a leading role in many of the polytechnics' national initiatives, and have expanded their volume of activity dramatically in the last two years, hoping to compete with the traditional universities.

Sports and student union facilities are good. Students value the university's proximity to London, but some find the immediate surroundings more quiet than they would like.

UNIVERSITY OF HUDDERSFIELD

Queensgate, Huddersfield HD1 3DH (tel. 0484 422288)

Royal charter 1992, formerly Huddersfield Polytechnic
Times ranking: 87

Enquiries: registrar
Full-time students: 2,985 (f), 3,899 (m)
4,262 **arts,** 2,622 **sciences**

Main subject areas: accountancy, law and management studies (BA, LLB); applied sciences, computing and mathematics (BSc); business (BA); human and health sciences, design technology (BCs); education (BEd); humanities and music (BA). Also a wide range of certificate and diploma courses.

Unlike most of the original polytechnics, Huddersfield leans towards the arts, although it tries to give them a vocational slant. Historical and political studies, for example, includes a six-week work placement.

The engineering courses are highly rated, and full-time degrees in textile design, communication arts and social sciences are all well regarded. More than half the students take sandwich courses.

Huddersfield is also one of only four centres training teachers for further education. Other education courses specialise in craft, design and technology, and retraining mature students with business experience to teach business studies in secondary schools.

The main campus is on a crowded site near Huddersfield town centre. The education department is two miles away. New buildings are planned to cater for continuing growth in student numbers over the next few years. Intakes have been rising by about 13 per cent a year, with special encouragement given to mature students without conventional qualifications, and applicants from under-represented social groups.

Among the new university's first major projects has been the provision of a new students' union, due to open in 1993. The union has had financial problems, but will now be able to supplement the university's overcrowded catering facilities.

As the university grows, so accommodation is also becoming more of a problem. Although there are 1,000 residential places, mostly within easy walking distance of the campus, the private housing market in Huddersfield is limited. First-years are given priority for the university's places.

Sports facilities are also relatively poor, consisting of a small sports hall and playing fields two miles from the campus. Some students prefer to use more extensive council facilities.

Town and gown relations are good, and Huddersfield students like the university's communal atmosphere. Their main concerns are over the pressure on space and the prospect of larger teaching groups.

UNIVERSITY OF HULL
Hull HU6 7RX (tel. 0482 46311)

Founded 1928, royal charter 1954
Times ranking: 54

Enquiries: academic registrar
Full-time students: 3,403 (f), 3,270 (m)
3,114 **arts,** 2,565 **sciences**

Main subject areas: arts (BA, BMus); science and mathematics (BSc); law and social sciences (BA, LLB); engineering and technology (BEng, BSc); education (postgraduate only).

Although neither would be considered fashionable, both the university and the city of Hull inspire strong loyalty among students. As Philip Larkin, once the university librarian, said: 'People are slow to leave it, quick to return'.

One reason is the low cost of living. Hall fees have been among the lowest in the traditional universities, and private accommodation is even cheaper. First-years are guaranteed one of the 2,750 residential places, some of which have en suite facilities.

The campus occupies 94 acres less than two miles from the centre of Hull. It includes a spacious and well-stocked library, and some valuable art in the Middleton Hall gallery, which is open to the public.

Strength in politics (BBC) is reflected in 13 graduates in the House of Commons, Euromindedness in the fact that every EC language except modern Greek can be taken at degree level. Electronic engineering (CCD) and engineering design manufacture (three Cs) are among the other top courses, although in general the university fared poorly in the December 1992 research rankings.

The university believes that a roughly equal balance between science and technology, arts, and social sciences helps promote a harmonious atmosphere. The absence of a medical school is being overcome, in collaboration with the local health authority, by the establishment of a postgraduate medical school with nine departments.

Hull finishes disappointingly low in *The Times* table largely because of the staffing economies the university has made in recent years. Having increased student numbers at the same time, Hull now relies more for its income on student fees than any of the traditional universities. There are few complaints from the students, however. A refurbished students' union and a new health-and-fitness centre have added to the leisure facilities. First-class degrees are hard to come by, but drop-out rates are relatively low. The university encourages visits from prospective applicants.

UNIVERSITY OF HUMBERSIDE

Cottingham Road, Hull HU6 7RX (tel. 0482 440550)

Royal charter 1992, formerly Humberside Polytechnic
Times ranking: 91

Enquiries: admissions office
Full-time students: 3,822 (f), 3,616 (m)
5,804 **arts,** 1,634 **sciences**

Main subject areas: art, architecture and design (BA); food, fisheries and environmental studies (BSc, BA); business (BA, BSc, BEng); social and professional studies (BA, BSc). Certificate and diploma courses are also offered.

A heavy preponderance of arts and social science students betrays the new university's origins as a collection of arts-based colleges in the 1970s. After only two years as a polytechnic, Humberside is relying on innovative teaching and international links to make its reputation.

BP has been sufficiently impressed to donate £1 million for the appointment of a professor of learning development. Computer-assisted learning and lectures via satellite are among the developments planned to cater for a fast-growing student population.

The university, which now has more than 9,000 students, including 3,000 part-timers, operates on four main sites in Hull and one in Grimsby. But growing numbers choose to spend part of their courses abroad. Six degree programmes carry the option of a year in the United States. There is even a link with the University of Technology, in Sydney, Australia.

Europe provides even more opportunities for Humberside students. The 60 formal links with European institutions outdoes even the continental accent of neighbour Hull University (see page 125). One in eight students is on a European course, and Humberside is one of the leading participants in EC higher education programmes.

Closer to home, the university has established good contacts with local companies, carrying out research and consultancy through its own trading company and providing a ready supply of work placements for sandwich courses.

Six local colleges run access courses for students who lack the necessary entry qualifications, and where possible courses are structured so that students can switch between full- and part-time attendance. Humberside is also one of the new universities experimenting with accelerated degrees, allowing students to take an honours degree in only two years by extending the academic year to 45 weeks.

If sports and student union facilities are limited, they are at least improving. Some students feel that the university is too spread out, and are concerned about the strains imposed by a rate of growth which reached 20 per cent in 1991.

UNIVERSITY OF KEELE
Staffordshire ST5 5BG (tel. 0782 621111)

Founded 1949 (as University College of North Staffordshire)
Times ranking: 54

Enquiries: director of academic affairs
Full-time students: 2,301 (f), 2,071 (m)
2,398 **arts,** 538 **sciences**

Main subject areas: humanities, history and American studies, human development, political and social sciences, management and economics (BA); science and engineering, earth sciences, computational, mathematical and neuro-sciences (BSc).

Keele is being steered firmly in the direction of teaching, rather than research, in spite of a 14 per cent real growth in external research income in each of the last three years. It received the largest increase in state funds for teaching of any traditional university in 1992–93, but among the lowest for research. The university topped a funding council 'worry list' in 1990 but is now out of the red and expanding fast.

New admissions were up by 20 per cent in 1991, and the university now has more than 4,500 students. However, the 617 acres of campus, among the most scenic in the country, can take many more. A small student body has had its advantages, but it has limited the variety of courses Keele has been able to offer and restricted the size of research groups. The objective now is to become established as the leading interdisciplinary university in Britain, with 7,500 students by the end of the decade.

The breadth of Keele's courses has always been its biggest selling point. About a third of the undergraduates are on four-year degrees with a general foundation year. Most students combine two main subjects with a subsidiary from the other side of the arts/science divide.

American studies (BBC), international relations (BCC) and the many dual honours degrees – especially those featuring politics and music – are among the university's strengths. Science subjects have been improving, as the university demonstrated by attracting two top scientists from ICI to run a new inorganic chemistry and materials science group.

October 1993 will see a switch to modular courses and two 15-week semesters, replacing the traditional academic year. The university is committed to ensuring that there is at least one member of staff for every 15 students throughout the period of expansion, a much more generous ratio than is expected in the new universities.

Keele also expects to continue accommodating at least 70 per cent of its full-time students. At present, it guarantees residential places on campus for all first-years. Students criticise the standard and size of the library, but the university has promised improvements.

UNIVERSITY OF KENT AT CANTERBURY
Canterbury CT2 7NZ (tel. 0227 764000)

Royal charter 1965
Times ranking: 32

Enquiries: admissions office
Full-time students: 2,510 (f), 2,802 (m)
3,071 **arts,** 1,191 **sciences**

Main subject areas: humanities (BA); social sciences (BA, LLB); information technology (BSc, BEng); natural sciences (BSc).

Kent has been a pioneer among the traditional universities in the adoption of flexible degree programmes and a strong European emphasis. Interdisciplinary study is encouraged, and a number of courses include the option of a year elsewhere in Europe. Almost a quarter of the undergraduates take a language for at least part of their degree, and European studies are among the most popular subject combinations. The theme carries through into research as well as teaching.

Like other universities established in the 1960s, Kent has always encouraged students to broaden their studies, allowing changes of specialism up to the end of the first year. The university also has a joint stake in 26 access courses throughout the county, giving more than 500 students the opportunity to upgrade their qualifications to degree entry standard.

The university is generally stronger in the arts than sciences. Social policy and administration (three Cs) is the top-rated research area, while the combination of sociology and social anthropology (also three Cs) has proved particularly successful.

Science subjects have not been neglected, however, and are being actively built up. Computer science and mathematics (both BCC), are well regarded, while degrees in the recently established business school (BBC for management science) are also in demand.

Students are attached to one of the four colleges, which include lecture theatres as well as study bedrooms and social facilities. Nine out of ten first-years, and more than half of all Kent's students, live in university-owned accommodation. All new students are offered a residential place.

The modern campus, overlooking Canterbury, has a cosmopolitan feel, enhanced by the presence of Chaucer College, an independent Japanese university, which opened in 1992. Though Kent is particularly popular with American students, those from other countries are also well represented. In 1991–92, there were students from 83 different countries at the university.

Students complain that the campus is often quiet at weekends, and worry about the effects of expansion on Canterbury's limited housing market. 1992's dramatic increase in student numbers may not be repeated, but growth is expected to continue for the next few years.

KINGSTON UNIVERSITY

Penrhyn Road, Kingston upon Thames, Surrey KT1 2EE (tel. 081-547 2000)

Royal charter 1992, formerly Kingston Polytechnic
Times ranking: 61

Enquiries: admissions officer
Full-time students: 3,181 (f), 4,744 (m)
4,022 **arts,** 3,903 **sciences**

Main subject areas: design (BA, BSc); business and law (BA, LLB); education (BEd, BA); technology (BSc, BEng); human sciences (BA); science (BSc). Certificate and diploma courses are also offered.

Having topped the polytechnics' quality ratings for two years in succession, Kingston is bullish about its prospects of competing with the traditional universities. Only the health and social services courses failed to score in 1991–92, despite the fact that the number of students had almost doubled in five years without appreciable growth in staff.

With student numbers having already passed 15,000, expansion will be slower in the next few years. The new university expects to extend its teaching day to 12 hours and the academic year to 50 weeks to cope.

Kingston also hopes to use its growing reputation in research to win a slice of the older universities' funds. Private research income is already healthy, as staff in all six faculties are encouraged to extend their interests beyond teaching. The business school has been especially successful. The Small Business Unit, for example, has won formal recognition as a national centre of excellence.

The four sites in southwest London are linked by an unusually extensive, 700-terminal computer network. Three of the four are close to Kingston town centre, while the business school is based in a stately home in 50 acres of woodland two miles away. A new technology block has replaced teaching accommodation once used to build Sopwith Camels and Hawker Hurricanes.

First-years are given priority for the 900 residential places, but many have to make use of the accommodation office's register of 2,500 places in flats and lodgings. Rents in the private market are notoriously high.

Sports facilities are adequate, and lectures are not held on Wednesday afternoons to encourage students to make use of them. The main students' union is lively, and there are branches on the other sites. But if most students like the university's location on the fringe of London, complaints about the high cost of living are frequent.

UNIVERSITY OF CENTRAL LANCASHIRE
Preston PR1 2QT (tel. 0772 201201)

Royal charter 1992, formerly Lancashire (originally Preston) Polytechnic
Times ranking: 76

Enquiries: access and student recruitment unit
Full-time students: 3,974 (f), 4,015 (m)
4,554 arts, 3,435 sciences

Main subject areas: business, cultural, legal and social studies (BA); design and technology (BA, BSc, BEng); health, science (BSc). Also a wide range of certificate and diploma courses.

Though ambitious construction projects have produced more teaching space and some 1,150 residential places, the new university is still struggling to cater for the extra students it is taking. Numbers have doubled in the last few years, and are due to carry on rising.

Pontin's holiday camp in Southport has become a regular feature of student life in Central Lancashire, having been used for emergency accommodation at the start of the last four academic years. Two new halls of residence should ease the problems in 1993.

The university has a single, predominantly modern campus in the centre of Preston. It is proud of its local commercial and community contacts, recruiting 40 per cent of its entrants locally.

It also claims largest proportion of mature students in the country. This is partly due to a well-established network of links with colleges throughout the Northwest, which enables students to take part of their degree near home. A number of access courses are available for candidates without traditional qualifications.

Looking increasingly outwards, Central Lancashire has now linked up with more than 30 partner institutions in Europe and the United States. Many courses offer the opportunity to study abroad.

The new university is strong in art, design and astronomy, with two observatories including Britain's most powerful optical telescope. Health-related activities are also being expanded through a partnership with the Royal Preston Hospital to establish a centre for medical studies.

Courses are now arranged on a credit system, although the amount of flexibility varies considerably between faculties. Where the system is fully operational, students choose their own units, which build into a degree. Electives are used to broaden the curriculum, with courses in subjects outside the student's normal range taking up to 15 per cent of his or her time.

Sports facilities are good, but the students' union is crowded. Students say that the institution would cater well for 7,000 rather than the 14,000 of them it now contains.

UNIVERSITY OF LANCASTER
University House, Lancaster LA1 4YW (tel. 0524 65201)

Royal charter 1964
Times ranking: 37

Enquiries: admissions office
Full-time students: 2,851 (f), 2,895 (m)
3,214 **arts,** 1,260 **sciences**

Main subject areas: science and engineering (BSc, BEng); management, social sciences (BA, BSc); humanities (BA).

Lancaster is another of the campus universities of the '60s. Like the others, it has always traded on its flexible degree structure. Undergraduates take three subjects in their first year. Only at the end of it must they select that in which they intend to specialise.

Combined degree programmes, including a relatively new range of combined sciences, are popular. Some degrees also offer 'active learning courses', in which work on outside projects counts towards final results.

Accountancy (BBC) has been rated the top department of its kind in Britain for research. Indeed, the seven top scores in 1992's research rankings was an outstanding performance. Religious study (BCD), bio-chemistry, sociology and environmental science (all BCC) are all highly regarded. The department of independent studies allows students to put together their own package of subjects.

A fifth of the entrants are mature students, a high proportion for a traditional university and the result in large part of an innovative scheme, subsequently developed in the polytechnics, which allows adults to join courses through their local college.

Lancaster also has a strong research record, especially in environmental subjects. This was reflected in a larger budget allocation in 1992–93 for research than for teaching. The business school took joint first place for business and management subjects in *The Times* table.

Half of the students are accommodated in the eight campus colleges, which have between 400 and 800 students each. All students and academic staff are attached to a college, whether or not they are residents. Non-scientific departments are also based in the colleges, but students are not matched to their host college's specialism.

First-years are guaranteed a residential place, but housing is becoming more of a problem for those who then move out, as most do. The university is planning to build more residences.

Students take full advantage of the nearby Lake District, although some find the campus, three miles out of Lancaster itself, more isolated than they expected. There are few complaints about the facilities, however. The students' union lacks a building of its own, but the campus is well equipped for sports.

UNIVERSITY OF LEEDS
Leeds LS2 9JT (tel. 0532 431751)

Founded 1874, royal charter 1904
Times ranking: 26

Enquiries: undergraduate admissions office
Full-time students: 5,901 (f), 7,708 (m)
5,365 **arts,** 5,971 **sciences**

Main subject areas: full range of subjects in seven faculties: arts (BA); science (BSc); engineering (BEng, MEng); medicine and dentistry (MBChB, MBChD); education (postgraduate only); economics and social studies (BA); law (LLB).

Among the biggest of the civic universities, Leeds occupies a 140-acre site near the city centre and the Metropolitan university (see page 133). It claims to have as wide a variety of courses as any British university.

English (ABC), education and mathematics (both BBC), mechanical engineering (three Cs) and geology (CCD) are among the top-rated subjects. The English department is one of the largest in the country, but those in search of something less traditional have plenty of choice, from Chinese (BBC) to colour chemistry (BCC).

The impressive Brotherton Library is one of the top university libraries, containing twice as many books as most of its counterparts. Students also have access to a particularly powerful computer network, with more than 1,400 terminals.

Leeds is an enthusiastic participant in European exchange programmes, with almost 100 Continental partners. One undergraduate in ten takes a language course, and there is a free-standing language unit.

First-year students are guaranteed a residential place, and most then move into the relatively cheap private sector, assisted by an efficient accommodation service. Most students find flats or houses close to the university.

The students' union is one of the biggest in Britain, and long famed as a venue for rock concerts. Sports facilities are also plentiful, although the playing fields are four miles away.

Students like the broad mix of backgrounds within the university, which includes more than 1,000 from overseas, and value the good town/gown relationship that has come with the city centre location. The cost of living is reasonable, and the city lively.

One blackspot last year was the unemployment rate for new graduates, which unexpectedly reached 14 per cent. Leeds may have suffered for its efficiency in keeping track of more job-seekers than some apparently successful rivals. When measured over a longer period, the university does not compare unfavourably with others for job prospects.

LEEDS METROPOLITAN UNIVERSITY
Calverley Street, Leeds LS1 3HE (tel. 0532 832600)

Royal charter 1992, formerly Leeds Polytechnic
Times ranking: 57

Enquiries: course enquiries officer
Full-time students: 4,668 (f), 4,646 (m)
5,370 **arts,** 3,944 **sciences**

Main subject areas: business (BA, LLB); environment (BSc); cultural and educational studies (BA, BEd); health and social care (BSc, BA); information and engineering systems (BEng, BSc). Also a full range of certificate and diploma courses.

Leeds Metropolitan finishes top among the new universities in *The Times* ranking, despite doing only moderately well in the polytechnics' last quality assessments. Its staffing levels and employment rating are among the main factors contributing to that success, but Leeds' secret lies in all-round strength.

Including part-timers, Leeds has 19,000 students. It expects to become even bigger in the next few years. As a result, large sums have been invested in new teaching methods. Students are likely to come face to face with a computer or video as often as a lecturer in the basic teaching sessions.

Personal contacts with academic staff are being reserved mainly for seminar groups and small group teaching. The system is supported by libraries that are larger than normal among the new universities, with more than 1,000 study spaces and 500,000 books.

Hotel catering, sport and recreation, personnel management and environmental studies are all well regarded. Both the business school and the engineering courses finished in the top 15 in their respective subject tables. Students are included on the committees that design and manage all courses.

The new university has two campuses: the main site close to the city centre and Leeds University (see page 132), and Beckett Park three miles away in 100 acres of park and woodlands. The latter boasts outstanding sports facilities and most of the university's residential places, as well as teaching accommodation for education, infomatics, and leisure and tourism.

Almost all the 800 hall places are allocated to first-years, but this by no means satisfies demand. Others rely on the accommodation agency run jointly with Leeds University.

Almost all the students are over 21 at entry, many living at home, which eases some of the pressure on accommodation. A minority are on conventional, full-time degrees because of the popularity of both sandwich and part-time courses.

Students praise the level of social and leisure facilities. The students' union is large and active, while the physical education college which formed part of the polytechnic has left a legacy of success in sporting competitition.

UNIVERSITY OF LEICESTER

University Road, Leicester LE1 7RH (tel. 0533 522522)

Founded 1918, royal charter 1957
Times ranking: 37

Enquiries: admissions office
Full-time students: 3,381 (f), 3,512 (m)
2,826 arts, 2,593 sciences

Main subject areas: arts (BA); science (BSc, BEng); social science (BA); law (LLB); medicine (MBChB); education (postgraduate only).

Leicester has been expanding more rapidly than most of the traditional universities, doubling its student numbers in recent years. After several decades of life as one of the smaller universities, it plans to have 10,000 places by the end of the decade.

Although only three departments reached the top rung of the research ladder in 1992's rankings, the university did well in the 1992–93 funding allocations for both teaching and research. It is a leader in space science (BCC with physics), while the medical school, built in the 1970s, is the newest in the country.

Though recent merger discussions with Loughborough University (see page 148), prompted by concern on the part of Leicester over its size rather than by worries about academic or financial weakness, have come to nothing, the two neighbours are to collaborate on a number of research projects.

There has been a proliferation of research centres at the university, including one for mass communications, which has spawned strong undergraduate courses in all aspects of the media. The siting of a medically based interdisciplinary research centre in Leicester is also a sign of growing strength in the medical school.

Apart from clinical medicine, most teaching and residential accommodation is concentrated in a leafy suburb little more than a mile from the city centre. The campus is a mixture of Georgian and modern architecture in sometimes uneasy combinations.

Computing facilities have been resited and modernised recently, with 1,000 microcomputers and 750 workstations for student use. An audio-visual centre is also widely used for teaching.

With some 3,000 residential places at its disposal, the university is well able to guarantee accommodation to first-years. A high proportion of undergraduates stay in university accommodation throughout their student life. Five of the six halls are in a complex at Oadby, two miles from the campus with which it is linked by a special bus service. The main sports ground and sports hall are also at Oadby. Social facilities, both in the halls and on campus, are good and reasonably priced.

Leicester has an equal opportunities code for admissions, which has helped to increase the proportion of mature students to almost one in five. Only a minority of departments interview candidates as a matter of course, but those offered places are invited to visit.

UNIVERSITY OF LIVERPOOL

PO Box 147, Liverpool L69 3BX (tel. 051-794 2000)

Founded 1881
Times ranking: 19

Enquiries: faculty admissions office
Full-time students: 4,871 (f), 5,553 (m)
4,023 arts, 4,598 sciences

Main subject areas: full range of degree courses in eight faculties: arts (BA, BMus); engineering (BEng, MEng); medicine and dentistry (MBChB, BDS); science and mathematics (BSc); social and environmental studies (BA, BSc, BArch); law (LLB); education (BA); veterinary science (BVSc).

Another big university to have experienced recent financial difficulties, Liverpool has now recovered sufficiently to appoint a series of new professors. Among them is a new vice-chancellor, Professor Philip Love, who hopes to build on a longstanding reputation for quality research.

Only six universities exceeded the £23 million external research income Liverpool attracted in 1992–93, while with the research councils alone the university achieved an indentical ranking. Liverpool has now been among the top dozen recipients of research council funds for the last 15 years.

Expansion has also brought more money for teaching in 1992–93. Postgraduate numbers have been increasing as quickly as undergraduate numbers. The growth is intended to continue for several years.

Hispanic studies (BCD), and physics, pharmacology and nursing (all three Cs) are highly rated, but the university prides itself on strength across all faculties. Interdisciplinary courses have been expanded, for example introducing engineering with management and European studies, law and German, and geophysics, mathematics and information studies.

Undergraduate courses are being divided into eight units per two-semester year. The three terms are to stay for the moment, but a more radical reorganisation is a possibility in the future.

Liverpool was among the first of the traditional universities to run access courses for adults without traditional academic qualifications. Now 15 per cent of undergraduates are over 21 at entry, and the proportion is still rising.

The university precinct, which includes the large and well-equipped guild of students, is only half a mile up the hill from the city centre. The 2,300 hall places, which can accommodate all first-years, are three miles away in a wooded suburb. Sports facilities are excellent. Both the university and the city, which, whatever its problems, remains vibrantly self-confident, are generally popular with students.

LIVERPOOL JOHN MOORES UNIVERSITY

Rodney House, 70 Mount Pleasant, Liverpool L3 5UX (tel. 051-231 2121)

Royal charter 1992, formerly Liverpool Polytechnic
Times ranking: 71

Enquiries: admissions
Full-time students: 5,139 (f), 5,885 (m)
4,585 **arts,** 6,439 **sciences**

Main subject areas: art, media and design, built environment (BA, BSc); business, social science (BA); education and community studies (BEd, BA); law, social work and social policy (BA, LLB); engineering and technology management (BEng, MEng, BSc); information science and technology, natural sciences and health sciences (BSc). Diploma courses are also offered.

Naming itself after a football pools millionaire is not the first gamble the former Liverpool Polytechnic has taken. In 1991 it launched Britain's first student charter, offering fee rebates if guarantees on library, teaching and accommodation services were not kept.

Later, while waiting for university status to arrive, JMU announced an ambitious plan to turn itself over 10 years and at a cost of £80 million into a huge, futuristic, multi-media institution. In the process, JMU set itself the task of transforming not only higher education in the city but the dilapidated city centre itself. Among the new initiatives are the replacement of many lectures by computer-based teaching methods, thus freeing teaching staff for face-to-face tutorials, and the goal of 22,000 students by the turn of the century.

It's a far cry from the recent past. Under local authority control in the dim, dark days of Militant, the polytechnic once came to the brink of closure. Perhaps in compensation, since gaining independence JMU has seemed to make a point of celebrating its escape with a series of showy occasions to mark new developments. Even before university status, the mission statement opened with a desire to be a 'prestigious' as well as progressive institution. There is, however, no intention of abandoning the range of diploma courses which have traditionally supplemented the largely vocational degree programmes.

The new university is scattered across Liverpool, the result of the gradual acquisition of a number of colleges. In keeping with its ambitions, it is already one of the biggest in the country, with more than 16,000 students, including part-timers.

A growing research reputation is a source of particular pride, and is reflected in an unusually large number of postgraduates for a new university. Engineering and education were the most highly-rated areas in polytechnic days, with pockets of top quality in science and art and design.

University-owned residential accommodation is scarce for the size of institution. There are only 320 hall places, although more than 1,000 places are available in self-catering flats. With little accommodation in the immediate vicinity of the university, students are expected to travel up to eight miles to lectures.

UNIVERSITY OF LONDON
Senate House, Malet Street, London WC1E 7HU (071 636 8000)

Founded 1836
Times ranking: 5

Enquiries: to individual colleges, institutes or schools.
Full-time students: 23,847 (f), 27,545 (m)

The federal university is Britain's biggest by far, although some of the most prestigious members are considering going their own way. Indeed its colleges and institutes have already seen their financial and academic autonomy increased considerably.

They are bound together by the London degree, which enjoys a high reputation worldwide. The colleges are responsible both for the university's academic strength, demonstrated again in *The Times* table, and its apparently precarious financial position.

London students have access to some joint residential accommodation, sporting facilities and the University of London Union. But most identify with their college, which is their social and academic base.

Colleges not listed separately but admitting undergraduates:
Birkbeck College, Malet Street, London WC1E 7HX (tel. 071-631 6561). Mainly part-time, 2,457 arts, 1,919 sciences.
Charing Cross and Westminster Medical School, Reynolds Building, St Dunstan's Road, London W6 8RP (tel. 071-846 7202). Degrees in medicine and BSc. 847 students.

Courtauld Institute of Art, Somerset House (North Block), The Strand, London WC2R 0RN (tel. 071-873 2645). History of art degree. 264 students.
Heythrop College, 11–13 Cavendish Square, London W1M 0AN (tel. 071-580 6941). Theological college. 228 students.
Jews' College, Albert Road, London NW4 2SJ (tel. 081-203 6427). Degree in Jewish studies. 20 undergraduates.
London Hospital Medical College, Turner Street, London E1 2AD (tel. 071-377 7000). Degrees in medicine and BSc. 877 students.
Royal Academy of Music, Marylebone Road, London NW1 5HT (tel. 071-935 5461). Music degree. 466 students.
Royal College of Music, Prince Consort Road, London SW7 2BS (tel. 071-589 3643). Music degree. 491 students.
Royal Free Hospital School of Medicine, Rowland Hill Street, London NW3 2PF (tel. 071-794 0500). Medical degree. 581 students.
Royal Veterinary College, Royal College Street, London NW1 0TU (tel. 071-387 2898). Degrees in veterinary medicine and BSc. 429 students.
St Bartholomew's Hospital Medical College, West Smithfield, London EC1A 7BE (tel. 071-982 6000). Degrees in medicine and BSc. 715 students.
St George's Hospital Medical School, Cranmer Terrace, London SW17 0RE (tel. 071-672 9944). Degrees in medicine and BSc. 627 students.
St Mary's Hospital Medical School, Norfolk Place, Paddington, London W2 1PG (tel. 071-723 1252). Degrees in medicine and BSc. 575 students.
School of Oriental and African Studies, Thornhaugh Street, Russell Square, London WC1H 0XG (tel. 071-637 2388). Arts and social science degrees. 1,332 undergraduates.
School of Pharmacy, 29–39 Brunswick Square, London WC1N 1AX (tel. 071-753 5830). Degrees in pharmacy and toxicology. 375 undergraduates.
School of Slavonic and East European Studies, London WC1E 7HU (tel. 071-637 4934). Arts degrees only. 421 undergraduates.
United Medical and Dental Schools (Guy's and St Thomas's), Lambeth Palace Road, London SE1 7EH (tel. 071-922 8013). Degrees in medicine, dentistry and BSc. 1,650 students.
Wye College, Ashford, Kent TN25 5AH (tel. 0233 812401). Degrees in agriculture, rural development and environmental studies. 752 students.

GOLDSMITHS' COLLEGE

Lewisham Way, New Cross, London SE14 6NW (tel. 081-692 7171)

Founded 1891, royal charter 1990
Times ranking: 46

Enquiries: registry
Full-time students: 2,357 (f), 1,269 (m)
2,339 **arts**, 397 **sciences**

Main subject areas: arts (BA, BMus); education (BA [Ed]); social and mathematical sciences (BSc, BA).

London University's newest college has a long history of community-based courses, mainly in education and the arts. Evening classes are still as popular as the conventional degree courses.

Determinedly integrated into its southeast London locality, the college precincts have a cosmopolitan character. More than 15 per cent of the students are over 21 on entry, many come from the area's ethnic minorities, and there is a growing proportion of overseas students. Goldsmiths' has also become highly fashionable among the trendier elements of the new left.

The older premises have been likened to a grammar school, with their long corridors of classrooms. But new building has included a purpose-built library with longer opening hours than those of many other university libraries.

Goldsmiths' has a well-established reputation in the visual arts (BBC for communications studies), numbering Graham Sutherland and Mary Quant among its alumni over the years. Education, which caters for primary teachers, is also well regarded.

The college's relatively low placing in *The Times* table reflects its open access policy for undergraduates and an accent on teaching, rather than research, in most departments. Its arts bias presents its own difficulties in comparisons of research income and graduate employment prospects.

Nine halls of residence accommodate most first-years from outside London. The college now has more than 1,000 residential places, and the New Cross area is cheaper than many in the capital for those who prefer to, or have to, live out.

The sports facilities which, in keeping with the college's overall philosophy, are also available to the public, are not outstanding. The main ground is eight miles away in Sidcup, Kent.

Social life revolves around a well-equipped and highly political students' union, which also has a reputation for attracting up-and-coming rock bands.

IMPERIAL COLLEGE OF SCIENCE AND TECHNOLOGY

South Kensington, London SW7 2AZ (tel. 071-589 5111)

Founded 1907
Times ranking: 3

Enquiries: senior assistant registrar for admissions
Full-time students: 1,306 (f), 4,570 (m)
3,842 sciences
Main subject areas: Engineering (MEng, BSc [Eng]); science (BSc).

Imperial rivals Oxbridge for the quality of its teaching and research across the range of science and engineering subjects. Indeed it outscored both the ancient universities for research in *The Times* table. More than 600 academic staff include Nobel prize-winners and many Fellows of the Royal Society. Most of the college's departments have been rated as internationally outstanding in the funding council's last two research assessments.

Engineering degrees (ABC for electrical, AAC for aeronautical engineering) have been strengthened by the addition of an extra year so that all students qualify for an MEng. Other subjects may go the same way when funding and government restrictions allow.

The addition in 1988 of St Mary's Hospital Medical School (see page 139) filled the last significant gap in the college's portfolio of scientific courses. The school has the status of a constituent college, and handles its own admissions.

Imperial itself is considering a change of status and severing its already loose link with London University. Having enjoyed more autonomy than others in the university, it may soon make the final break. That will be a decision for a new rector, who takes up the post in autumn 1993.

He is likely to continue the expansion of courses that give the opportunity of a year's study abroad. Imperial now operates exchange programmes with a variety of prestigious technological institutions on the Continent, and runs a European office to handle the administration.

The campus, in the museum district of west London, includes almost 1,000 residential places, enough to guarantee accommodation for all first-years from outside London. Women are given priority in the allocation of hall places. Private housing is expensive.

Excellent indoor sports facilities are available on campus, but it is 15 miles to the outdoor pitches, which are served by coaches on Saturdays and Wednesday afternoons, when there are no lectures. There is also a boathouse at Putney.

The students' union is well equipped and largely apolitical. Imperial is not recommended for academic slouches, but tough entry requirements ensure that they are a rare breed in any case.

KING'S COLLEGE LONDON

The Strand, London WC2R 2LS (tel. 071-836 5454)

Founded 1829

Times ranking: 15

Enquiries: registry

Full-time students: 3,789 (f), 3,667 (m)

1,984 arts, 3,592 sciences

Main subject areas: arts and music (BA, BMus); medicine and dentistry (MBBS, BDS, BSc); education (BSc); engineering (BEng, MEng); law (LLB); life sciences, mathematics and physical sciences (BSc, BPharm); theology (BA).

Following a merger with Chelsea and Queen Elizabeth colleges, King's is now the second largest of London's colleges. More than 60 departments offer almost 200 degrees in a wide range of subjects.

The merger was followed by a series of complex and unluckily timed property deals, however, as the sites of Chelsea and Queen Elizabeth were disposed of to be replaced by a new base south of the Thames. The resulting financial problems were severe. However, the college seems now to have put the worst of its money problems behind it. The medical school will remain in Camberwell in south London. The original college's distinguished Georgian buildings on the Strand, masked by a modern entrance, will also be retained.

Residential places are more widely spread, but are sufficiently plentiful to allow many undergraduates two years in hall. A new student village in Hampstead should enable the college to continue guaranteeing accommodation for first-years who accept places before the end of May.

War studies (BCC), theology and classics (both three Cs), education, philosophy and the creative arts are among the top-rated research departments. Science students remain in the majority, however, and are now able to take some novel interdisciplinary combinations, such as chemistry and philosophy.

King's was an early convert to modular degrees, and also flirted with the possibility of two-year degrees during a turbulent period which saw the resignation of the principal. Though the two-year option was dropped, a rationalisation of departments nonetheless caused unrest in 1992.

The college has been successful at attracting external research income, and is a solid bet for a good degree for those who can satisfy the demanding entry requirements. More than half of those graduating in 1991 were awarded a first or upper-second class degree.

Students' union facilities are good, those for sport adequate, if distant for outdoor sports. There will be more pressure on both if the college meets its target of adding another 1,500 students by the end of the decade.

LONDON SCHOOL OF ECONOMICS AND POLITICAL SCIENCE
Houghton Street, London WC2A 2AE (tel. 071-405 7686)

Founded 1895
Times ranking: 5

Enquiries: undergraduate admissions office
Full-time students: 1,701 (f), 2,454 (m)
2,268 **arts,** 94 **sciences**

Main subject areas: accounting and finance, anthropology, economic history, economics, geography, government, industrial relations, international history, international relations, language studies, law, philosophy, logic and scientific method, social psychology, social science and administration, sociology, statistical and mathematical sciences (BA, BSc, LLB).

Rebuffed by the government in its bid to move into County Hall, the LSE still hopes to break out from its cramped site near London's Law Courts, though the option of a move to Docklands has been rejected. The school urgently requires more space to expand its student numbers.

Proposals to divide the institution into undergraduate and graduate schools have been dropped, but John Ashworth, the school's high-profile director, still wants to concentrate on masters, rather than bachelors, degrees. He also wants to follow Imperial College's lead to take the school out of London University.

If the planned 50 per cent expansion in student numbers over the next four years should on the face of it make entry easier, the emphasis on postgraduate study will nonetheless ensure that the LSE retains its distinctly elite character. Only Oxbridge and Durham have higher average entry scores. Plans for further expansion stretching 20 years into the next century are also in place.

The school already has the highest proportion of overseas students in the country, with the nationals of more than 100 countries taking up half of the places. They have helped to generate foreign currency earnings of £12.5 million in four years. Alumni are in influential positions all over the world, not forgetting Britain, where 50 sitting MPs are LSE graduates.

Areas of study range much more broadly than the school's name implies. Law, economic and social history, anthropology, social policy, and history are all internationally recognised, as are pure economics and politics. A highly successful research assessment saw these departments given the maximum score in December 1992.

Most of the 1,000 residential places, which are enough to guarantee accommodation for all first-years from outside London, are within a mile of the school. Those who rely on the private market must either travel long distances or scour one of the most expensive areas in the country.

Like the teaching accommodation, the students' union and indoor sports facilities were designed for fewer people. The main sports ground is spacious enough, but takes 40 minutes to reach.

QUEEN MARY AND WESTFIELD COLLEGE

Mile End Road, London E1 4NS (tel. 071-975 5555)

Founded 1882 Westfield, 1887 Queen Mary, merged 1989
Times ranking: 39

Enquiries: admissions office
Full-time students: 2,230 (f), 3,224 (m)
2,101 arts, 2,401 sciences

Main subject areas: arts (BA); engineering (BEng, MEng); law (LLB); physical and biological sciences, informatics and mathematical sciences (BSc); social studies (BA, BSc [Econ]).

Though the arts-based Westfield and scientific Queen Mary seemed ideal partners for a merger, all has not been plain sailing since. With complications over the disposal of Westfield's valuable property in Hampstead, financial worries have never been far below the surface. Furthermore, a controversial rationalisation of departments has seen the scientists from Queen Mary emerge in something of a dominant position, with Westfield's staff reduced to fighting a less than successful rearguard action to preserve at least some of the distinctive flavour of their college. In the process they have found themselves obliged to lose the once highly rated Mediterranean Studies.

Leading subjects today include mathematics and aeronautical engineering (both BCC), Spanish (three Cs) and law (three Bs). A new faculty of basic medicine caters for pre-clinical medical students from two of London's top teaching hospitals.

There has also been growing interest in outer space, with new courses in astronomy and aerospace materials. Encouragement for inter-disciplinary study has continued with the combination of languages, the study of European institutions and a specialism in science or technology.

The college is one of the five designated areas for expansion of the sciences within London University, and there is no talk here of a breakaway. Student numbers have been increasing, and are expected to continue to do so.

Most degree courses are organised in units to offer maximum flexibility. The majority of students take at least one course in departments other than their own, some arts students even migrating to another college.

A new arts building for 1,000 students opened in 1992, by which point the college had already expanded its catering and residence facilities as part of the post-merger development plan. Most of the halls are a 20-minute tube journey away, but first-years from outside London are guaranteed accommodation.

There is a new students' union building on campus and good sports facilities, although the main sports ground is several miles away in Essex.

ROYAL HOLLOWAY AND BEDFORD NEW COLLEGE

Egham Hill, Egham, Surrey TW20 0EX (tel. 0784 434455)

Founded 1849 Bedford, 1886 Royal Holloway, merged 1985.

Times ranking: 28

Enquiries: academic registrar
Full-time students: 1,993 (f), 1,722 (m)
1,942 **arts,** 1,442 **sciences**

Main subject areas: classics, drama and theatre studies, modern languages, history (BA); music (BMus); social policy and social science (BA); biochemistry, biology, psychology, geography, geology, management, mathematics, physics, computer science (BSc).

A 100-acre wooded campus between Windsor Castle and Heathrow mixes classic Victoriana with less distinguished modern architecture. The Founder's Building, modelled on a French chateau for Thomas Holloway, is one of Britain's most remarkable university buildings.

Nearby, a £24-million building programme carried out in the 1980s has added new buildings for the earth sciences, life sciences, mathematics and computing, history and social policy. There is also a new students' union, assured of heavy use given the college's rural setting.

Royal Holloway is another of the colleges in which London University intends to expand science teaching and research, although arts students are still in the majority. That is partly the legacy of the arts-oriented Bedford College, like Royal Holloway originally for women only.

The top-rated departments are also on the arts side, with English (ABC), Italian (BCC) and theatre studies (ABC) all nationally prominent. Geology (three Cs), classics (BCC) and physics (BCD) are also strong. The 18 departments encourage interdisciplinary work, and the college also takes advantage of the university's inter-collegiate teaching arrangements.

Like other parts of London University, the college has had financial problems. A proposal to cure them by disposing of part of Holloway's valuable art collection met with stiff opposition and a challenge in the courts, though a Turner seascape eventually went for £11m.

A new hall and flats have brought the number of residential places to almost 2,000, ensuring that every first-year and about half of those in their final year can be accommodated. Private housing is scarce and expensive.

Sports facilities are being upgraded over five years, and at least they are close at hand. The college fairly describes itself as 'London University's country campus', and has a reputation for attracting upmarket students from the Home Counties. It can seem empty at weekends.

UNIVERSITY COLLEGE LONDON
Gower Street, London WC1E 6BT (tel. 071-387 7050)

Founded 1826
Times ranking: 4

Enquiries: director of schools and colleges liaison.
Full-time students: 4,269 (f), 4,757 (m)
3,221 **arts**, 3,407 **sciences**

Main subject areas: full range of disciplines in seven faculties: arts (BA); science (BSc); engineering (BEng, MEng); law (LLB); environmental studies, life sciences (BSc); clinical sciences (MBBS, BSc).

Another of London's academic powerhouses, UCL describes itself as 'a university within a university', the result of its size and breadth of expertise. It is the largest of London's colleges, with a history of pioneering subjects that have later become established features of higher education. Modern languages, geography and the fine arts are examples.

UCL is a thoroughly modern institution, however, with lucrative links with Japanese companies, among others. It is another college to have considered breaking away from London University, although recent reforms appear to have eased its restlessness.

Anatomy (three Cs), anthropology, several branches of engineering, geography and pharmacology (all BCC), law (ABC), modern languages, anthropology, archaeology (all BCD), history and the creative arts are among the 22 subjects to receive top ratings for research. A growing number of degrees now take four years. Science courses and some in the arts are divided into modular units for greater flexibility.

The college incorporates the Slade School of Fine Art and the Institute of Archaeology. The University College and Middlesex School of Medicine, formed from a merger in 1988, was among the top-ranked medical faculties in *The Times* table.

The college already has more than 3,000 residential places, and the number is due to increase over the next few years. Though some were disappointed at the start of the 1992–93 academic year, almost all first-years are guaranteed accommodation even if they live in London. Many undergraduates are also able to stay on in hall, thus avoiding the expensive central London housing market.

The students' union is cramped for the size of college, but UCL is on the doorstep of the spacious and under-used University of London Union. Indoor sports facilities, which are also open to the public, are conveniently placed and good, but the 60-acre athletic ground is a coachride away at Shenley.

LONDON GUILDHALL UNIVERSITY
117–119 Hounsditch, London EC3A 7BU (tel. 071-320 1000)

Founded 1992, formerly City of London Polytechnic
Times ranking: 71

Enquiries: Admissions office, City Poly, India House, 139 Minories, London EC3N 2EY.
Full-time students: 2,556 (f), 2,951 (m)
4,193 **arts,** 1,314 **sciences**

Main subject areas for degrees and diplomas: arts, design and manufacture (fine and applied art, furnishing and interior design, furniture, general studies, music technology, silversmithing, jewellery and allied crafts); business (accounting and finance, business studies, economics, financial services and law); life, social and communication sciences (civil aviation, computing and information studies, geography, languages, politics and government, psychology and sociology).

Disputes with City University, with which London Guildhall had on/off merger negotiations, over keeping the name 'City' in its new title meant that the one-time City of London Polytechnic was the last of the new universities to acquire a new name to accompany its new status. But by opting in the end for London Guildhall as its new name, honour seems to have been satisfied all round, with the new university still able to make clear its links with the City of London.

University status is to be used as the springboard for a build-up of strengths in engineering, the social sciences and craft subjects. Guildhall will also continue to expand its burgeoning part-time courses in business studies, modern languages and art.

Though based in the heart of the City of London, much of the institution spills over into Docklands and the East End. Mature students and part-timers are in the majority. They range from City suits to secretaries and the ethnic minorities of East London.

Among the highest-fliers are commercial pilots being ground trained on the only such course offered by a British university. The transport links date back to the polytechnic's beginnings as a nautical college. Also worthy of note are Europe's first furniture restoration and conservation degree, and one of the continent's biggest silversmith and jewellery departments.

Credit accumulation is well established, allowing almost any combination of subjects to be studied. Undergraduates also have the option of delaying specialisation, or of taking combined honours courses, if they do not like the conventional pattern of degrees.

Almost a third of Guildhall's students are on further education courses, but research and postgraduate work has also been growing in the business field. Expansion is to be concentrated on business and professional courses and on vocational degrees, especially in management training, information technology and languages.

There are only 500 residential places, and private accommodation is expensive and difficult to find. Students complain that much of the teaching accommodation is crowded and in poor condition, but they rate the teaching standards highly.

UNIVERSITY OF LOUGHBOROUGH
Loughborough, Leicestershire LE11 3TU (tel. 0509 263171)

Founded 1909, royal charter 1966
Times ranking: 18

Enquiries: undergraduate admissions office
Full-time students: 2,155 (f), 4,815 (m)
2,942 **arts,** 2,965 **sciences**

Main subject areas: engineering (BEng, MEng); applied science, human and environmental studies (BSc); education and humanities (BA, BSc).

Best known for its successes on the sports field, Loughborough is acquiring a growing academic reputation, as reflected in its top 20 placing in *The Times* table, where it matches Manchester and Bristol in thirteenth place. Based on a former college of advanced technology, the university has developed a strong portfolio of courses in a limited range of subjects.

Although arts undergraduates are almost as numerous as those on the science side, it is in physical education and technology that the university has made its name. There were more than 1,100 applications to study physical education, sports science and recreation management (BBC) in 1991. Electronic (BCC) and automotive (BBC) engineering are also popular, as is European business (also BBC). Sociology (three Cs) was the other top research subject in 1992.

Now that a merger with Leicester University is no longer an option, Loughborough is going for modest growth on its own. There were only 150 more new students last year than in 1991, but even that was slightly more than the university was aiming for.

The funding council has endorsed further expansion with a budget settlement for the 1992–93 academic year that pointed the university in the direction of specialisation in teaching, rather than research. The council has also given Loughborough £51,000 to develop new teaching methods. Top consultants will monitor progress across all departments.

All but 100 first-years were accommodated by the university, thanks to the addition of 600 hall places during 1991–92. More than £3 million has been committed to another residential project, which should provide 267 more places in 1993.

Almost 80 per cent of the students live on campus, a mile from the small town of Loughborough, with Leicester and Nottingham both within easy reach. Private accommodation is in short supply for those who prefer to live out.

The indoor and outdoor sports facilities are arguably the best in Britain, and the representative teams have a tradition second to none. The students' union is large, more political than the technological and sporting bias might suggest, and serves as the centre for most students' social activity.

UNIVERSITY OF MANCHESTER
Manchester M13 9PL (tel. 061-275 2000)

Founded 1851, royal charter 1903
Times ranking: 11

Enquiries: registrar
Full-time students: 5,708 (f), 7,401 (m)
5,636 **arts**, 5,819 **sciences**

Main subject areas: full range of degree courses in nine faculties: arts (BA, MusB); theology (BA); economics (BA[Econ], BSoc Sci); law (LLB); education (BEd); medicine (MBChB); science (BSc, BEng, MEng); biological sciences (BSc); dentistry (BDS).

Though Manchester has been through a rocky period, including a lengthy spell without a permanent vice-chancellor, it still ranks among the top universities in *The Times* table. In other days it would have expected a still higher placing.

A decision not to expand too rapidly beyond its already considerable size backfired in the funding regime of the start of the 1990s. With neither teaching nor research budgets keeping pace with inflation, valuable ground was lost.

Nevertheless, the university's reputation ensures that applicants are of high quality across the full range of disciplines. Manchester also remains sixth on the research councils' list of favoured institutions.

Anthropolgy (three Bs), mathematics (ACC), and dentistry, computation and nursing (all BCC) are among the top-rated courses. The business school, although not an undergraduate base, has been ranked among the best in Europe.

The university precinct, shared with UMIST (see page 151), the teaching hospitals and the headquarters of the Metropolitan University, boasts some of the best facilities in Britain. The campus library and the John Ryland's Library in the city centre together make one of the largest in any university, with 3.4 million books, one-million manuscript or archival items and space for more than 2,000 students.

The imaginatively run Whitworth Art Gallery houses valuable collections, especially of English watercolours, as does the award-winning Manchester Museum. The university also runs the Jodrell Bank observatory, and even has a share in an ageing nuclear reactor, safely out of the way at Risley.

Student accommodation is shared with UMIST, and is based on Owens Park, Britain's biggest student village. First-years are guaranteed a residential place if they apply by the end of August.

Facilities in the two sports centres are excellent and conveniently placed. There is a new students' union building, which has eased previous overcrowding. Manchester students tend to be fiercely loyal to their university and their adopted city, lured by the nightlife as well as the academic pedigree.

UNIVERSITY OF MANCHESTER INSTITUTE OF SCIENCE AND TECHNOLOGY

PO Box 88, Manchester M60 1QD (tel. 061-200 4043)

Founded 1824, part of Manchester University since 1905
Times ranking: 26

Enquiries: registrar's department
Full-time students: 1,472 (f), 3,754 (m)
930 **arts,** 2,999 **sciences**

Main subject areas: biological and physical sciences, mathematics and computation, business, social sciences and languages (BSc); engineering and technolgy (BEng, BScMEng, MEng).

Although technically a faculty of Manchester University, UMIST sees itself as an institution in its own right, with its own principal and most of its own facilities. It has a number of recent successes to underline its separate identity.

Not least among these was a 35 per cent expansion in the latter years of the 1980s, achieved against a background of continuing recruitment difficulties in scientific and technological subjects. While other universities fear that their expansion plans, based on the arts and social sciences, will have to be reined in, UMIST faces no such restrictions.

Part of the reason for such success has been the favourable employment record of UMIST's graduates, who were rated employers' favourites in one business survey in 1992. A Queen's Award for export achievement was another reflection of high quality.

UMIST has always had close links with industry and the business community, one crucial side-effect of which is the highest level of research income of any university in the country. One of UMIST's own companies, which specialises in diagnostic testing for the food and medical industries, has a 1992 valuation of £27.5 million.

Engineering (BBC for chemical courses) and metallurgy (CCD) are two of the top-rated areas. Social sciences, linguistics and management are available, as well as technological subjects.

The students have access to Europe's largest computer centre and a £4-million library that is one of the most high-tech in the country. A third of the 600 study places have computer facilities.

All first-years are guaranteed a residential place. New residences are due to open in the autumn of 1993, by which time UMIST's pool of accommodation will have grown by 600 places, or 47 per cent, in two years.

Students have access to Manchester University's sports facilities, as well as a ground of their own. Student union facilities were modernised in 1992.

MANCHESTER METROPOLITAN UNIVERSITY

All Saints Building, Oxford Road, Manchester M15 6BH (tel. 061-247 2000)

Royal charter 1992, formerly Manchester Polytechnic
Times ranking: 61

Enquiries: academic registrar
Full-time students: 6,240 (f), 4,527 (m)
7,848 **arts,** 2,919 **sciences**

Main subject areas: art and design (BA); community studies and education (BA, BEd), clothing design and technology (BSc), hotel catering and tourism management, humanities, law and social sciences (BA, BSc, LLB), management and business (BA), science and engineering (BSc, BEng). Certificates and diplomas, as well as degrees.

The largest of the new universities grew even larger in 1992 with the addition of Crewe and Alsager College. Including the many part-timers, Manchester Metropolitan now has more than 26,000 students, a total exceeded only by London University.

More than half of the students are over 21 at entry, and the university prides itself on keeping a balance between the sexes. The 300 courses at degree level and below cover 50 subject areas, mostly linked directly with business, industry or the professions.

Among the teaching strengths are engineering, hotel and catering and retail marketing. The addition of Crewe and Alsager has enhanced the university's already substantial reputation in education. The social sciences narrowly missed a place in *The Times* top 10, while the business courses went one better, finishing ninth.

Overseas links have expanded rapidly, both in Europe and farther afield. Law courses, for example, are being taught in Hong Kong, with a return of £500,000 for the university over the next three years. The university also encourages students to take language courses, whatever their specialism, under its Uniwide scheme. Demand for places outstrips supply, but 800 students now take advantage of the system.

Although the main campus is in the university area of Manchester, four of the five main faculties are out of the city centre. That in Didsbury, where a former college campus caters for 3,500 education and community studies students, is the farthest flung.

A third of the students come from the Manchester area, easing some of the pressure on accommodation. There are more than 2,000 residential places, mostly reserved for first-years, but the city's huge student population makes for fierce competition in the private sector.

The students' union is a well-organised, multi-million pound operation serving all sites. The university has two sports centres, on the main site and at Didsbury. Manchester's image as a vibrant, youth-oriented city is a great attraction to would-be students. Though some are daunted by the metropolitan university's sheer size, individual courses and sites are not necessarily impersonal.

MIDDLESEX UNIVERSITY
White Hart Lane, London N17 8HR (tel. 081-362 5000)

Royal charter 1992, formerly Middlesex Polytechnic
Times ranking: 60

Enquiries: course enquiries office
Full-time students: 4,851 (f) 4,407 (m)
7,731 **arts**, 1,521 **sciences**

Main subject areas: art and design, business studies and management (BA); education and performing arts (BEd, BA); engineering (BEng); science and mathematics (BSc); humanities and social science (BA). Certificate and diploma courses also offered.

While it was waiting to shed its polytechnic title, Middlesex took to styling itself 'The European university'. And in fact its international links are strong. One in five students is from overseas and large numbers of undergraduates take parts of courses abroad.

Almost a third of undergraduates are on sandwich courses, with work placements ranging from a few weeks to a full year. A modular degree system offers 35 areas from which to construct a study programme, and should take in the entire network of subjects by autumn 1993. The system also gives students the option of an extra five-week session during July and August, during which they can try out new subjects or add to their credits.

Although Middlesex was famous at one time for the largest philosophy department in the country, 90 per cent of students are on vocational courses, many at sub-degree level. More than 60 per cent are over 21 at entry.

The university continued its recent expansion in 1992, accepting an extra 1,250 students to bring the total to 12,500. A teaching campus was reopened at White Hart Lane, in Tottenham, with room for 900 initially. By 1994 it will have places for 2,000.

The additional space was sorely needed. Students staged a lengthy sit-in at the end of 1991 to protest about overcrowding and worsening staffing levels. Both were the result of financial problems that ruled out substantial improvements.

There are now eight sites dotted around London's North Circular

Road, which gives its name to the university newspaper. They include a country estate at Trent Park, an innovative warehouse conversion at Bounds Green, and a house in Hampstead which was once the home of the ballerina Anna Pavlova.

Middlesex is heavily involved in applied research, and has pioneered a number of degrees, including performance arts and European business administration. Its engineering courses only narrowly missed a place in *The Times* top 10.

The students' union operates on all the main sites, and sports facilities are good. First-years have first call on the 600 residential places, but most have to live out.

NAPIER UNIVERSITY
219 Colinton Road, Edinburgh EH14 1DJ (tel. 031-444 2266)

Royal charter 1992, formerly Napier Polytechnic of Edinburgh
Times ranking: 76

Enquiries: information office
Full-time students: 2,293 (f), 3,127 (m)
2,812 **arts,** 2,608 **sciences**

Main subject areas: accountancy, business studies, communication studies, economics, hotel and catering management, design, languages, photography, law (BA); biology, chemistry, computing, information technology, mathematics, physics, surveying (BSc); civil, mechanical, electrical and electronic engineering (BEng). A number of diploma courses are also offered.

Napier was Scotland's first and largest polytechnic. Now a university of more than 10,000 students, including part-timers, it is aiming to develop from a local institution into one that ranks with the best in Britain. Though *The Times* table suggests that there is a long way to go, Napier sits comfortably ahead of the other new universities north of the border.

The university has its roots as a college of science and technology which merged with a college of commerce, and it remains strongly and avowedly vocational. Most courses include a work placement of up to a year.

One result of the close relationship with industry and commerce is consistent success in the employment market for new graduates. Another is a flourishing consultancy business, which ploughs money back into departments.

Particular strengths include a degree in energy engineering, which includes social and political aspects of the subject, a communications degree aimed at marketing, advertising and public relations, and a BA in photography. A new degree in business information management, combining management with information technology, is also proving popular.

Movement between courses of different levels is facilitated by a modular system, which now takes in all degree subjects. The range of independent study has also been increased.

The university, like the polytechnic before it, was named after John Napier, the inventor of logarithms. The tower where he was born still sits among the concrete blocks of the Merchiston site, in the student district of Edinburgh. Two other sites are linked by university minibus and public transport: Sighthill, a 1960s building in the west of the city; and the stately Craiglockart, once a military hospital where the war poets Siegfried Sassoon and Wilfred Owen met.

Napier still lacks a central students' union, though plans are afoot to rectify this. There are only 200 residential places, although the high proportion of home-based students slightly improves the chances of accommodation for first-years.

UNIVERSITY OF NEWCASTLE UPON TYNE
Newcastle upon Tyne NE1 7RU (tel. 091-222 6000)

Founded 1834 (as part of Durham University), royal charter 1963
Times ranking: 23

Enquiries: admissions officer
Full-time students: 4,170 (f), 5,562 (m)
3,694 **arts**, 4,629 **sciences**

Main subject areas: wide range of disciplines in eight faculties: medicine (MBBS, BDS); arts (BA); science (BSc); engineering (BEng, MEng); social and environmental science (BA, BSc); law (LLB); education (mainly postgraduate); agriculture (BSc, BEng).

Newcastle now vies with its former parent university, Durham, for recognition as the top university in the Northeast. The civic university has a big advantage in terms of size, and came well out of the latest allocations of funding for both teaching and research. The £24.5 million in research grants and contracts it was awarded in 1991–92 was easily a record.

An eight per cent increase in new students in 1992–93 saw total numbers top the 10,000 mark for the first time. An extra 640 residential places almost kept pace with the expansion, and ensured that every first-year who wanted accommodation could have it. Most of the halls are within easy reach of the city-centre campus.

Originally a medical school, Newcastle has maintained its reputation in that field, sharing the fourth place in *The Times* rankings. It has also long been one of the top centres for agriculture. But only four top ratings in 1992's research assessment was something of a disappointment. Highly-rated degrees include computing science (BCD), civil engineering (three Cs), economics (BBC) and classical studies (three Bs). The fine art degree (two Es plus portfolio) is one of the few single honours courses in the traditional universities, attracting more than 700 applications for 47 places in 1991.

The campus itself is spacious and varied, occupying 45 acres close to the main shopping area, Northumbria University and the Newcastle United's ground, which is overlooked by one of the halls. The university boasts two theatres, an art gallery and three museums.

Newcastle has become an increasingly fashionable university among students from the south, as well as from the Northeast. The city has plenty of social facilities, and is generally welcoming towards students. Sports facilities are excellent, and include a new sports centre, three grounds within the city limits and access to the university's country estate in Northumberland. The students' union is large and lively.

UNIVERSITY OF NORTHUMBRIA AT NEWCASTLE

Ellison Place, Newcastle upon Tyne NE1 8ST (tel. 091-232 6002)

Royal charter 1992, formerly Newcastle Polytechnic
Times ranking: 71

Enquiries: registrar's department
Full-time students: 4,927 (f), 4,709 (m)
6,668 **arts,** 2,968 **sciences**

Main subject areas: arts and design, business and management (BA); social sciences (BA, BSc, LLB, BEd); engineering, science and technology (BSc, BEng, MEng). A wide range of certificate and diploma courses are also offered.

One of the largest of the new universities, Northumbria now has more than 15,000 students, two-thirds of them full-timers. Like most of the new universities, numbers are rising and scheduled to go on doing so.

Northumbria has also been expanding geographically, both at home and abroad. A campus opened last year in Carlisle, serving a county without a university of its own. The Carlisle campus, listed as an ancient monument, is intended to have 800 students within five years. Initially, it will offer only business courses and act as a link for Cumbrian firms seeking academic expertise. Considerably farther afield, smaller centres have also been established in Hong Kong and Moscow.

In Newcastle itself, the polytechnic nurtured its relations with the local community through a special centre, and encouraged applications from students without traditional qualifications. One result is that a third of the students are over 21 at entry. The university would have liked to underline its local roots still more by calling itself Newcastle City University, but government restrictions forced it to adopt its present unwieldy title instead.

The fashion school is perhaps Northumbria's best-known feature, though the school of art is also well regarded. As a polytechnic, the institution had more quality awards than most of its rivals in 1992. Science, business, arts and humanities all achieved maximum scores.

The main campus is in the centre of the city, within sight of Newcastle University. Another site, three miles away, contains the bulk of the 1,500 residential places, for which first-years are given priority.

Both the sports and social facilities are adequate, although rising numbers are inevitably adding to the pressure on them. Students have complained of overcrowding and worsening staffing levels, but inspectors' reports have continued to be favourable.

UNIVERSITY OF NORTH LONDON

166–220 Holloway Road, London N7 8DB (tel. 071-607 2789)

Royal charter 1992, formerly Polytechnic of North London
Times ranking: 84

Enquiries: marketing communications office (courses)
Full-time students: 3,167 (f), 2,917 (m)
4,434 **arts,** 1,650 **sciences**

Main subject areas: business and management (BA); humanities and teacher education (BA, BEd); science, computing and engineering (BSc, BEng); environmental and social sciences (BA, BSc, LLB). Certificate and diploma courses are also offered.

North London is shaking off a reputation for student militancy, replacing it with one for spreading higher education into ethnic communities otherwise little seen in the university system. As a polytechnic, it pioneered access courses aimed at the local black population. Its success can be measured by the fact that today more than a third of North London's students are black.

The new university has dedicated itself to more of the same, rather than trying to compete with the traditional universities. Its mission statement stresses a commitment to widening educational opportunities and expanding international and business links.

Nevertheless, some departments are heavily involved in research, as well as teaching. Chemistry, which won a glowing reference from Her Majesty's Inspectorate, is one example.

Sandwich and part-time degrees in electronic engineering are highly rated, as are health studies, teacher education and leisure and tourism. About half the students are on sub-degree or professional courses. Many programmes at all levels are designed for mature students, who account for two-thirds of all entrants. North London has a series of modular degree schemes operating on a faculty basis. Some students feel that the full flexibility of the system is not generally understood and that the system is consequently underused.

The university's chief drawback is the scale and standard of some of its facilities. The three main sites, in Holloway, Highbury and Kentish Town, are crowded and run down in parts. Major building projects are under way, and will be sorely needed if a planned 40 per cent expansion is to take place by 1995–96.

Sports facilities are reasonable, if distant for outdoor games, and the students' union is especially active politically. Residential accommodation is scarce, with first-years taking priority in the allocation of North London's 400 hall places. The university advises those who miss out on a hall place to make arrangements well before term starts, such is the scramble for affordable housing.

UNIVERSITY OF NOTTINGHAM

University Park, Nottingham NG7 2RD (tel. 0602 484848)

Founded 1881, royal charter 1948
Times ranking: 23

Enquiries: registrar
Full-time students: 4,080 (f), 5,440 (m)
3,488 **arts**, 4,326 **sciences**

Main subject areas: wide range of disciplines in seven faculties: arts (BA); law and social sciences (BA, LLB); education (mainly postgraduate), science, agricultural and food sciences (BSc); engineering (BEng, MEng); medicine (MBBS).

Nottingham's landscaped campus is one of the most attractive in Britain and the university one of the most popular, with 16 applicants to every place in 1991. Indeed Nottingham is widely regarded as a rising star soon likely to improve upon an already respectable place in the top 25 universities in *The Times* ranking. Its 11 top ratings in the 1992 research assessment exercises represented one of the success stories of the year.

Though Nottingham sees itself as a 'research-led university', it is still planning to expand its undergraduate intake. Its strength across the board was demonstrated in placings in the top 15 of all but one of *The Times*'s separate subject rankings, business and management being the only exception. The university is best known for its sciences. These, developed from an association with the Boots family, attract a larger proportion of students than most non-specialist institutions. There are also strong faculties in agriculture, law and medicine.

Pharmacy (three Bs) and chemistry (BCD) are highly rated, while arts degrees are acquiring a growing reputation with the aid of a new £5-million arts centre. There are pockets of excellence, too, in the social sciences: politics (three Bs) had more than 500 applications for 31 places in 1991.

The university went over to a modular course structure in 1992, taking in almost all first degrees. Students also have access to a new computer network, which is intended to take much of the teaching load as expansion continues.

The main campus is three miles west of the city centre, its 330 acres, donated by Jesse Boot, containing 12 halls of residence as well as the teaching accommodation. Agricultural and food sciences are on a separate site at Sutton Bonington, eleven miles south of Nottingham. All first-years are guaranteed a residential place.

Sports facilities are extremely good and conveniently placed. Much of the social life centres on the halls, but the students' union is also well equipped. Town/gown relations are good, and the cost of living relatively low.

NOTTINGHAM TRENT UNIVERSITY
Burton Street, Nottingham NG1 4BU (tel. 0602 418418)

Royal charter 1992, formerly Nottingham (originally Trent) Polytechnic
Times ranking: 81

Enquiries: academic registrar
Full-time students: 4,644 (f), 6,334 (m)
7,260 **arts**, 3,718 **sciences**

Main subject areas: art and design, business and management, humanities (BA); education (BEd); engineering, environmental studies (BEng, MEng, BSc); law, economics and social sciences (BA, LLB); science (BSc). Certificate and diploma courses are also offered.

Nottingham Trent is another of the new universities which would have preferred a 'city university' title but which was obliged to return to its roots with its new name (the wrangle over the name did little for inter-varsity relations in the city). Nonetheless, the new university has set itself the target of challenging its older established rivals in research within five years without compromising the values that it championed as a polytechnic. Part-timers will continue to make up about a third of the student population.

The research effort predates university status by several years. The strategy is to focus on interdisciplinary combinations, such as business and engineering and overlaps between the academic world and private enterprise. Research teams have been established to compete with the traditional universities in areas of particular strength such as business, textiles and engineering. The hope is that undergraduates will benefit both from the funding the university thereby expects to attract and the high-calibre research staff that should follow in its wake.

Degree courses were highly rated as a polytechnic: Nottingham won more quality awards than any other institution in the last funding council assessments. Only the mathematics and computer science courses missed out. Nottingham was also one of the most popular polytechnics in terms of applications and grew steadily in recent years to more than 14,000 students, many of whom are on sandwich courses. All courses will soon have a 'computer appreciation' component.

The university has two sites. Most faculties are based on the main, city-centre campus. Humanities and science students are five miles away in a former teacher training college with education in a Georgian mansion nearby.

Almost 1,000 residential places are not enough to accommodate all first-years, but they are given priority. Sports and social facilities are good on both sites.

UNIVERSITY OF OXFORD

University offices, Wellington Square, Oxford OX1 2JD (tel. 0865 741111)

Founded 1096

Times ranking: 1

Enquiries: admissions office
Full-time students: 5,578 (f), 8,876 (m)
5,762 **arts,** 4,361 **sciences**

Main subject areas: full range of disciplines in five faculties: arts, social sciences, engineering and technology, medicine, science and mathematics.

Oxford is the oldest and probably the most famous university in the English-speaking world. *The Times* table suggests that it is effectively inseparable from Cambridge in terms of quality, and still head and shoulders above the rest.

The arts faculties have been the envy of other universities for centuries and topped *The Times* subject rankings, while the new Magdelen College science park epitomises a drive to enhance Oxford's reputation in the sciences. Like Cambridge, the university has also added a management school, based on Templeton College.

The 28 undergraduate colleges continue to teach students in small tutorial groups, with lectures an optional extra which some find only marginally useful. With more than 14,000 students, Oxford is already one of the largest of the traditional universities. It is expected that future growth will focus on postgraduates.

BALLIOL

Balliol College, Oxford OX1 3BJ (tel. 0865 277777)

Students: 365

Famous as the alma mater of many prominent post-war politicians, including Harold Macmillan, Denis Healey and Roy Jenkins, the university's current Chancellor, Balliol has maintained a strong presence in university life and is usually well represented in the Union. Academic standards are formidably high, as might be expected in the college of Wyclif and Adam Smith, notably in the classics and social sciences. Applicants for the notoriously over-subscribed PPE course are strongly advised to sit the entrance examination rather than to seek a conditional offer. For the joint school of English and modern languages the college only considers those offering French. Library facilities are good and include a 24-hour law library.

Balliol began admitting overseas students in the 19th century and has cultivated an attractively cosmopolitan atmosphere, of which the lively JCR is a natural focus.

Most undergraduates are offered accommodation in college for three years, while the 130 graduate students are usually lodged in the Graduate Centre at Holywell Manor.

BRASENOSE
Brasenose College, Oxford OX1 4AJ (tel. 0865 277823)

Students: 340

Brasenose may not be the most famous Oxford college but it makes up for its discreet image with a consistently healthy academic performance, an advantageous position in the centre of town, and lesser known attractions such as Gertie's Tea Bar. Brasenose was one of the first colleges to become co-educational in the 1970s, although men still outnumber women by more than two to one. In its defence, the college prospectus points out that the major undergraduate office, President of the JCR, has been filled as often by a woman as a man.

Named after the door knocker on the 13th-century Brasenose Hall, the college has a pleasant, intimate ambience which most find conducive to study. Law, PPE and history are traditional strengths and competition for places in these subjects is intense. Sporting standards are as high as at many much larger colleges and the college's rowing club is the oldest in the university. Accommodation is under review, with the college currently restructuring charges for its 340 students. Most third-years live in the Brasenose annex at Frewin Court, just a few minutes' walk away.

CHRIST CHURCH
Christ Church College, Oxford OX1 1DP (tel. 0865 276150)

Students: 425

The college founded by Cardinal Wolsey in 1525 and affectionately known as 'the House' has come a long way since Evelyn Waugh mythologised its aristocratic excesses in *Brideshead Revisited*. The social mix at Christ Church is much more varied than most applicants suspect and the college has gone out of its way recently to become something of a champion of political correctness. The male/female ratio is improving steadily and a code of practice on sexual harassment is being implemented.

Academic pressure at Christ Church is reasonably relaxed, although natural high-achievers prosper and the college's history and law teaching is highly regarded. The magnificent 18th-century library, housing 100,000 books, is one of the best in Oxford. It is supplemented by a separate law library.

Sport, especially rugby, is an important part of college life. The playing fields are a few minutes' walk away through the Meadows. The river is also close at hand for the aspiring oarsman, and the college has good squash courts.

Accommodation is rated by Christ Church students as 'excellent' and includes flats off Iffley Road as well as a number of beautifully panelled shared sets (double rooms) in college. The newly opened bar adds to the lustre of a college justly famous for its imposing architecture and cathedral, the smallest in England.

CORPUS CHRISTI
Corpus Christi College, Oxford OX1 4FJ (tel. 0865 276700)

Students: 217

Corpus, Oxford's smallest college, is naturally overshadowed by its Goliath-like neighbour, Christ Church, but makes the most of its intimacy, friendly atmosphere and exquisite beauty. Like 'the House' it has an exceptional view across the Meadows.

Although the college has less than 300 students all told, it has an admirable library open 24 hours a day. Academic expectations are high and English, PPE and medicine are especially well established. Despite this, the undergraduate prospectus asserts that it is 'considered much more important to be sociable than to get good results'. Corpus is able to offer accommodation to all its undergraduates, one of its many attractions to those seeking a smaller community in Oxford.

EXETER
Exeter College, Oxford OX1 3DP (tel. 0865 279600)

Students: 325

Exeter is the fourth oldest college in the university and was founded in 1314 by Walter Stapeldon, Bishop of Exeter. Nestling halfway between the High Street and Broad Street, site of most of the city's bookshops, it could hardly be more central. The college boasts handsome buildings, the exceptional Fellows' garden and attractive accommodation for most undergraduates for all three years of their university careers.

Exeter's academic record is strong and the college was a consistent high performer in the days of the Norrington Tables. It is, however, often accused of being rather dull. Given its glittering roll-call of alumni, which includes Martin Amis, JRR Tolkien, Alan Bennett, Richard Burton and Tariq Ali, this seems an accusation that on the face of it at least is hard to sustain.

College food is not rated highly by students. The proximity of the Covered Market with its excellent sandwich stalls partly compensates, however.

HERTFORD
Hertford College, Oxford OX1 3BW (tel. 0865 279400)

Students: 334

Though tracing its roots to the 13th century, Hertford is determinedly modern. It was one of the first colleges to admit women and now has one of the better ratios of men to women in the university. Hertford also helped set the trend towards offers of places conditional on A level (known as Mode N) which many state-school pupils prefer.

The college lacks the grandeur of Magdalen or Christ Church but has its own architectural trade-mark in the Bridge of Sighs. The undergraduate prospectus also mentions proximity to the History Faculty library (Hertford's neighbour), the Bodleian and the King's Arms, perhaps Oxford's most popular pub.

Academic pressure at Hertford is not high but the quality of teaching, especially in English, is generally thought admirable. Accommodation is improving, thanks in part to the new Abingdon House Complex, and the college can now lodge 85 per cent of its undergraduates at any one time. Like most congenial colleges, Hertford is often accused of being claustrophobic and inward-looking – a charge most Hertfordians would ascribe simply to jealousy.

JESUS
Jesus College, Oxford OX1 3DW (tel. 0865 279700)

Students: 312

Jesus, the only Oxford college to be founded in the reign of Elizabeth I, suffers from something of an unfair reputation for insularity. Its students, whose predecessors include T E Lawrence and Harold Wilson, describe it as 'friendly but gossipy' and shrug off the legend that all its undergraduates are Welsh.

Close to most of Oxford's main facilities, Jesus has three compact quads, the second of which is especially enticing in the summer. Academic standards are high and most subjects are taught in college. Physics, chemistry and engineering are especially strong. Rugby and rowing also tend to be taken seriously.

Accommodation is almost universally regarded as excellent and relatively inexpensive. New self-catering flats in north and east Oxford have enabled every graduate to live in throughout his or her Oxford career.

The range of accommodation available to undergraduates is similarly good. The college's Cowley Road development is described by the student union as 'some of the plushest student housing in Oxford'.

KEBLE
Keble College, Oxford OX1 3PG (tel. 0865 272727)

Students: 414

Keble, named after the leader of the Oxford Movement, was founded in 1870 with the intention of making Oxford education more accessible and the college remains proud of 'the legacy of a social conscience'. That said, the student union has had cause recently to complain that 'college life is still definitely male dominated'. With 400 undergraduates, Keble is one of the biggest colleges in Oxford, while its uncompromising Victorian Gothic architecture also makes it one of the most distinctive. Once famous for the special privileges it extended to rowers, the college is now academically strong, particularly in the sciences where it benefits from easy access to the Science Area, the Radcliffe, the Science Library and the Mathematical Institute. At the same time, the college's sporting record remains exemplary.

Undergraduates are guaranteed accommodation in their first two years, although rent increases in recent years have been the cause of some friction between undergraduates and the college authorities. Students who live in must eat in Hall 30 times a year, a ruling mildly resented mainly because of the quality of the food.

LADY MARGARET HALL
Lady Margaret Hall, Oxford OX2 6QA (tel. 0865 274300)

Students: 357

Lady Margaret Hall, the first college for women in Oxford, has been co-educational since 1978 and today has a 50/50 male-female split. For many students, LMH's comparative isolation – the college is three-quarters of a mile north of the city centre – is a real advantage, ensuring a clear distinction between college life and university activities, and a refuge from tourists. Although the neo-Georgian architecture is not to everyone's taste, the college's beautiful gardens back onto the river, which allows LMH to have its own punt house. The students union describes academic life at the college as 'fairly lax' while commending its record in English, history and law.

Accommodation is guaranteed for all first- and third-years and for most second-years. The college's two tower-blocks have the remarkable attraction of private bathrooms in all their rooms. LMH shares most of its sports facilities with Trinity College though has squash and tennis courts on site.

LINCOLN
Lincoln College, Oxford OX1 3DR (tel. 0865 279800)

Students: 243

Small, central Lincoln cultivates a lower profile than many other colleges with comparable assets. The college's 15th-century buildings and beautiful library – a converted Queen Anne church – combine to produce a delightful environment in which to spend three years. Academic standards are high, particularly in arts subjects, although the college's relaxed atmosphere is justly celebrated. Accommodation, rated 'excellent' by the student union, is provided by the college for most undergraduates throughout their careers and includes rooms in the Mitre Hotel, a medieval inn. Graduate students have their own centre a few minutes' walk away in Bear Lane.

Lincoln's food is outstanding, among the best in the university. Sporting achievement is impressive for a college of this size, in part a reflection of the college's good facilities.

MAGDALEN
Magdalen College, Oxford OX1 4AU (tel. 0865 276000)

Students: 380 students

Perhaps the most beautiful college in Oxford or Cambridge, Magdalen is known around the world for its tower, its deer park and its May morning celebrations. The college has shaken off its public school image to become a truly cosmopolitan place, with a large intake from overseas and an increasing proportion of state-school pupils. Magdalen's record in English, history and law is second to none, while its new science park at Sandford is bound to bolster its reputation in the sciences. Library facilities are excellent, especially in history and law.

First-year students are accommodated in the Waynflete Building and allocated rooms in subsequent years by ballot. Sets in cloisters and in the palatial New Buildings are particularly sought after. Magdalen is also conveniently placed for the wealth of rented accommodation in east Oxford.

The college is a pluralistic place, proud of its drama society and choir. Enthusiasm on the river and sports field makes up for a traditional lack of athletic prowess.

MERTON
Merton College, Oxford OX1 4JD (tel. 0865 276310)

Students: 254

Founded in 1264 by Walter de Merton, Bishop of Rochester and Chancellor of England, Merton is one of Oxford's oldest colleges and one of its most prestigious. Quiet and beautiful, Merton has high academic expectations of its 250-plus undergraduates. History, law, English, physics and chemistry all enjoy a formidable track record. The medieval library is the envy of many other colleges.

Accommodation is cheap, of a good standard and offered to students for all three years. Merton's food is probably the best in the university; formal Hall is served six times a week. No kitchens are provided for students who live in college.

Merton's many diversions include the Merton Floats, its dramatic society, an excellent Christmas Ball and the peculiar Time Ceremony, which celebrates the return of GMT. Sport facilities are excellent, although participation tends to be more important than the final score.

NEW COLLEGE
New College, Oxford OX1 3BN (tel. 0865 248541)

Students: 410

New College is large, old (founded in 1379 by William of Wykeham) and much more relaxed than most expect when first confronting its daunting facade. It is a bustling place, as proud of its excellent music and its bar as of its strength in law, history and PPE. The ratio of women to men is high and the college openly invites applications from schools that have never sent candidates to Oxford. The Target Schools Scheme, designed to increase applications from state schools, is well established.

Accommodation is good and guaranteed for the first two years, after which most live out. The college's library facilities are impressive, especially in law, classics and PPE. The sports ground is nearby and includes good tennis courts. Women's sport is particularly strong.

The sheer beauty of New College remains one of its principal assets and the college gardens are a memorable sight in the summer. In spite of these traditional charms, the college has strong claims to be considered admirably innovative.

ORIEL
Oriel College, Oxford OX1 4EW (tel. 0865 276555)
Students: 276

In spite of its forbidding reputation as a bastion of muscular privilege, Oriel is a friendly college with a strong sense of identity and has adjusted rapidly to co-educational admissions (women were admitted for the first time in 1985). Indeed, the student union describes this much-maligned institution as 'one of the most community-minded colleges in the university'. Academic standards are better than legend suggests and the college's well-stocked library is open 24 hours a day. But Oriel's sporting reputation is certainly deserved and its rowing eight is rarely far from the head of the river. Other sports are well catered for, even if their facilities are considerably farther away than the boathouse, which is only a short jog away.

Accommodation is of variable quality but Oriel can usually provide rooms for all three years for those students who require them. Scholars and Exhibitioners chasing firsts in their final year are given priority in the ballot for college rooms. An extensive modernisation programme is underway to improve accommodation standards. Oriel also offers a lively drama society and a termly undergraduate newspaper.

PEMBROKE
Pembroke College, Oxford OX1 1DW (tel. 0865 276444)
Students: 332

Although its alumni include such extrovert characters as Dr Johnson and Michael Heseltine, Pembroke is one of Oxford's least dynamic colleges. Those who seek a steady, quiet undergraduate career or whose university ambitions extend beyond college life will be most at home in its low-key atmosphere. Academic results are solid, and the college has Fellows and lecturers in almost all the major university subjects.

Pembroke promises accommodation to 'a fair proportion' of undergraduates throughout their courses. The new Geoffrey Arthur building on the river, 10 minutes' walk from the college, offers excellent facilities. College food is reasonable, though some find formal Hall every evening rather too rich a diet.

Rowing and rugby are strong and squash and tennis courts are available at the nearby sports ground.

QUEEN'S
Queen's College, Oxford OX1 4AW (tel. 0865 279120)

Students: 280

One of the most striking sights of the High Street, Queen's has now shed its exclusive 'northern' image to become one of Oxford's liveliest and most attractive colleges. The college's academic record is good. According to the student union, 'the general attitude to work is fairly relaxed and seems to bring good results'. Modern languages, law and mathematics are reckoned among the strongest subjects. Queen's does not normally admit undergraduates for the honour school of English language and literature. The library, open till 10 pm, is as beautiful as it is well stocked.

The college's 280 students are guaranteed accommodation in their first and final years, and most are found rooms for their second if they require them. The college's beer cellar is one of the most popular in the university and the JCR's facilities are also better than average.

ST ANNE'S
St Anne's College, Oxford OX2 6HS (tel. 0865 274800)

Students: 430

St Anne's, about three-quarters of a mile from the city centre, began life as 'The Society of Oxford Home Students' in 1879, became a university college for women in 1952 and has admitted men since 1979. Though lacking the heavyweight tradition of many other colleges, it is a happy, successful community. Its academic standing is never less than respectable. Indeed, St Anne's boasts that it is 'top in a number of subjects'. The library is particularly rich in law, Chinese and medieval history texts. Opening hours are long.

Accommodation is guaranteed to first- and third-years and to many second-years. Those living out are helped by the new Battels Equalisation Scheme, which shares the costs of commercial rents among students. A new accommodation block will provide larger rooms, including two for disabled students.

ST CATHERINE'S
St Catherine's College, Oxford OX1 4AR (tel. 0865 279000)

Students: 451

Arne Jacobsen's modernist design for 'Catz', Oxford's youngest undergraduate college and one of its largest, has attracted much attention as the most striking contrast in the university to the lofty spires of Magdalen and

New College. Close to the university science area and the pleasantly rural Holywell Great Meadow, St Catherine's is nevertheless only a few minutes' walk from the city centre.

Academic standards are especially high in mathematics and physics though the college's scholarly ambitions are far from having been exhausted. The undergraduate prospectus complains that Fellows are 'increasingly eager to apply more academic pressure in college'. The well-liked Wolfson library (famous for its unusual Jacobsen chairs) is open till 1 am on most days.

Accommodation is available for first- and third-years. Rooms are small but tend to be warmer then in other, more venerable colleges. Squash, tennis and netball courts are all on the main college site. St Catherine's has one of the best JCR facilities in Oxford.

ST EDMUND HALL
St Edmund Hall, Oxford OX1 4AR (tel. 0865 279000)

Students: 406

St Edmund Hall – 'Teddy Hall' – is one of Oxford's tiniest colleges but also one of its most populous with no less than 400 undergraduates swarming through its medieval quads. The male-to-female ratio of 40/60 has done much to dispel the ingrained image of St Edmund Hall as a rough, hearty college. The college has gone out of its way to tone down younger members' rowdier excesses. Nonetheless, the sporting culture at St Edmund Hall is still vigorous and the college usually does well in rugby, football and hockey.

Academically, the college has some impressive names among its fellowship as well as a marvellous library, originally a Norman church. The student union reports that 'a laid-back approach [to work] is the norm'. Accommodation is reasonable and is guaranteed to first- and third-years though most second-year students live out. The college has two annexes, one near the University Gardens, the other in Iffley Road, where many of the rooms have private bathrooms. Hall food is better than average.

ST HILDA'S
St Hilda's College, Oxford OX4 1DY (tel. 0865 276884)

Students: 363

St Hilda's, founded in 1893 by Dorothea Beale and celebrating its centenary in 1993, may soon be Oxford's last single-sex college if Somerville becomes co-educational. In spite of its variable academic record, the college is a distinctive part of the Oxford landscape and is usually well represented in university life. The 50,000-volume library is growing fast and plans for its extension are being considered. St Hilda's also boasts one of the largest ratios of independent to state-school undergraduates in Oxford. Accommodation is guaranteed to first-years and for one of undergraduates' remaining two years. Many of the rooms offer some of the best river views in Oxford. The standard of food is high.

ST HUGH'S
St Hugh's College, Oxford OX2 6LE (tel. 0865 274900)

Students: 370

One of Oxford's lesser-known colleges, St Hugh's was criticised by students in 1987 when it began admitting men. There are now fewer women than men at the college, although the male/female ratio is better balanced than at most Oxford colleges.

Like Lady Margaret Hall, St Hugh's is a short bicycle ride from the city centre and has a picturesque setting. It is an ideal college for those seeking a place to live and study away from the madding crowd, and is well liked for its pleasantly bohemian atmosphere. Academic pressure remains comparatively low, although the student union says there are signs that this is changing.

St Hugh's is one of the few colleges which guarantees accommodation to undergraduates for all three years, although the standard of rooms is variable. Sport, particularly football, is taken quite seriously.

ST JOHN'S
St John's College, Oxford OX1 3JP (tel. 0865 277300)

Students: 371

St John's is one of Oxford's powerhouses, excelling in almost every field and boasting arguably the most beautiful gardens in the university. Founded in 1555 by a London merchant, it is richly endowed and makes the most of its resources to provide undergraduates with an agreeable and challenging three years. The work ethic is very much part of the St John's ethos, and academic standards are formidably high, with English, chemistry and history among the traditional strengths, though all students benefit from the impressive library. The proportion of state-school undergraduates is still low but the college compensates to some extent by offering generous hardship funds to those in financial difficulty.

As might be expected of a wealthy college, the accommodation is excellent and guaranteed for three or four years. St John's has a strong sporting tradition and offers good facilities.

ST PETER'S
St Peter's College, Oxford OX1 2DL (tel. 0865 277300)

Students: 274

Opened as St Peter's Hall in 1929, St Peter's has been an Oxford college since 1961. Its medieval, Georgian and l9th-century buildings are close to the city centre and most of Oxford's main facilities. Though still young and comparatively small, St Peter's is well represented in university life and has pockets of academic excellence. There are no fellows in classics at the college. Women are still under-represented at St Peter's.

Accommodation is offered to students for the first year and for one year thereafter and is generally of a high standard. A new residential block, opened in 1988, has added to the stock of rooms and the college's facilities are impressive, including one of the university's best JCRs.

SOMERVILLE
Somerville College, Oxford OX2 6HD (tel. 0865 270600)

Students: 335

Somerville became the subject of a national debate in 1992 when the college announced plans to admit men after more than a century of single-sex education. The row made headlines for months and forced an intervention by the the college's visitor, Lord Jenkins. The strength of feeling generated by the plans (still likely to go ahead) illustrates the impressive Somervillian tradition, whose beneficiaries have included Margaret Thatcher, Indira Ghandi and Shirley Williams. But if academic pressure can be considerable it nonetheless leaves undergraduates with enough time to thrive on the university scene.

Accommodation, including 30 small flats for students, is of a high standard, and is guaranteed for the first and third year. Sport is strong at Somerville and the rowing eight usually finishes near the head of the river. The college's new hockey pitches and tennis courts are nearby. The 100,000-volume library is open 24 hours a day and is one of the most beautiful in Oxford.

TRINITY
Trinity College, Oxford OX1 3BH (tel. 0865 279900)

Students: 274

Architecturally impressive and boasting beautiful lawns, Trinity is one of Oxford's least populous colleges. It is ideally located, beside the Bodleian, Blackwell's book shop and the White Horse pub. Cardinal Newman, an alumnus of Trinity, is said to have regarded Trinity's motto as 'Drink, drink, drink'. The student union today describes the academic pressure tactfully as 'not overbearing'. Nonethless, the college produces its fair share of firsts, especially in arts subjects.

Sport is not a priority at Trinity but the William Pitt debating society and Trinity Players, the college drama group, provide other forms of diversion. Accommodation is of a reasonable standard and most undergraduates can live in for three years if they wish.

UNIVERSITY
University College, Oxford OX1 4BH (tel. 0865 276602)

Students: 372

University is the first Oxford college to be able to boast a former student in the Oval Office. Indeed, the college seems certain to benefit from its unique links with President Clinton, a Rhodes Scholar at University in the late '60s. The college is probably Oxford's oldest, though highly unlikely to have been founded by King Alfred, as legend claims.

Academic expectations are high and the college prospers in most subjects. Biochemistry, geology and psychology are particularly strong. That said, University has fewer claims to be thought a powerhouse in the manner of St John's, arguably its greatest rival. Accommodation is guaranteed to undergraduates for all three years, with third years lodged in an annexe in north Oxford about a mile and a half from the college site on the High Street. The student union complains that facilities are poor. Sport is strong and University is usually successful on the river.

WADHAM
Wadham College, Oxford OX1 3PN (tel. 0865 277946)

Students: 409

Founded by Dorothy de Wadham in 1610, Wadham is known in about equal measure for its academic track record – the college generally ranks in the top third in examination performance – and its progressive politics. The JCR is famously dynamic and politically active, although the breadth of political opinion is greater than its left-wing stereotype suggests. And for somewhere supposedly unconcerned with such fripperies, its gardens are surprisingly beautiful. The somewhat rough-hewn chapel is similarly memorable. The college has a good 24-hour library.

Accommodation is guaranteed for at least two years and there are many large, shared rooms on offer. Journalism and drama play an important part in the life of the college, although sport is there for those who want it.

WORCESTER
Worcester College, Oxford OX1 2HB (tel. 0865 278300)

Students: 337

Worcester is to the west of Oxford what Magdalen is to the east, an open, rural contrast to the urban rush of the city centre. The college's rather mediocre exterior conceals a delightful environment, including some characteristically muscular Baroque Hawskmoor architecture, a garden and a lake. Though academic pressure has been described as 'tastefully restrained', law, theology and engineering are among the college's strengths. The 24-hour library is strongest in the arts.

Accommodation varies in quality from the ordinary to the conference standard in the Linbury Building but the shortage of cooking facilities is a common complaint. The ratio of bathrooms to students (about 1 to 6) is better than in many colleges.

OXFORD BROOKES UNIVERSITY
Gipsy Hill, Headington, Oxford OX3 0BP (tel. 0865 741111)

Royal charter 1992, formerly Oxford Polytechnic
Times ranking: 66

Enquiries: academic secretary
Full-time students: 4,153 (f), 3,458 (m)
4,073 **arts,** 3,538 **sciences**

Main subject areas: arts, humanities (BA); education BEd; built environment, social sciences (BA, BSc); sciences (BSc); engineering (BEng); law (LLB). Certificates and diplomas available in most areas.

The new university had more trouble than most in finding a name that avoided confusion with an illustrious neighbour. The title, chosen after months of deliberation, celebrates the achievements of John Brookes, who having headed the college which spawned the polytechnic is regarded as a founding father.

Always one of the top polytechnics, Oxford pioneered the modular degree system that is sweeping British universities. There are now 1,000 units from which to choose, allowing students to dip into the arts, education, humanities and sciences in building up a degree.

Students can call a halt at nine modules and collect a Certificate in Higher Education, qualify for a diploma at 17 modules, take an ordinary degree with 25, or an honours degree with a full 27 modules. There are examinations every term.

With one site fully developed and another stifled by Green Belt restrictions, the new university has called a temporary halt to expansion to stave off problems of overcrowding. Students have complained that lecture theatres are packed and that the library, creche and computer suites struggle to meet demand. Open University-style learning packages have been introduced to help staff and students cope with larger classes. Most courses make some use of computers, and several of the workstation rooms are open 24 hours a day.

The computing facilities have won a national award, while planning, architecture and estate management all garnered high praise from Her Majesty's Inspectorate. The polytechnic scored heavily in funding council quality assessments.

Additional residential accommodation has been added recently, but although there are now more than 2,200 places and first-years get priority there is room for only half in hall. Private accommdoation is scarce and expensive, and the university advises an early visit to Oxford for those hoping to find it.

Oxford Brookes attracts more independent school pupils than any other new university. The active students' union, which operates on both sites, is critical of the sports facilities, but a new sports hall is planned.

PAISLEY UNIVERSITY
High Street, Paisley, Renfrewshire PA1 2BE (tel. 041-848 3000)

Royal charter 1992, formerly Paisley College
Times ranking: 87

Enquiries: public relations office
Full-time students: 1,307 (f), 2,581 (m)
1,472 **arts,** 2,416 **sciences**

Main subject areas: engineering (BEng, BSc); information, social and management sciences (BA); science and technology (BSc). Sub-degree courses are aslo offered.

Paisley, only seven miles from Glasgow, is Scotland's largest town. Many of the new university's 5,000 students come from the surrounding area. Student numbers have grown rapidly in recent years, but class sizes still compare favourably with those of rival institutions.

Most courses are strongly vocational, with a technological thrust. There are close links with industry and commerce, notably with the computer giant IBM. All students are offered hands-on computer training.

Courses are flexible. Science and technology students, for example, can choose from 11 interlinked degrees. More than 600 students are on the credit accumulation and transfer scheme, which covers some 800 subject units for day or evening classes. First-year science courses are also franchised to three further education colleges in the west of Scotland, with admission to Paisley in mid-course. A high proportion of students are on sandwich degrees.

Research and consultancy is concentrated on six specialist units in areas such as alcohol and drug abuse, and non-destructive testing. The newest is the Centre for Environmental and Waste Management, set up in 1991 with industrial support.

The campus covers 20 acres in the middle of Paisley. Recent building developments have included the modernisation of the library, central computing facilities and chemistry laboratories, and the addition of an interactive video suite.

There are only 720 residential places, with preference given to first-years whose homes are more than 25 miles away. There are plans for another 60 places in a student village two miles from the campus but most undergraduates will still have to rely on the relatively cheap private accommodation available locally.

The students' association building is a ten-minute walk from the campus. Though not intended for the university's current 5,000-strong student body, it has at least been refurbished recently. Sports facilities, situated on the edge of town, are limited.

UNIVERSITY OF PLYMOUTH
Drake Circus, Plymouth, PL4 8AA (tel. 0752 600600)

Royal charter 1992, formerly Polytechnic South West, originally Plymouth Polytechnic
Times ranking: 79

Enquiries: registry
Full-time students: 3,826 (f), 5,207 (m)
1,841 arts, 4,672 sciences

Main subject areas: agriculture, food and land use (BSc); art and design, business and management (BA); education BEd); science, human sciences (BSc); technology (BEng, MEng, BSc). Certificates and diplomas also offered.

Having taken over an art college in Exeter, an agricultural college near Newton Abbot and a college of education at Exmouth in recent years, in its new guise Plymouth is the largest university in the Southwest by some margin. In addition, it is responsible for Dartington College of Art outside Totnes and also franchises courses to a number of colleges in the region. One result is that though the authorities do their best to create a university identity, the component parts are too diverse and widely spread for them to have had much success yet.

Having gone out of its way to reinforce its regional image as a polytechnic, the new university has gone in the opposite direction in choosing its new name, however, at any rate in part on the basis of the marketing men's creed that city titles attract applicants. In fact Plymouth has never had trouble finding students, even though the majority of courses are in science and technology. Unlike many other new universities, 90 per cent of the students are on full-time or sandwich courses, mostly degrees.

As a polytechnic, the institution collected a shoal of quality awards in the funding council's last quality assessments. The sciences, mathematics and computing, social sciences and environmental courses all came out well. Today, the university is best known for a variety of marine studies, which also have an established research record. Having actively sought university status for many years, Plymouth is determined not to shrink from wider competition now that it has arrived.

Prospects of securing a residential place vary between the campuses. There are 700 places reserved for first-years in Plymouth, where 9,000 students are based. Accommodation is guaranteed on the Rolle College campus, in Exmouth, and at Seale Hayne, at Newton Abbot, but students have to rely on the private sector in Exeter. Inevitably, social and sporting facilities also vary between campuses. Plymouth is the best provided for.

UNIVERSITY OF PORTSMOUTH

University House, Winston Churchill Avenue, Portsmouth PO1 2UP (tel. 0705 827681)

Royal charter 1992, formerly Portsmouth Polytechnic
Times ranking: 59

Enquiries: assistant registrar
Full-time students: 3,404 (f), 5,249 (m)
4,692 **arts,** 3,961 **sciences**

Main subject areas: business and management (BA); environment studies (BSc, BA); engineering (BEng, MEng); humanities and social sciences (BA). Certificate and diploma courses are also offered.

Portsmouth only narrowly missed university status before the polytechnics were created, and never gave up the chase. Degree work goes back more than 70 years, and now four out of five students are taking degrees. Postgraduate numbers have also been growing steadily.

Placed in the top three among the new universities in *The Times* table, Portsmouth is in the throes of further expansion. It is also building on a reputation for research that was singled out in a national report on the polytechnics.

Staffing levels are among the most generous in the new universities, and none of the former polytechnics in England can match its library spending. The recently extended library is among the best in the new universities, taking 3,500 journals, stocking 500,000 volumes and providing room for 1,000 readers. Completion rates are also among the best in the sector, and the graduate employment rate is good, especially for a university where arts students are in the majority.

The main body of the university consists of about 30 buildings spread around Portsmouth and Southsea. There is a second campus for the business school three miles away, at Milton. A university minibus service links the two.

Languages are a particular strength. One student in five takes a language course, and the facilities rival those in many of the traditional universities. Science courses achieved the highest ratings in the last quality assessments for the polytechnics. Engineering and health subjects also did well.

Six halls, some overlooking the sea, provide about 1,000 residential places, three-quarters of which are reserved for first-years. Private rented accommodation is plentiful out of the holiday season, but all-year lets are more difficult to find and can be expensive.

Sports facilities are good, especially for water sports enthusiasts. The students' union, which operates on both sites, tends to be the focus of social activity.

UNIVERSITY OF READING
Whiteknights, PO Box 217, Reading RG6 2AH (tel. 0734 875123)

Founded 1892, royal charter 1926
Times ranking: 32

Enquiries: registrar
Full-time students: 4,152 (f), 4,092 (m)
3,642 **arts**, 2,295 **sciences**

Main subject areas: letters and social sciences (BA, LLB); agriculture and food, science (BSc, BEng); urban and regional studies, education and community studies (BA, BA[Ed]).

Best known for its agricultural courses (CDD), which have always attracted large numbers of overseas students, Reading is also strong in subjects as diverse as Italian (three Cs) and environmental sciences (BCC). A merger with Bulmershe College has strengthened education courses, as well as enabling the university to introduce film and drama (BBC) and American studies (BCC).

The university will have a new vice-chancellor, Professor Roger Williams, in the autumn of 1993. The former Manchester University professor of government is committed to breaking down the barriers between the arts and sciences. Reading has already taken some steps in this direction, notably in a joint initiative with the Open University to develop standardised course materials to help underqualified students cope with physics degrees. The programme will be used to diagnose the gaps in students' knowledge and to provide work to bring them up to the standard of other undergraduates. The scheme won a prize for innovation in 1992, and Reading was also one of nine institutions chosen to lead a new national project to widen access to physics degrees. A four-year degree in the subject, including an access year, is being introduced in 1993–94.

Arts and social science students take three subjects for their first two terms. Science degrees are modular, but late changes of specialism are possible on most courses. Reading had five top ratings in the 1992 research assessment. It also has the highest score in our 'value added' rating in the main ranking table.

The main campus is set in 300 acres of parkland on the outskirts of Reading, but the old college less than two miles away has its own facilities. Although the university has 13 halls of residence, first-years are guaranteed a place only if they are holding Reading as a firm choice by the end of May. The university likes to mix students in terms of subjects and seniority.

Sports facilities are good, although there is a nominal fee for their use. The main students' union is large, and has a well-equipped branch at Bulmershe.

THE ROBERT GORDON UNIVERSITY
Schoolhill, Aberdeen AB9 1FR (tel. 0224 633611)

Royal charter 1992, formerly the Robert Gordon Institute of Technology
Times ranking: 83

Enquiries: admissions office
Full-time students: 2,185 (f), 2,415 (m)
2,359 **arts,** 2,241 **science.**

Main subject areas: architecture (BSc); art and surveying, business, management, librarianship and information studies, public administration and law (BA); food and consumer studies, health and social work, pharmacy, applied sciences, computer and mathematical sciences (BSc); electronic and electrical engineering, mechanical and offshore engineering (BEng). Also linked diplomas.

Early links with the North Sea oil and gas industries exemplify Robert Gordon's commitment to vocational education. All offshore workers must have a certificate from its Survival Centre, and a number of longer courses are tailored to the industry's needs. Fire engineering is the latest addition to the university's service for its major employer. Other strengths include engineering, pharmacy, business and management, architecture and art and design.

Courses are flexible. Membership of the SCOTCAT credit accumulation and transfer system allows easy transfer in and out of the university, which also takes large numbers of students without the standard entrance qualifications.

There are now more than 40 degree courses, and fleeting talk of a merger with Aberdeen University is long forgotten. Students from the two institutions mix easily, and there is a healthy academic rivalry in some areas.

Robert Gordon has been expanding, and the Scottish Office is providing £10 million to cater for further growth. The offshore courses draw students from all over Britain, as well as overseas, but Scots are very much in the majority.

The main city-centre campus adjoins Aberdeen art gallery. As well as four other sites in the city, the university runs an attractive field study centre in the Highlands at Cromarty.

Residential accommodation has long been a problem in the city, but the university is adding places every year. Four-hundred additional places are planned for the autumn of 1993, bringing the total to almost 1,500. Though half are reserved for first-years, there are still not enough for all new undergraduates.

The students' association, based in the city-centre union building, is active, despite the absence of a bar. Sports facilities are unremarkable.

UNIVERSITY OF ST ANDREWS
College Gate, North Street, St Andrews KY16 9AJ (tel. 0334 76161)

Founded 1411
Times ranking: 19

Enquiries: schools liaison office
Full-time students: 2,155 (f), 2,046 (m)
2,145 **arts**, 1,683 **sciences**

Main subject areas: arts and social science (MA); divinity (BD, MTheol); science (BSc); medicine (MB, BSc).

St Andrews is the oldest Scottish university and the third oldest in Britain. The town is steeped in history, as well as being the centre of the golfing world. The university is set in the heart of St Andrews, and accounts for about a quarter of the town's 16,000 inhabitants. There are close relations between town and gown, particularly on the cultural and social side.

Many colourful traditions remain. New students acquire third- and fourth-year 'parents' to ease them into university life, and on Raisin Monday give their academic guardians a bottle of wine in return for a Latin receipt, which can be written on anything. Every Sunday, students wearing red undergraduate gowns process along the pier of St Andrews harbour.

The preponderance of students from south of the border has earned St Andrews the nickname of Scotland's English university. Today, Scottish numbers have now crept up to almost half the undergraduate total and more than half the postgraduates. Although small, St Andrews maintains a wide range of courses. It rates highly for languages (ABB for English), psychology (ABB), philosophy and ancient history (both three Bs).

The university's reputation has always rested primarily on the humanities. It has the largest medieval history department in Britain, for example. But a full range of physical sciences are available, with sophisticated lasers and the largest optical telescope in the United Kingdom.

There is room for three-quarters of St Andrews students in university residences, so accommodation is no problem for first-years. A new residence of 350 rooms with en suite facilities should be available in autumn 1993, making almost 3,000 residential places.

Sports facilities are excellent. There are even two £1,000-bursaries awarded by the Royal and Ancient Club to promising golfers. Social facilities are sufficient for the size of university. St Andrews is a tight-knit community much favoured by independent schools and much loved by most of its students but not to everyone's taste.

UNIVERSITY OF SALFORD
Salford M5 4WT (tel. 061-745 5000)

Royal charter 1967
Times ranking: 50

Enquiries: admissions office
Full-time students: 1,701 (m), 3,219 (m)
1,402 **arts,** 2,998 **sciences**

Main subject areas: aeronautical and mechanical, civil, electronic and electrical engineering, orthopaedic mechanics (BEng); biological sciences, chemistry, physics, mathematics, computing, business and management, economics, sociology (BSc); geography, modern languages, politics (BA).

The main victim of the university cuts of the early 1980s, Salford has bounced back as the prototype decentralised, customer-oriented university. It is often cited approvingly by ministers and, although not in the top rank of universities, is generally regarded as stronger now than before the cuts.

Originally a College of Advanced Technology, Salford has retained its technological bias despite adding a limited portfolio of social science courses. About 40 per cent of the students are on sandwich degrees, many going abroad for their placements.

The modern landscaped campus is only two miles from the centre of Manchester and has a mainline railway station. At its centre is a municipal park, a haven of lawns and shrubberies on the banks of the River Irwell.

European studies and engineering (three Cs for mechanical) are among Salford's strengths. The university is rated in the top 25 for engineering in *The Times* subject tables.

Salford is among those traditional universities being steered towards teaching, rather than research, in its funding allocation for the 1993–94 academic year. Its teaching budget has been increased substantially, while poor ratings in the previous research assessment exercise led to an effective freeze in that part of the university's income.

A rationalisation of research activity is about to take place to direct funds into areas of strength. The creation of research schools has been mooted to ensure that the best teams of academics are able to compete on an equal footing with leading rivals elsewhere.

First-years are guaranteed places in mostly purpose-built accommodation close enough to walk or cycle to lectures. Private rents are relatively low, although the size of Manchester's student population creates some problems.

The students' union has plenty of facilities and sports enthusiasts are well catered for. Students generally like the university, which also has one of the highest proportions of overseas students.

UNIVERSITY OF SHEFFIELD

Sheffield S10 2TN (tel. 0742 768555)

Founded 1828, royal charter 1905
Times ranking: 19

Enquiries: undergraduate admissions office
Full-time students: 4,459 (f), 6,270 (m)
3,972 **arts,** 4,669 **sciences**

Main subject areas: full range of disciplines in eight faculties: architectural studies (BScTech); arts (BA, BMus); educational studies (postgraduate); engineering (BEng, BScTech, MEng); law (LLB); medicine and dentistry (BMedSci, MBChB, BDS); pure science (BSc); social science (BA).

Sheffield suffered in the first *Times* rankings for an outstanding performance in 1991, when it topped the traditional universities' allocations for both teaching and research. There was little room for improvement in 1992, although the university turned in another good showing in that year's research assessment exercise.

Sheffield consistently features in the top three for the volume of student applications, and has expanded more rapidly than most of the traditional universities. It has moved into the top ten institutions for research council grants, and was in *The Times* top 20 for medicine, science, engineering and the humanities.

Psychology (three Bs), mechanical engineering and archaeology (both BCC), social policy (BBC) and law (ABB) are especially strong. Almost 200 undergraduate courses are being moulded into a modular system, and semesters are being introduced.

The university also offers courses in a network of further education colleges, mainly but not exclusively in the north of England. A £100-million university college is planned for the Dearne Valley, 12 miles north of Sheffield.

First-years are almost certain of one of the 3,750 residential places, which are within walking distance of the main university precinct, itself less than a mile from the city centre. Most departments are in the same area, on the affluent side of the city.

The students' union is well equipped and run; it even has its own pub near the halls. Sports facilities are excellent, the World Student Games having transformed the city's amenities and complementing the already impressive range run by the university.

Students invariably like Sheffield. It is said that a quarter stay in the city after graduation. One blackspot in 1992 was the graduate employment rate, but job prospects over a longer period have not been poor compared with other universities.

SHEFFIELD HALLAM UNIVERSITY

Pond Street, Sheffield S1 1WB (tel. 0742 720911)

Royal charter 1992, formerly Sheffield Polytechnic
Times ranking: 66

Enquiries: enquiry office
Full-time students: 5,137 (f), 6,998 (m)
6,862 **arts**, 5,611 **sciences**

Main subject areas: computing and management science (BSc); cultural studies (BA); education (BEd); construction, engineering, information technology (BEng, MEng, BSc); financial studies and law (LLB, BA); health and community studies, leisure and food management (BA); science (BSc); business, urban and regional management (BA). Certificate and diploma courses are also offered.

The new university is undergoing an £80-million transformation designed both to alter its image and cater for an even bigger student population, as well as to revitalise the city centre. As a polytechnic, it considered moving to a less central development area, but will now keep its main site in the heart of Sheffield. Campus 21, as the redevelopment programme is known, will reduce the number of sites from five to two by the end of 1996. The project is the largest in higher education since the 1960s, and should ease the growing pressure on facilities.

For the moment, business students will continue to be based at Totley, on the outskirts of Sheffield, while others are in buildings closer to the main site. There is free transport between sites.

Sheffield Hallam now has almost 20,000 students, including part-timers, making it one of the largest of the new universities. It was one of the first three polytechnics to be established, and can trace its origins in art and design back to the 1840s.

Business and industry are closely involved in developing the 100 full-time and 150 part-time courses, most of which are applied, rather than theoretical. There is also growing strength in applied research, which provides more income than most of the new universities can command.

Sheffield was consistently successful in the polytechnics' quality ratings. Engineering, education, mathematics and computing, business and managenent (which finished a creditable eighth in *The Times* table) did particularly well in the last exercise.

Almost half of the students are over 21 on entry. That many live at home gives first-years looking for accommodation about a one-in-three chance of being offered one of the 2,100 residential places. For those who have to fend for themselves in the private sector, rents are relatively low.

The university's sports facilities are limited, but those built for the World Students Games are on the doorstep. The students' union is adequate, and should acquire more space in the new developments.

SOUTH BANK UNIVERSITY

103 Borough Road, London SE1 0AA (tel. 071-928 8989)

Royal charter 1992, formerly South Bank Polytechnic
Times ranking: 81

Enquiries: central registry
Full-time students: 3,682 (f), 5,113 (m)
2,745 **arts,** 6,050 **sciences**

Main subject areas: built environment (BA, BSc, BEng); engineering (BEng, BSc); management and policy studies (BA, LLB); science, technology, health and society (BSc, BEng). A wide range of certificate and diploma courses are also offered.

South Bank has styled itself 'the university without ivory towers'. Those looking for *Brideshead Revisited* will not find it at the Elephant and Castle, London SE1. The new university's links with the local community are such that 70 per cent of students are from the area, many coming from south London's wide range of ethnic groups. Out of 17,000 students, 40 per cent are part-time, and one in five is on a sandwich course.

South Bank has stayed closer than most of the new universities to the technological and vocational brief given to the original polytechnics. Strengths include engineering, accountancy, business and the built environment. The design students regularly rake in national prizes. Unusual features include the National Bakery School and a Centre for Chinese Studies.

Certificate, diploma and degree courses all run in parallel, so that students can move up or down if another level of study is found to suit them better than their original choice. Diploma courses, as well as degrees, can be taken as sandwich courses.

The main site is in Southwark, not far from the riverside arts complex with which the university shares a name. There are five smaller bases nearby, with management and continuing education three miles away at Clapham Common.

Academic facilities include a new library, which is one of the most technologically advanced in the country. All students have access to language courses, mainly through programmed tapes in a manned self-service language laboratory.

Sporting prowess is a particular source of pride. Facilities include two gymnasia and a large sports ground in nearby Dulwich. Students' union facilities are due to be expanded.

The university warns prospective students that it does not accept responsibility for finding accommodation, although first-years are given priority in the three halls of residence. The usual London housing problems apply for those who have to fend for themselves.

UNIVERSITY OF SOUTHAMPTON
Highfield, Southampton SO9 5NH (tel. 0703 595000)

Founded 1862, royal charter 1952
Times ranking: 11

Enquiries: assistant registrar
Full-time students: 3,202 (f), 4,712 (m)
2,592 arts, 3,836 sciences

Main subject areas: wide range of disciplines in seven faculties: arts (BA); engineering and applied science (BEng, MEng, BSc); law (LLB); mathematical studies (BSc); medicine (BM, BSc); science (BSc); social sciences (BA, BSc[Social Sciences]).

Though Southampton is outgrowing its compact campus three miles from the city centre, red tape has slowed expansion plans. With the university favouring a second campus on a wooded site capable of taking teaching and residential accommodation for the next 40 years and the local authorities backing an urban solution, the result has been stalemate.

In the meantime, electronics and computer science have acquired new premises on the original campus at a cost of £12 million, while work is under way on a dockside campus for oceanography, geology and some engineering work. By 1994, Southampton expects to have Europe's most comprehensive ocean study centre.

Chemistry (BCC), electronic engineering (three Bs), economics (BBC) and ship science (CCD) are among the top-rated degrees. Medicine (three Bs) offers clinical training even in the first two years, allowing fourth-year students to specialise.

Arts, mathematical studies, science and social science degrees are modular. Students may take in units from other departments to broaden their studies. Engineering, law, mathematics and social sciences also postpone specialisation until the second year.

Vice-chancellor Sir Gordon Higginson retires at the end of the 1993–94 academic year. In eight years, he has seen the university move back into the top ten for research council grants and begin a period of concerted growth at undergraduate level.

Almost 40 per cent of Southampton's students live in university accommodation, although first-years are only guaranteed a place if they accept by the end of May. The university has set itself the target of adding 500 residential places in the first half of the decade. One existing hall has been designed specifically for disabled students.

Sports facilities are good, and include a climbing wall on the side of the students' union building. The union itself has the usual range of amenities.

UNIVERSITY OF STAFFORDSHIRE
College Road, Stoke-on-Trent ST4 2DE (tel. 0782 744531)

Royal charter 1992, formerly Staffordshire (originally North Staffs) Polytechnic
Times ranking: 91

Enquiries: academic registrar
Full-time students: 2,941 (f), 4,392 (m)
4,066 **arts**, 3,267 **sciences**

Main subject areas: ceramics, fine art, design, history of art (BA); applied science, mathematics, computing (BSc); mechanical and computer-aided engineering, electrical and electronic engineering (BEng); economics, business and management (BA, BSc); law (LLB); humanities, politics, geography, recreation studies and sociology (BA). Diplomas are also offered.

Despite its low placing in *The Times* table, the new university has been growing in confidence and attracting applicants in ever-increasing numbers. A massive rationalisation programme, designed to cope with rapid and continuing expansion, has seen two-thirds of Staffordshire's staff move offices.

There are two centres, a relatively small, predominantly male site in Stafford, and the headquarters in Stoke. The larger of the two Stoke sites features the new Octagon Centre, in which lecture theatres, offices and walkways surround a huge concourse containing more than 300 advanced computer workstations.

The business school, which did well in the polytechnics' last quality ratings, straddles the two sites in a deliberate attempt to foster links with the private sector. Courses are being developed in enterprise, innovation and communications.

Computing and engineering were the polytechnic's traditional strengths, but arts and social science courses have seen the greatest new growth. Extensive language laboratories are open to all students, and are heavily used.

Good sports facilities, coaches and courses have been attracting growing numbers of top sportsmen and women, including three who won medals at the World Student Games in 1991. Stoke is much better provided for than Stafford. Expansion is placing a strain on student union facilities on all sites.

Hundreds of residential places have been added since a much-publicised accommodation shortage in 1990. The university now has more than 1,700 beds, although finding accommodation was still a struggle for some at the start of the 1992–93 academic year. One compensation is that private rents are lower than in most other student areas.

UNIVERSITY OF STIRLING
Stirling FK9 4LA (tel. 0786 73171)

Royal charter 1967
Times ranking: 40

Enquiries: student recruitment officer
Full-time students: 1,900 (f), 1,900 (m)
2,250 **arts,** 750 **sciences**

Main subject areas: biological and environmental sciences, education, psychology, sociology, accountancy, computer science and mathematics, economics, business and management, marketing, English, film and media studies, modern languages, music, philosophy, political and religious studies (BA, BSc, BAcc, BEd).

One of the most beautiful campuses in Britain features low-level, modern buildings in a loch-side setting beneath the Ochil Hills. Even after a 30 per cent expansion over four years, Stirling will still be among the smallest universities in Britain and likely to remain so.

Although highly rated in some research fields – notably in the world-renowned Institute of Aquaculture – the university is being encouraged to concentrate on teaching rather than research. A 20 per cent increase in this year's teaching budget was the sixth highest in the traditional universities.

Stirling was the British pioneer of the semester system, now growing in popularity in other universities. The academic year is divided into two 15-week terms, with short mid-semester breaks. Successful completion of six semesters will bring a general degree, eight for honours.

The emphasis on breadth of study is such that there are no faculties. Undergraduates can switch the whole direction of their studies as they progress. Each student has an academic adviser to help plan a programme of courses.

Film and media studies (ABB) is particularly popular, and the Scottish Centre for Japanese Studies, which offers the language with a range of other subjects, is beginning to break new ground. Business and management courses (three Bs) are also well regarded, and finished in *The Times* top 15 in the subject tables. Social work (BCC, for a new course in 1993) was the top-rated research area.

First-years are guaranteed one of the 2,600 residential places on campus. Additional accommodation is planned both on the campus and in Stirling itself before the university reaches its peak size.

Students' union and social facilities are more than adequate for a small university, while sports enthusiasts have access to an Olympic-size pool and the Scottish National Tennis Centre. The campus also features the MacRobert Arts Centre, which is open to the public and has a management committee chaired by Diana Rigg.

UNIVERSITY OF STRATHCLYDE
Richmond Street, Glasgow G1 1XO (tel. 041-552 4400)

Founded 1794, royal charter 1964
Times ranking: 40

Enquiries: schools and colleges liaison service
Full-time students: 3,550 (f), 5,325 (m)
4,066 **arts**, 3,266 **sciences**

Main subject areas: arts and social science (BA, LLB, BEd); science (BSc); engineering (BEng, MEng); business (BA, BSc).

Even as Anderson's University in the 19th century, Strathclyde concentrated on 'useful learning'. Some Glaswegians still refer to it as 'the tech'. But if the nickname does less than justice to the current portfolio of courses, the university has never shrunk from its technological and vocational emphasis.

Strathclyde aims to offer courses that are both innovatory and relevant to industry and commerce – hence civil engineering with European studies, or mathematics with languages. One of the most popular courses is the five-year BA in international business and modern languages (BBC), which combines three business subjects with two languages and offers a year in an overseas business school.

The business school is one of the largest in Europe, and was ranked joint fourth in *The Times* subject rankings. Its European focus is matched elsewhere in the university, which has encouraged all departments to adapt their courses to the needs of the single market.

Strathclyde runs a credit-based modular degree system, which has proved especially attractive to mature students. They now account for 30 per cent of the student population, and have a special group to look after their interests.

A merger with Jordanhill College of Education in summer 1993 will widen study options, and increase the size of the university to more than 13,000 students. Among the benefits may be the establishment of a music department, bringing together expertise from both partners.

Strathclyde has also formed an association with Bell College of Technology, in Hamilton, to offer degrees in engineering and biological sciences. The initiative is partly in response to the closure of Ravenscraig steelworks.

The university is losing its image as a 'nine-to-five' institution thanks to a student village on campus, complete with pub. The large union building attracts students from all over Glasgow. The sports facilities are also good.

First-years are given priority in the allocation of 2,500 residential places, most of which are on the campus, bordering Glasgow's chic Merchant City. The rest are in the city centre, where half the first-years find private accommodation.

UNIVERSITY OF SUNDERLAND
Edinburgh Building, Chester Road, Sunderland SR1 3SD (tel. 091-515 2082)

Royal charter 1992, formerly Sunderland Polytechnic
Times ranking: 85

Enquiries: admissions officer
Full-time students: 3,173 (f), 3,982 (m)
2,046 **arts,** 3,577 **sciences**

Main subject areas: arts and social studies (BA); business, management and education (BA, BEd); science (BSc); technology (BSc, BEng). Certificates and diplomas are also offered.

The new university is aiming to double its student numbers over the 1990s. To make room, a second campus is being added. Dr Anne Wright, one of only two female vice-chancellors, is aiming for 18,000 students by 2001.

Four of the eight schools will move to the new site, although of those applying in 1993 only business and computing students will be affected as undergraduates. The business school and part of the school of computing and information systems will be in new premises from 1994, with the rest of the computing specialists following in 1996.

Eventually, education and art, design and communications will follow, filling the 24-acre riverside site. There will also be a working heritage centre for the glass industry, as part of a £90-million regeneration of a former shipyard area.

The university's 900 residential places are already inadequate, and will become progressively more so as expansion really takes off. Nonetheless, for the moment a high proportion of home-based students coupled with low private-sector rents are keeping the lid on accommodation problems. Another 200 places should be available by autumn 1993, while 1,000 more are to be added in four stages a mile from the new campus. Most university halls of residence are within walking distance of the two existing town-centre sites.

Sunderland is pioneering a scheme to extend access to higher education to local people without A-levels. Students who have reached the required level of numeracy, literacy and other basic skills will be admitted to degree courses by interview on the recommendation of their colleges.

Only the teacher training and part-time business courses received awards in the polytechnics' last quality assessments. However, Sunderland is active in European higher education networks, and has links with more than 60 Continental universities and colleges.

The students' union does not have a building of its own, but sports facilities are adequate for the moment. The majority of students are over 21 at entry and from the Northeast, although that may change as numbers rise.

UNIVERSITY OF SURREY
Guildford, Surrey GU2 5XH (tel. 0483 300800)

Founded 1891, royal charter 1966
Times ranking: 23

Enquiries: undergraduate admissions office
Full-time students: 1,857 (f), 2,346 (m)
1,074 **arts,** 2,328 **sciences**

**Main subject areas: engineering (BEng, MEng, BSc); science (BSc);
human studies (BSc, BA, BMus).**

Surrey has remained true to the technological legacy of its institutional predecessor, Battersea Polytechnic Institute. Even some of the arts courses carry a BSc and are highly vocational. It's a subject bias which has helped the university to a regular spot at or near the top of the graduate employment league, as well as paving the way to a healthy research income. That said, arts courses have been growing.

Surrey hit the headlines in 1992 when it accepted a 13-year-old as an undergraduate, the youngest of modern times. But its real priorities are work experience and language competence. Most degrees last four years, one (or two half-years) of which are spent in work placements, often abroad.

All students are encouraged to enrol for a course at the language centre, and new engineering degrees have a language component (three Bs for information systems engineering with a European language). With more than 1,000 workstations, computers are also common to all Surrey's courses.

The compact campus is a ten-minute walk from the centre of Guildford. Most of the buildings date from the late 1960s, when the university was developing. The campus includes two lakes, playing fields and residential accommodation.

A neighbouring 70-acre site houses the Surrey Research Park, which is attracting tenant companies rapidly. Successes in technology transfer contracts abroad and, in particular, in attracting overseas students won the university a Queen's Award for Export Achievement in 1991.

Some 2,500 campus residential places, plus another 350 in a university development not far away, enable Surrey to offer accommodation for the first and final years of a degree course. The service is welcome: Guildford is an extremely expensive area for renting in the private sector.

Sports and social facilities on campus are good. The proximity of London, little more than half an hour away by train, is an attraction to many students, but can also make the university less lively at weekends.

UNIVERSITY OF SUSSEX
Falmer, Brighton BN1 9RH (tel. 0273 678416)

Royal charter 1961
Times ranking: 19

Enquiries: admissions officer
Full-time students: 2,883 (f), 2,800 (m)
2,433 **arts,** 2,006 **sciences**

Main subject areas: biological sciences, physical sciences, mathematics and computing (BSc); engineering (BEng, MEng); social sciences, languages, humanities (BA).

Though the glitter which seemed synonomous with Sussex in the 1960s, with the then-new university a self-proclaimed champion of innovation and determinedly fashionable, had become distinctly tarnished by the 1980s, the tide appears to have turned again in Sussex's favour. From a regular spot near the foot of the graduate employment tables in the 1980s, for example, in 1991 hugely improved graduate employment figures lifted Sussex to a place in the top 20 in the first *Times* rankings, a position bettered by only two technological universities.

This was by no means the only factor in its revitalisation, however. Despite taking students with lower average entry grades than any other university in the top 20 and having markedly lower staffing levels, a strong performance against virtually all the other indicators pulled Sussex up. Research income is especially buoyant for an arts-dominated institution, library spending is high and the proportion of overseas students substantial.

With one in five undergraduates spending a year abroad and established favourites such as American studies (BBC) still highly rated, demand for places remains strong. Applications rose by 45 per cent in three years at the start of the decade, and there should be no difficulty in finding the candidates for a planned expansion from 6,000 to 7,500 students. Six departments, including dentistry (three Cs) and computer science (BCC), won top ratings in the 1992 research ratings.

More than 600 new residential places are being added, at a cost of £19 million, to accommodate the extra students. First-years and the many overseas students have first call on campus places. Most second- and third-year undergraduates choose to live in Brighton itself.

The university's initial concern for breadth of study survives, together with an interest in professional courses. Sussex has the region's first Common Professional Examination in law, as well as centres for social work and legal studies.

Sports facilities are good, while the active students' union has the usual amenities. Almost a quarter of the students are over 21 on entry. They and their younger colleagues may criticise the university, but few would choose to go elsewhere.

UNIVERSITY OF TEESSIDE
Borough Road, Middlesbrough, Cleveland TS1 3BA (tel. 0642 606755)

Royal charter 1992, formerly Teesside Polytechnic
Times ranking: 94

Enquiries: student administration section
Full-time students: 1,967 (f), 3,444 (m)
2,980 **arts,** 2,431 **sciences**

Main subject areas: computing and mathematics, health (BSc); social and policy studies (BA, LLB); science and technology (BSc); business and management, design, humanities (BA). Certificates and diplomas are also offered.

The new university has made good use of its links with multinational corporations with bases in the area such as ICI. It is no coincidence that chemical engineering and computing are two of the strongest subjects. Although one of the smaller universities, Teesside has a good range of courses, including nursing and welfare studies. Art and design is another of the highly rated areas.

Dr Derek Fraser, the new vice-chancellor, is keen for the university to expand, and has already created a new management structure to put his ideas into practice. The corporate plan he inherited envisaged another 1,000 full-time students over the next three years, bringing the total to 6,500.

On top of that, the university has gone into partnership with Durham University to open a new Joint University College at nearby Stockton. The first 180 students are already in their first year of European studies, human sciences and environmental technology courses. The college has its own management and facilities.

The university is based mainly in Middlesbrough, with an outpost four miles away at the foot of the Eston Hills. Almost a third of the students are on certificate or diploma courses, and about half are over 21 on entry.

Teesside has begun franchising courses to further education colleges, and intends to do more of this in future, attracting more local students at the same time. More than 90 per cent of courses should be within the university's modular credit accumulation scheme by autumn 1993.

Residential accommodation is scarce. There are plans to increase the 1,300 places, but for the time being most first-years have to rely on the private sector. The sports facilities are reasonably good, and the large students' union is the centre of social life for most undergraduates.

THAMES VALLEY UNIVERSITY

St Mary's Road, Ealing, London W5 5RF (tel. 081-579 5000)

Royal charter 1992, formerly The Polytechnic of West London
Times ranking: 85

Enquiries: Sue Hirst
Full-time students: 3,300 (f), 2,900 (m)
4,000 **arts**, 1,200 **sciences**

Main subject areas: accountancy, law and economics, business and information studies, humanities and languages, hospitality studies, management (BA); nursing and midwifery, technology (BSc). Certificates and diplomas are also offered.

Thames Valley is another of the new universities to have enjoyed a meteoric rise up the pecking order of higher education, this despite having been granted polytechnic status only in 1991. The breakthrough came when Ealing and Thames Valley colleges agreed to merge, producing an institution of sufficient size to become a polytechnic at the most opportune moment.

The restyled institution would have liked to adapt its polytechnic title to become West London University, but eventually settled for a title which reflects its geographical spread. TVU London, as it likes to be known, will continue to occupy town-centre sites in Ealing and Slough.

The university is eager to expand its Ealing base, which was built for far fewer students and has been suffering from overcrowding. Limited construction projects have eased the problem, the latest development being a £2.2-million law building.

Dr Mike Fitzgerald, the youthful vice-chancellor, sees a more realistic solution in students' doing much of their studying off campus via computer. The move towards an electronic university already sees students issued with bar codes that set out timetables, for example, and give access to the library.

The addition of the London College of Music and Queen Charlotte's College of Health Care Studies has widened the scope of the university, which has a long-established reputation in languages and some social sciences.

Although research is not TVU's first priority, Ealing was accredited for postgraduate degrees before most of the polytechnics. One in eight of the academics were entered for last December's research assessment exercise.

Both the students' union and sporting facilities leave something to be desired, although the Slough multi-gym is impressive. There are plans to provide more university accommodation, but most first-years have to rely on expensive private housing.

UNIVERSITY OF ULSTER

Coleraine, County Londonderry BT52 1SA (tel. 0265 44141)

Royal charter 1984, formerly the New University of Ulster and Ulster
Polytechnic (merged 1984)
Times ranking: 58

Enquiries: admissions officer
Full-time students: 5,557 (f), 4,497 (m)
4,758 **arts,** 3,003 **sciences**

**Main subject areas: art and design, business and management,
education, humanities (BA); informatics (BSc); science and technology
(BSc, BEng); social and health sciences (BSc). A wide range of
certificate and diploma courses are also offered.**

Ulster suffers in *The Times* rankings for concentrating on the character-
istics that made the polytechnic the stronger partner when the university
was formed. Its charter was unique in stipulating that there should be
courses below degree level. Community consciousness has done the
university's reputation no harm in Ireland, however. Almost 40 per cent of
the students come from blue-collar backgrounds, more than twice the UK
average, while the student profile also mirrors the religious balance of the
province.

A third of the university's students are part-time, a proportion that has
been growing steadily and now includes 2,600 on degree courses alone.
Mature students are strongly represented, and one in 12 of first-class
graduates in 1992 was over 40.

A new corporate plan stresses both continuing commitment to such
diversity as well as some significant change. For instance, semesters are
being introduced in the 1993–94 academic year, with an added summer
teaching period, and all courses will be modular by the end of 1993.

The main sites inherited from the polytechnic in and near Belfast have
never been busier, and the expanded Magee College in Londonderry
attracts students from both sides of the border. The original university at
Coleraine is more traditional.

Although research is not the university's principal strength, Ulster is to
be the site of a prestigious new Centre for Conflict Resolution, formed in
collaboration with the Tokyo-based United Nations University. The
centre, which will study ethnic conflict worldwide, will be based initially at
Coleraine, but is destined for a permanent home at Magee.

High technology brings the university together for teaching purposes, but the sites are 80 miles apart at the farthest point, and very
different in character. Jordanstown, seven miles out of Belfast, has the
most students, Coleraine still has an isolated feel, and Magee, for many

years the poor relation confined to adult education, is now a thriving centre.

The university has little more than 1,000 residential places between the three centres, but a high proportion of students live at home with the result that a majority of first-years can be accommodated. The sporting and students' union facilities inevitably vary between sites.

UNIVERSITY OF WALES
Cathays Park, Cardiff CF1 3NS (tel. 0222 32656)

Founded 1893
Times ranking: see individual colleges

Enquiries: to individual colleges
Full-time students: 12,817 (f), 13,147 (m)

The university is second only to London, its federal counterpart, in terms of full-time student numbers. Like London, it is also surrendering more power to its colleges. At the same time, however, inter-collegiate links have been increasing, especially in research. A grant of £250,000 to strengthen research was shared between 19 collaborative projects involving all six colleges. All six can now be linked up for videoconferences as well. The university has yet to feel the effects of administration by a separate funding council for the Principality.

November 30 1993 marks the centenary of the University of Wales.

Not listed separately: **University of Wales College of Medicine**, Heath Park, Cardiff CF4 4XN (tel. 0222 747747). Founded 1931. Full-time students: 1,059 (BMedSci, BSc, BDS, BN). Based at the University Hospital of Wales, two miles from the centre of Cardiff.

UNIVERSITY COLLEGE OF WALES

PO Box 2, Aberystwyth, Dyfed SY23 2AX (tel. 0970 623111)

Founded 1872

Times ranking: 52

Enquiries: admissions officer

Full-time students: 2,020 (f), 2,155 (m)

2,202 **arts**, 1,135 **sciences**

Main subject areas: arts (BA); law (LLB); science (BSc); economics and social studies (BA, BScEcon); rural studies, information and library studies (BSc, BA); education (postgraduate only).

Although the oldest of the Welsh university colleges, Aberystwyth has long adopted a pioneering approach. Autumn 1993 sees the completion of the college's move to modular degrees, the culmination of a longstanding policy of flexibility in undergraduate programmes. Even before this development, Aberystwyth students were not required to nominate an honours subject when applying. The choice could be left until the end of the first year, during which students could try out at least three subjects. Vocational and academic courses all benefit from the same arrangement.

In spite of its rural surroundings, 'Aber' is as keen as its big city rivals to tailor courses to the needs of business and industry. It was among the recipients of a £1-million government grant to promote business awareness among staff and students, and is working closely with the Welsh Medium Enterprise Agency to promote self-employment among Welsh speakers. The collaboration has resulted in a new degree course in Welsh and accountancy (BCC).

Traditional strengths have included Celtic studies (CCD), and international politics and environmental science (both BCC). Applied mathematics (CCD) was the top-rated department in December 1992's research rankings, the only area considered internationally outstanding.

A bracing seaside location does the college no harm when the applications season comes around. Aberystwyth was heavily oversubscribed for 1992–93, with 10,500 applicants chasing 1,350 places, a record for the college.

There are plans to increase the intake and to provide more residential places to meet rising student demand without the accommodation problems experienced in 1991. Another 600 hall places have been added for the 1992–93 academic year, and a student village with 1,000 beds next to the campus should be ready soon. Most first-years who need accommodation will be offered a place.

Sports facilities are good, and the students' union is the focus of social life. Aberystwyth itself is small and travel to other parts of Wales and to

England slow, so applicants should be sure that they will be happy to spend three years or more in a tight-knit, remote community.

UNIVERSITY OF WALES, BANGOR
Bangor, Gwynedd LL57 2DG (tel. 0248 351151)

Founded 1884
Times ranking: 55

Enquiries: registrar
Full-time students: 1,859 (f), 2,088 (m)
1,633 **arts,** 1,508 **sciences**

Main subject areas: accountancy and banking, biological and environmental sciences, health studies, pure and applied sciences, mathematics and computing (BSc); electrical and electronic engineering (BEng); arts, social sciences and languages (BA, BMus).

Bangor has emerged from major restructuring in the late 1980s as a leaner, fitter institution. Departments such as philosophy and physics have closed to enable the college to develop strengths in a range of different subjects.

The aim is to expand from 4,500 students to 6,000 by the end of the decade, launching new courses in popular disciplines. European financial management (BCC), mathematics with insurance, and marine biology (both three Cs) are recent examples. There were 2,000 applications for 40 places on a new sport, health and physical education degree (BCC).

Other initiatives have seen the health studies faculty, which includes nursing, offer new courses in radiography and speech therapy. And the agriculture, forestry and biology departments are coming together in an Institute of Environmental Studies.

Longer-established favourites include a unique course in agroforestry (CCD), electronic engineering (three Bs) and psychology (BCC). Ocean sciences students (CCD) have the benefit of two research ships.

Bangor is one of the university's two centres for Welsh-medium teaching. It also offers a single honours degree in the subject (CCD). Almost one in ten of the students speak Welsh and several departments now offer tuition in the language. One of the seven halls of residence is also Welsh-speaking.

An extra 500 hall places will bring the total to more than 2,000 in the autumn of 1993, with another 400 to come in 1994. First-years are guaranteed accommodation, although private housing is in short supply for those who choose to live away from the college.

The students' union is spacious for the size of college, and has a separate Welsh union. Sports facilities are also good, especially for outdoor pursuits and watersports. The university is the focus of social and cultural life in the small town (officially a city) of Bangor.

UNIVERSITY OF WALES COLLEGE OF CARDIFF
PO Box 68, Cardiff CF1 3XA (tel. 0222 747747)

Royal charter 1988, formerly University College (founded 1883) and University of Wales Institute of Science and Technology (founded 1866), merged 1988
Times ranking: 43

Enquiries: admissions officer
Full-time students: 4,587 (f), 5,260 (m)
3,980 **arts,** 4,097 **sciences**

Main subject areas: Business studies and law (BA, LLB); health and life sciences (BSc, BD, BPharm); humanities and social studies (BA, BScEcon, BMus, BEd); engineering and environmental design (BEng, BSc); physical sciences (BSc).

Now recovered from the financial crisis which brought the merged institution into being, Cardiff has established itself as the frontrunner in Welsh higher education. Not only is it the university's largest college by far, it also won pride of place in December 1992's research assessment exercise.

The five top ratings it received for architecture (BBC), city and regional planning (BCD), civil engineering (three Cs), English (three Bs) and psychology (BBC) led the way to a big improvement over the college's performance in 1989. Almost a third of the areas assessed were judged excellent by national standards.

The previous assessment caught Cardiff in some disarray, not to mention debt, following the 1988 merger. Since then, research teams have been reorganised and new staff brought in. As a result, research council income increased by 60 per cent in 1991–92, while undergraduate courses have also benefited.

Cardiff now has more than 11,000 students and is planning for 16,000 by the end of the century. A new £30-million engineering complex, including state-of-the-art physics and astronomy facilities, will free teaching space to cater for more arts students.

Many of the 400 degree schemes feature a common first year, allowing students to defer their choice of specialism. Preliminary years are available in engineering and biology for students with arts qualifications.

The college is hoping for a new academic and residential complex in Cardiff Bay to complement its city-centre site. Recently, however, it has been concentrating on improving and expanding its residential stock.

More than £6 million has been spent refurbishing accommodation, and extra hall places have left the college with more than 3,500 beds. First-years are guaranteed a place.

The merger has left the students' union with some of the best facilities in Britain, and sports enthusiasts are equally well provided for, especially with the opening of a £1.5-million sports hall. Little more than a third of the students are Welsh, and many come from overseas.

ST DAVID'S UNIVERSITY COLLEGE

Lampeter, Dyfed SA48 7ED (tel. 0570 422351)

Founded 1822, part of University of Wales since 1971
Times ranking: 48

Enquiries: deputy registrar
Full-time students: 551 (f), 503 (m)
1,005 **arts,** 8 **sciences**

Main subject areas: archaeology, classics, English, geography, history, informatics, library and information studies, modern languages, Near East and Islamic studies, philosophy, Welsh studies (BA); religious studies, theology (BD).

In the whole of England and Wales, only Oxford and Cambridge were awarding degrees before Lampeter. Yet only Buckingham University is smaller today.

Based on an ancient castle site, the college was established to train young people for the Anglican ministry in Wales. The original building, with a quadrangle at its centre, was modelled on a Cambridge college and now houses the chapel, students' union and main offices.

Bachelors of arts and divinity are the only undergraduate degrees, although informatics has been added to give students some experience of computers. There are 75 workstations between the 1,000-plus students.

The BA degree, taken by most students, is divided into two parts. The first year is taken up with three humanities subjects, and students are encouraged to try a new language such as Swedish, Greek, Arabic or Welsh. Part two normally takes a further two years, though modern languages, Welsh and philosophy take three.

There are exchange schemes with Canadian and Swedish universities. For those who stay behind, an archive of 20,000 historical books and manuscripts supplememts the main library of 175,000 volumes.

Most of the students are English, but a number of departments offer the option of tuition in Welsh. Lampeter is deep in Welsh-speaking west Wales, and both the college and students' union have strong bilingual policies.

The college's isolation would be a problem for the unprepared. The town has only 4,000 inhabitants, and the nearest station is at Camarthen, more than 20 miles away. A high proportion of the students run cars. Most students live in college accommodation, and first-years are guaranteed a place. New residences are being built to cope with planned expansion over the next few years.

For the moment, the student union facilities are adequate, and are the centre of social life at the college. The sports hall is modern and outdoor pitches close at hand.

UNIVERSITY COLLEGE OF SWANSEA
Singleton Park, Swansea SA2 8PP (tel. 0792 205678)

Royal charter 1920
Times ranking: 29

Enquiries: deputy registrar
Full-time students: 3,207 (f), 2,684 (m)
2,945 **arts,** 2,026 **sciences**

Main subject areas: Arts, social sciences (BA); science (BSc); engineering (BEng, MEng).

The college has embarked on a phased expansion with a target of 10,000 students by the end of the decade. As part of the plan, 25 new courses were introduced in 1992, many with a language component.

Swansea takes its European interests seriously, with 84 links with Continental institutions. Science students, as well as those on arts courses, are being encouraged to undertake some of their studies abroad.

A number of inter-faculty courses combine languages with subjects such as management and engineering. The new law school will also offer options in European and international law, as well as the British legal system.

The college counts European business management (three Bs) and modern languages (BCD for German) among its strengths. Civil engineering (CCD) was the top-rated department in the latest research assessment. Computer science and marine biology (both BCC) are also popular.

For all of the concentration on international activities, Swansea has not forgotten its local responsibilities. In 1992 it launched a 'University of the Valleys' scheme, offering part-time courses for mature students in an area hard hit by pit closures and the decline of the steel industry.

The college's immediate locality is far from depressing, however. A coastal position two miles from the centre of Swansea offers quick access to excellent beaches on the Gower Peninsula, and the campus itself occupies an attractive parkland site.

Apart from Singleton Abbey, the neo-Gothic mansion which houses the administration, most of the buildings are modern. More than 2,700 students live in college rooms, and all first-years from outside the area are guaranteed accommodation. Half of the halls are on campus, the rest 20 minutes' walk away in a well-equipped student village. Both the students' union and sports facilities are good. Swansea has a good record in competitive sport, particularly rugby.

The college makes a particular effort to cater for disabled students. There are facilities for blind, deaf and wheelchair-bound students, and a member of staff who is himself disabled looks after their needs.

UNIVERSITY OF WARWICK
Coventry CV4 7AL (tel. 0203 523523)

Royal charter 1964
Times ranking: 8

Enquiries: academic registrar
Full-time students: 3,493 (f), 3,812 (m)
4,045 **arts,** 2,147 **sciences**

Main subject areas: arts, educational studies, social studies (BA, LLB); science (BSc, BEng, MEng).

Now the most successful of what used to be the new universities until the polytechnics' promotion, Warwick was derided by some in its early years for its close links with business and industry. Few are critical today. Ranked joint eighth in *The Times* league table, Warwick, with York, is the highest placed English university outside Oxbridge and London. Eleven top ratings in December 1992's funding council rankings confirmed the quality of its research. The overall standard of the 34 departments has also brought Warwick a top European award. And the science park, which was one of the first in Britain, is among the most successful.

One of the secrets of Warwick's success has been its ability to concentrate on its strengths. While other universities have tried to cover the whole range of academic disciplines, it has pursued a selective policy. Without the expense of medicine, dentistry or veterinary science to bear, the university has invested shrewdly, especially in business, science and engineering.

The business school, which was one of 11 areas to be rated of international standing for research, acquired a £1-million wing in November 1992. It can now take more than 3,000 students, compared to only 500 a decade ago.

Expansion in other areas has been less dramatic. Warwick sees itself primarily as a research university, and has been building up its post-graduate courses, but has no wish to endanger its present character and standing.

Biological sciences (three Cs), mathematics (AAB), computer science, history of art, and economics (all three Bs), engineering (BCC) and sociology (BCC) are among the other strengths. There is now a separate postgraduate school, although all students still mix on the 500-acre campus three miles south of Coventry.

There are 3,500 residential places on campus, many with en-suite facilities. First-years are guaranteed accommodation, and about half of those in their final year also live in, although restrictions on cars put some off. Sports and students' union facilities are both good.

UNIVERSITY OF WESTMINSTER
309 Regent Street, London W1R 8AL (tel. 071-911 5000).

Royal charter 1992, formerly Polytechnic of Central London
Times ranking: 75

Enquiries: central admissions unit
Full-time students: 3,510 (f), 4,290 (m)
4,080 **arts,** 3,720 **sciences**

Main subject areas: business, management and social studies (BA); engineering and science (BSc, BEng); environment (BA, BEng, BSc); law, languages and communication (BA, LLB). Certificate and diploma courses are also offered.

Westminster hit the jackpot in December 1992's research assessment exercise as the only new university to achieve a top rating for any of its units. There were only five academics involved, but the value in terms of prestige and publicity was immeasurable. A number of other new universities achieved a better than average rating for research and had more academics assessed, but the Centre for Communication and Information Studies enabled Westminster to claim a triumph. Entry to the already popular degree in media studies may become considerably more difficult.

Even in polytechnic days, research was always given a high priority. But teaching, both on full- and part-time courses, will continue to be Westminster's bread and butter. The university's main base in the heart of London's West End brings in large numbers of part-timers: 12,500 as against 7,800 full-time students at the last count.

Language teaching is one of the main strengths, with courses available from the most basic level to postgraduate. The School of Communications claims to teach the largest number of languages (26) in any British university.

Art and design, engineering, computing, architecture and other environmental subjects were all rated highly in the polytechnic's last teaching rankings. The university is also a leader in the Enterprise in Higher Education initiative, which weaves work-related skills into degree programmes.

What was Britain's oldest polytechnic (established in 1838) occupies 19 sites that sprawl across central London to Harrow, in the northern suburbs, where major development is to take place. Academic blocks, 400 residential places and a new sports hall are planned in a £40-million development. By the end of the century, the former higher education college campus will take 7,500 students, compared with the present 4,000.

But for the moment accommodation remains a problem, although first-years are given priority in the allocation of halls of residence. Only a minority of the full-time students live at home and, despite the purchase of more halls in 1991, the university has more students per residential place than most others.

UNIVERSITY OF WOLVERHAMPTON
Wulfruna Street, Wolverhampton WV1 1SB (tel. 0902 321000)

Royal charter 1992, formerly Wolverhampton Polytechnic
Times ranking: 74

Enquiries: academic registrar
Full-time students: 4,793 (f), 4,022 (m)
6,007 **arts,** 2,808 **sciences**

Main subject areas: applied sciences (BSc); art and design (BA); business and management (BA, BSc, BABE); computing and information technology (BSc); construction, engineering and technology (BEng, BSc); education (BEd); health sciences (BSc); humanities and social sciences, languages and European studies (BA); legal studies (LLB). Certificate and diploma courses are also offered.

Wolverhampton pioneered the high street higher education shop, bringing in thousands of students who might otherwise never have continued their education. The shop is part of the university's open-door policy to widen access to higher education across the west Midlands. There are big 'outreach' programmes, taking university courses into the work-place. The business school for example, the largest of Wolverhampton's 10 schools, is running a management development programme for Birmingham City Council's 50,000 employees.

Business courses were praised by Her Majesty's Inspectorate in 1992, particularly for an innovative one-year BA in Business Enterprise (BABE), designed mainly for mature students with diploma qualifications and potential for further progress. Eastern European universities are among those involved in student exchanges.

The inspectors were less impressed by an example of Wolverhampton's franchising operation, which is increasing the number of students the university can take by running the first year of some degrees at further education colleges. Hotel, tourism and licensed retail management was found to be patchy, although satisfactory overall.

A more direct form of expansion has come with the opening of a campus in Telford, given a separate identity as The University in Shropshire. Business, computing and teacher training courses are being offered, appropriately in an enterprise zone, to serve a county without its own university.

The new base gives the university five campuses. In addition to that in Telford, there are two in Wolverhampton itself, one in Walsall for teacher education, and one in Dudley for humanities and social sciences. There are now more than 16,000 students, including part-timers. The university now plans to increase its student intake by six per cent a year.

Residential accommodation is limited, but first-years are given priority and many students live at home. Social and sporting facilities vary considerably between sites, the best being in Wolverhampton.

UNIVERSITY OF YORK

Heslington, York YO1 5DD (tel. 0904 430000)

Royal charter 1962
Times ranking: 8

Enquiries: undergraduate admissions office
Full-time students: 2,062 (f), 2,564 (m)
1,967 **arts,** 1,691 **sciences**

Main subject areas: 20 departments covering arts and social science, philosophy, economics and politics (BA); science and mathematics (BSc, MSci); and engineering (BEng, MEng, BSc).

York was another university to demonstrate both in *The Times* rankings and the December 1992 research assessment exercise that youth is no bar to academic excellence. Four top research ratings have helped the university to a place in our top 10.

Like Warwick, the only one of York's contemporaries to rate as highly in our table, York has chosen its subjects carefully and has no plans for dramatic growth. But if there is no medicine, dentistry, veterinary science or law, the available subjects are offered in a range of unusual combinations.

Still one of the smaller universities, York plans to expand only to 5,000 students by 1994–95, and 6,000 by the end of the century. It suffered for the policy in the first *Times* rankings because other universities' growth brought them bigger budget increases for teaching.

Applicants for degree courses also felt the effects. There were 13,800 applications for 1,100 undergraduate places in 1990, and even more in the two subsequent years. Only eight universities have higher average entry requirements.

Unlike many universities, York's main growth over the past decade has been in science and technology, balancing an initial bias towards the arts and social sciences. Most of the top-rated courses are still in the established areas, however. Economics (BBC), social policy (BCC) and computer science (three Bs) are among the strengths.

Since 1990, the university has begun reviewing its courses every three years. Its first external 'academic audit' was generally complimentary about quality assurance procedures, and found students satisfied with the tuition arrangements.

The seven colleges (one reserved for postgraduates) mix academic and social roles. First-years are guaranteed a residential place on the lakeside campus, two miles from the centre of York, where three-quarters of all the university's students can be accommodated.

Social life is based mainly on the colleges, and there is no separate students' union building. The sports facilities are patchy: 40 acres of playing fields on campus, some indoor facilities, but no university swimming pool.

The data gathered for the *Times* survey covers a wide range of issues. This diversity poses immediate questions of consistency. It would be easier to reduce the number of variables. It was decided not to take this option for several reasons. The first was the desire to go as far as possible in reflecting the diverse nature of the universities. The second was the wish to minimise the biases which might emerge from a narrower range of factors. Some inconsistency is a price worth paying for this.

Sources
The information came from a host of sources. Where possible, these were cross-checked with other sources. Among the sources of information were: the Universities Statistical Record 'University Statistics' Volumes I & II; the Committee of Vice Chancellors and Principals 'University Management Statistics and Performance Indicators in the UK'; and the Polytechnic and Colleges Funding Council 'Macro Performance Indicators'.

All universities and colleges were sent the raw data for the bulk of the variables for their institution. Many used this opportunity to check or amend figures. Others felt the form or nature of the material did not lend itself to checking by them.

Official statistics were used extensively. All institutions were asked to supply copies of their annual reports and institutional plans. Where these were made available, they were used extensively. In some cases individuals in institutions added a perspective or a view on the data relating to their institution. Although the most recent consistent figures available were used, many nonetheless date from 1990. In some cases the data refers to several years. This is especially true in the case of the research assessment undertaken by the Funding Council.

The material in the tables is derived almost entirely from published or secondary statistics. It was decided for two reasons not to undertake primary research such as the reputational survey undertaken by *US News*. First, there is a large volume of material available on higher education in the UK. Much of this is based on figures which examine the relative achievements of institutions of the type used here. Second, those preparing *The Times Guide* are acutely aware of the number and scale of the enquiries which have been undertaken into universities over the last few years. The Funding Council's research assessment alone involved 2,700 submissions from 170 HEIs (Higher Education Institutions) across the 72 units of assessment. The work of over 43,000 full-time equivalent academics was included in the submissions. The submissions were assessed by 63 panels and sub-panels with 450 members and 50 assessors.

Against this background it was decided not to add another survey to the demands placed on academics in 1992.

A poll of polls
The final figures in the tables should be thought of as a poll of polls. This is useful in getting an overview but is built around a series of key assumptions. Perhaps the most important – after the choice of variables – are the weightings for different variables. It was decided to publish these weightings so that users who want to allocate a different weighting, for instance less to research and more to employment or student accommodation, can do so. In some instances, the interpretation of a variable can vary between users. For some, a low student/staff ratio indicates success in mobilising resources so that there are lots of staff available for teaching and related duties. For others, a high student/staff ratio shows success in making teaching methods more efficient.

Care should always be taken in interpreting figures. Some of those employed here cause particular problems. For example, it was decided to look at the qualifications of academic staff. It seems that staff with doctorates list these as a matter of course in staff handbooks, research reports, calendars or yearbooks. This does not seem to be the case with professional qualifications. There may be significant under-reporting of these figures.

The form of data analysis raises other questions. The poll-of-polls method exaggerates some differences and reduces others. This former is especially true in the figures on completion rates, ie the proportion successfully completing their studies. UK universities have probably the highest completion rates in the world. The difference between Durham, say, which has one of the highest completion rates, and a mid-range institution probably reflects a difference of less than 10 per cent. The latter will probably still see more than 75 per cent of all entrants graduate successfully.

Some important issues, for example increasing access to different groups within the community, are not covered. Similarly, other indicators of success are also not featured. They include the range of local support and advisory services, support for the arts, and a host of other contributions locally, nationally and internationally. The reasons for these omissions are largely practical. It is hoped that future versions of *The Times Guide* will find ways to cover these areas.

INDEX